Roots of the Revival

MUSIC IN AMERICAN LIFE

A list of books in the series appears at the end of this book.

Roots of the Revival

American and British Folk Music
in the 1950s

RONALD D. COHEN AND
RACHEL CLARE DONALDSON

UNIVERSITY OF ILLINOIS PRESS
Urbana, Chicago, and Springfield

1 2 3 4 5 C P 5 4 3 2 1

∞ This book is printed on acid-free paper.

Library of Congress Cataloging-in-Publication Data
Cohen, Ronald D., 1940- author.
Roots of the revival : American and British folk music in the
1950s / Ronald D. Cohen and Rachel Clare Donaldson.
pages   cm. — (Music in American life)
Includes bibliographical references and index.
ISBN 978-0-252-03851-8 (hardcover : alk. paper) — ISBN 978-
0-252-08012-8 (pbk. : alk. paper) — ISBN 978-0-252-09642-6
(e-book)
1. Folk music — United States—History and criticism. 2. Folk
music — Great Britain — History and criticism. I. Donaldson,
Rachel Clare. II. Title.
ML3545.C64   2014
781.62'13009045—dc23   2013048531

To Josh Houston and Alan Cohen

Contents

Acknowledgments   ix

Introduction   1

1. Background in the United States and Great Britain to 1950   5

2. The Weavers and the Resurgence of Folk Music, 1950–1953   25

3. Blacklisting and Folk Developments, 1953–1954   51

4. Popular Folk Music Comes of Age, 1955–1956   71

5. Further Developments, 1957–1958   93

6. The Decade Ends, 1959–1960   115

Notes   153

Index   175

Acknowledgments

Much thanks to many colleagues, particularly Bob Riesman, as well as Will Kaufman, Richard Carlin, and Jim Lane for their astute editorial assistance. Laurie Matheson has been a wonderful friend and editor who deserves our highest praise, along with our terrific copy editor, Julie Gay.

Roots of the Revival

Introduction

The accepted wisdom is that the period between the commercial success of the Weavers in the early 1950s and the explosion of the Kingston Trio in 1958 was rather a dead zone for popular folk music in the United States. "In the 1950s, a burgeoning commercial folk revival was stamped out by the anticommunism hysteria," the folk journalist Scott Alarik has explained in *Revival: A Folk Music Novel*. Certainly the anticommunist movement had a chilling effect, but not to such an extent.[1]

Folk music was only a small part of the cultural and social explosion during the 1950s, a complex era that has too long been wrongly characterized as "the bland leading the bland." The pervasive political miasma led to the blacklisting, firing, and investigating of numerous performers, writers, teachers, labor organizers, government employees, and so many others. Hollywood films felt the cultural sting, yet many great movies were produced. The same was true in other areas of culture throughout the decade, such as plays, radio, and television programs, comic books, novels, poetry, paintings, and music, not only folk music but rhythm and blues, rockabilly, doo-wop, country, and other streams that culminated in rock 'n' roll. This was a complex time of cultural repression as well as efflorescence and rebellion.

The 1950s was an age of unprecedented affluence for millions of American families who could afford a house in the burgeoning suburbs and a middle-class existence. There were some egregious problems at home, however, such as poverty for the minority, particularly in the South, along with rampant racism and segregation—although there were important victories for the civil rights movement—as well as Cold War tensions with the Soviet Union, which fueled a nuclear arms race as well as the fear of domestic communism. All was not sweetness and light, but there was enough prosperity to go around for the white majority, particularly in contrast to the devastating years of depression and world war.[2]

Folk music was part of the pervasive culture, as well as the emerging counterculture, during the decade. Popular folk performers such as John Jacob Niles, Burl Ives, Josh White, Harry Belafonte, and the early Weavers easily entered the musical mainstream, while others existed more on the fringe but still attracted a loyal following. In addition to the commercial performers, there were also folk festivals, radio programs, record collectors, small record labels, and a host of organizations and venues. Indeed, folk music remained widespread and accessible, despite its often-perceived left-wing taint.

Even school children were somewhat exposed. In 1951 the California State Department of Education published a small booklet, *Folk Songs of the United States: For Enriched Social Living in School, Home, and Community.* "The purpose of this collection of folk songs of the United States is to encourage spontaneous singing in school, home, church, and community, with the hope that the youth of our country may possess, appreciate, and proudly enjoy a common stock of tradition and in turn become intelligent carriers of our culture to our own future generations and to people of other countries," the preface explained. The dozens of songs included "All the Pretty Little Horses," "Buffalo Gals," "Go Tell Aunt Rhody," "Jacob's Ladder," "New River Train," "Skip to My Lou," and other standards. Teachers were encouraged to accompany the singing with an autoharp, although a guitar was also acceptable, but there was little classroom spontaneity. Folk songs also accompanied the widespread teaching of square dancing in elementary schools. Folk songs for children appeared on numerous recordings, particularly those issued by Folkways Records as well as Young People's Records/Children's Record Guild.[3]

Historians and folklorists have essentially written off the decade because folk musicians seemingly suffered from the anticommunist crusade. Robert Cantwell's insightful *When We Were Good* does salvage something, however, when he comments: "In the crucial years, then between the blacklist and the appearance of the Kingston Trio's 'Tom Dooley,' the folksong movement was becoming in schools and camps a folk revival." He deftly captures some crucial aspects of the story, but he also leaves much out. Dick Weissman, who began his folk music career in the mid-1950s, has also depicted some aspects of folk music at the time. "When the Weavers were blacklisted and thus effectively removed from any national exposure as either performers or recording artists, many Americans identified folk music with radical, 'un-American' causes," he explains. "Nevertheless, folk music did not disappear from the American popular musical scene." Weissman mentions Harry Belafonte, the Tarriers, the Easy Riders, Stan Wilson, Odetta, and a few other commercial performers, as well as some of the record companies and the Greenwich Village scene, but there was so much else.[4]

While a burgeoning folk revival made headway in the United States, across the Atlantic a similar, although smaller, movement became visible. Moreover, they were increasingly connected: American folk music had a definite influence on the British scene. In this context Alan Lomax, who moved to London in 1950 and remained until his return to the United States in 1958, played a significant role. Exploring the transatlantic connections highlights the complexity and vibrancy of folk music during the decade. In addition to Lomax, Jack Elliott, Peggy Seeger, Ralph Rinzler, Guy Carawan, and other Americans played an important role in promoting folk music in the British Isles, which bounced back to the United States in the 1960s in the form of rock 'n' roll.

The popularity of folk music, particularly among young people, is a bit confusing. While the baby boom generation, those born after 1945, did not reach their teen years until the late 1950s and particularly in the 1960s, there was certainly a rush in college attendance through the decade. Here was a middle-class audience with disposable income to purchase clothing and magazines, attend movies, and particularly shop for popular music recordings. A teenage consumer culture had taken hold, particularly with the invention of 45 RPM records in the late 1940s as well as magazines aimed at the youth market. While young people generally preferred to dance to rock 'n' roll and the popular slow ballads, by the late 1950s folk music increasingly appeared on the new 10" and 12" long-playing 33⅓ RPM albums, pioneered by Columbia Records in 1948, which contained more than forty minutes of music and was designed to be listened to while a person was seated. RCA Victor's 7" 45 RPM record, geared to a teen audience and jukebox sales, soon followed. Square dancing and other interactive styles had long been accompanied by folk musicians, but this was no longer the case with contemporary folk music. Moreover, folk music had long appealed mostly to an adult audience but would now increasingly become a popular young people's sound, even before the baby boom generation entered college, until its full-blown emergence during the folk revival years of the early 1960s.

While a rich folk music community developed in the 1950s, it had emerged from earlier decades of development and experimentation. Chapter 1 traces this background, followed by five chronological chapters, each covering both the United States and Great Britain, with their fascinating musical and political interactions, drawing on a wide variety of primary and secondary sources. The influential role of folklorist and musician Alan Lomax is woven through the chapters, along with that of Pete Seeger and numerous other performers, promoters, activists, record company executives, folklorists, record collectors, and journalists. By 1960 the stage was set for the folk revival (aka great folk scare) of the 1960s.

1

Background in the United States and Great Britain to 1950

Folk music has had many definitions and incarnations throughout the twentieth century in the United States and Great Britain. The public has been most aware of its commercial substance and appeal, with the focus on recording artists and their repertoires, but there has been so much more, including a political agenda, folklore theories, grassroots styles, regional promoters, and discussions on what musical forms—blues, hillbilly, gospel, Anglo-Saxon, pop, singer-songwriters, instrumental and/or vocal, international—should be included. These contrasting and conflicting interpretations were particularly evident during the 1950s.

Alan Lomax

Alan Lomax (1915–2002) began his career as a music collector on a field trip through the South with his father, John, in 1933; a mere four years later, at age twenty-two, Lomax was named Assistant in Charge of the Archive of American Folk Song at the Library of Congress, where he remained until 1942, when he joined the Office of War Information (OWI). He entered the Army in April 1944, and was finally discharged in March 1946, at which point he resumed his left-wing and folk music activities. Lomax believed in preserving as well as promoting vernacular music, while reaching out to the masses through his radio shows on the Mutual network and work with the Henry Wallace presidential campaign on the Progressive Party ticket in 1948. Before the war he had two programs on CBS, one during the day aimed at school children, the other at night for adults.

In July 1950, Lomax joined a stellar list of folklorists from around the world for "Four Symposia on Folklore" held at Indiana University in Bloomington. Along with regaling the attendees with a concert of folk songs, he engaged in the sometimes-heated discussions of the current state of folklore and its possible future. "In the last ten years . . . the ballad has become part of the big entertainment industry in America," he explained. "There are now usually one or two programs on the air, where ballads are sung, and out of this has come one other thing which has been very, very important. A number of commercial record albums have been published and these have taken the songs to the people who really wanted them, and were active consumers and learners of ballads. This has been a much more slow, solid, and healthy sort of growth." Lomax had always preferred vernacular musicians, but he also promoted commercial presentations through influencing the careers of Josh White, Pete Seeger, Woody Guthrie, and Burl Ives. He did so following World War II by producing Decca record albums by Ives, Carl Sandburg, and others, organizing numerous concerts, as well as hosting and designing various radio programs throughout the 1940s. "I have felt the last two years," he said in Indiana, "that I have really been a folklorist for the first time, a functioning folklorist, using folklore for the benefit of the people." While Lomax had some praise for commercial performers, he pointed out to his colleagues that, in New York, "our professional singer is a bore to most of the people who five years ago took up the call to ballads with him. They want to hear real oral musicians and it's when those people now step out to sing that the roof goes off and the audience gets there almost at once."[1]

Lomax had presented a range of musicians during a series of concerts during 1946–47 for People's Songs at Town Hall, to which he was apparently referring in his Indiana remarks. "Blues at Midnight" featured Big Bill Broonzy, Pete Johnson, Sonny Terry, and Brownie McGhee, "Calypso at Midnight" had the Duke of Iron and Lord Invader, while "Honkytonk Blues at Midnight" presented Broonzy, Memphis Slim, and Sonny Boy Williamson. By decade's end, despite his varied activities, Lomax still had no regular job and, in addition, felt the pressure of the country's mounting anticommunist fervor, including the publication in June 1950 of *Red Channels: The Report of Communist Influence in Radio and Television* by a group of ex-FBI agents. In the company of dozens of prominent Americans, he rated less than a page listing his work with People's Songs and other suspect activities. Nevertheless, on September 24, 1950, Lomax left the United States heading for Brussels, Belgium; he soon settled in London, however, where he would reside for the next eight years, promoting and collecting folk music throughout the British

Isles, as well as in Spain and Italy. During his sojourn abroad he would have a major influence on folk music in both the United States and Great Britain, tying together what had come before and what would follow.

Collectors, Collections, and Publications

Lomax was one of the most active folk music collectors, radio promoters, and organizers during the 1940s. He was not alone, though, and he had a rich trove of material to draw upon, including songbooks, recordings, and academic studies. Ballad and folk song collecting had existed in the British Isles since the eighteenth century, highlighted by Francis James Child, a professor of medieval studies and English literature at Harvard, whose five volumes of *The English and Scottish Popular Ballads* (1882–1896) was the capstone. There was little interest in the United States in folk song collecting until the twentieth century, although William Wells Newell published two articles on "Early American Ballads" in the *Journal of American Folklore* (1899–1900). Phillips Barry contributed an article, "The Ballad of the Demon Lover," to *Modern Language Notes* in 1904, the first of his many academic contributions, quickly followed by Henry M. Belden's "The Study of Folk-Song in America" in *Modern Philology* (1905). The next year Belden organized the Missouri Folklore Society, where local teachers spearheaded song collecting that resulted in the later publication of *Ballads and Songs Collected by the Missouri Folk-Lore Society* (1940), with a wide range of Child ballads, Irish songs, French language tunes, and much else.[2]

The search for variants of the ballads collected by Child—always referred to as the "Child ballads"—in the United States would long fascinate the collectors, but a source of native folk songs was quickly discovered that deftly altered the field. In 1910 John A. Lomax, Alan's father, published *Cowboy Songs and Other Frontier Ballads*, which made a strong case for looking inward for a unique musical style and substance. Lomax was not the first to publish cowboy songs, since brief articles had appeared in the *Journal of American Folklore* and other publications as early as 1901. N. Howard "Jack" Thorp's *Songs of the Cowboys* was published in 1908, which included "Old Paint," "The Cowboy's Lament (Streets of Laredo)," and "The Old Chisholm Trail," but he received scant circulation. Only Lomax grabbed the public's imagination and put cowboy songs on the country's musical map.[3]

By 1910 Olive Dame Campbell, the wife of a missionary schoolteacher, had assembled a collection of native white songs from Kentucky, Georgia, and Tennessee, but she could find no publisher. She was not the only woman in the South with an interest in local song lore. Katherine Pettit and May Stone, the founders of the Hindman Settlement School in Knott County, Kentucky, in 1902, had been collecting songs from the children at their school; George Lyman Kittredge, a Child protégé and one of John Lomax's professors at Harvard while he was briefly a student in 1906–1907, published some of their collection as "Ballads and Rhymes from Kentucky" in the *Journal of American Folklore* in 1907. From 1912 to 1915 E. C. Perrow's "Songs and Rhymes from the South" appeared in the *Journal of American Folklore*, which included 270 texts from the Appalachian region. In 1916 Loraine Wyman and Howard Brockway issued *Lonesome Tunes: Folksongs of the Southern Mountains*, quickly followed by Josephine McGill's *Folk-Songs of the Kentucky Mountains* (1917). Wyman's *Twenty Kentucky Mountain Songs* appeared in 1920.

While Child, an American, set the standard for future collectors of British ballads, in late 1914 as war had broken out in Europe, Cecil Sharp first traveled to the United States with his assistant Maude Karpeles to promote English folk dance. Born in London in 1859, Sharp reversed the process established by Child by doing much of his collecting in the southern United States. After briefly working in Australia, he returned to England and began teaching, writing about, and collecting British folk songs and dances. The five volumes of his *Folk Songs from Somerset* (1904–1909) quickly became influential. Sharp, accompanied by Karpeles, returned to the United States in 1916 and began collecting in earnest, with the assistance of Olive Dame Campbell. They collected four hundred songs from 67 informants in North Carolina, Tennessee, and Virginia, of which forty Child ballads, seventy local songs, and two dozen other English ballads appeared in *English Folk-Songs of the Southern Appalachians* (1917). The following year, as war raged, they returned to gather six hundred songs, and in 1918 they compiled another 625 tunes before returning again to England. Back in England Sharp gave a series of lectures based on his Appalachian collecting, such as one at Aeolian Hall on May 13, 1919, accompanied by Owen Colyer singing "Young Hunting," "The Wife Wrapt in Wether's Skin," "The False Young Man," and three others, while members of the English Folk Dance Society performed "The Kentucky Running Set." Sharp died in 1924, and in 1932 Karpeles produced a final volume of their southern collection, with another 274 songs. Along with the bulk of American collectors, Sharp had the romantic and highly fanciful notion that the backwoods southern singers were essentially cut off from the hustle and bustle of modern society and therefore were able to preserve and pass on traditional British ballads and songs. A gross exaggeration, this attitude would continue even as radio programs and phonograph records reached into southern mountain and rural areas in the 1920s. Moreover, Sharp believed that returning these ballads to England would rejuvenate his country's musical and cultural legacy, then in jeopardy of being corrupted by modern society.[4]

While Sharp and others were gathering songs and ballads from southern white singers, a separate group of collectors began focusing on African American musicians and songsters. Shortly after the Civil War, William Francis Allen, Charles Pickard Ware, and Lucy McKim Garrison published *Slave Songs of the United States* (1867). They focused on spirituals, also known as jubilee songs, although they realized there were also secular songs dealing with work experiences. Howard Odum, born in Georgia and a graduate of Emory College in 1904, entered the University of Mississippi as a graduate student and soon discovered a wealth of African American songs. He first published "Religious Folk Songs of the Southern Negroes" in the *American Journal of Religious Psychology and Education* in 1906. Soon armed with a cylinder record player, he collected and published 115 secular songs in the *Journal of American Folklore* in 1911. Odum's major study with Guy B. Johnson, *The Negro and His Songs*, was issued in 1925, quickly followed by *Negro Workaday Songs* (1926); 1925 also saw the release of Dorothy Scarborough, *On the Trail of Negro Folk-Songs*. The older spirituals were not forgotten, however, with Frederick Work's booklet *Folk Songs of the American Negro*, published in 1907.

African American songs appeared in print as well as on phonograph records beginning in the 1890s. The Unique Quartet began recording as early as 1890, with their Edison cylinders of "Mamma's Black Baby Boy" appearing in 1893. The popular team of Bert Williams and George Walker began recording secular songs in 1901. In 1909 a quartet, part of the Fisk Jubilee Singers, visited the Victor studios in Camden, New Jersey, and recorded ten cylinders. An increasing number of black performers entered the recording studios from 1910 to 1920. Mamie Smith recorded "Crazy Blues" on the Okeh label in 1920, which initiated the enthusiasm for blues and other African American secular recordings. The collectors Lawrence Gellert, Howard Odum, and Dorothy Scarborough, followed by John and Alan Lomax in the 1930s, scoured the South for African American blues, field hollers, sacred tunes, and other songs with Anglo-African roots. The Lomaxes headed for southern prison camps in 1933, believing that their informants were cut off from modern musical influences and therefore had an unsullied, vernacular sound. When they began recording Huddie Ledbetter, aka Lead Belly, at the Angola camp in Louisiana, they thought they had found such an example, but they soon discovered that his repertoire included a wide range of popular songs as well as his own compositions. There was no such thing as musical purity by the 1920s in southern prisons and mountain settlements, or anywhere else. When Alan Lomax conducted his field trips to Coahoma County, Mississippi, with John W. Work, Lewis Wade Jones, and Samuel C. Adams in 1941–42, they discovered that the local jukeboxes were filled with the popular tunes of Count Basie, Louis Jordan, Fats Waller, and even Artie Shaw, while the recordings of Delta bluesmen were quite scarce. Moreover, Robert Johnson and Son House, for example, had aspirations to be commercial musicians, rather than folk musicians playing only for local audiences.[5]

Among the other roots collectors, Robert Gordon explored a variety of interesting musical sources. Born in Maine in 1888 and instructed by the ballad scholars at Harvard, he taught in the English Department at the University of California-Berkeley, 1918–1924. His interest in folk songs led to his editing the "Old Songs That Men Have Sung" column in *Adventure* magazine, beginning in 1923 for more than four years, which reached two million readers nationwide. This was similar to such music features in *Railroad Man's Magazine* and *Sea Stories*. Because of his column, Gordon received a broad range of song texts from his readers. He particularly liked collecting songs along the San Francisco waterfront, working with Frank Kester, who ran the sea songs and stories column "The Dogwatch" in the *Oakland Tribune*. Gordon used a cylinder record player to record more than two hundred local songs. He returned east in 1924 and soon began a recording trip to the South, where he lived for some years. During 1927 into 1928 he published a series of articles in the *New York Times Magazine* based on his collecting, then in 1928 he was appointed head of the newly created Archive of American Folk Song at the Library of Congress, which received part of his extensive collections. He left the library in 1932; a year later he was replaced by John Lomax. Gordon was unable to publish a book based on his pioneering collecting and had faded from memory by the time of his death in 1961.[6]

In 1938 the National Service Bureau, a branch of the Federal Theater Project, Works Progress Administration (WPA), published Gordon's *Folk-Songs of America*, a compilation of his *New York Times* articles. "Of folk-song alone, America has a body perhaps greater in extent than that possessed by any other nation, and certainly unsurpassed in interest and variety of types," he wrote in the article originally published on January 2, 1927. In addition to the British and Scottish ballads, Gordon included "mountain ballets," "play-party" songs, "songs of the Plains, of the great Western trek, of the trials and hardships of pioneer days," creole songs, Spanish-American songs,

African American songs—"The negro of the south is perhaps our best folk-singer"—"sailor chanteys," and so much more. "Folk-song is a body of song in the possession of the people, passed on by them often for generations by word of mouth, from singer to singer, not learned from books or from print," Gordon argued. With this romantic tinge, he was not interested in contemporary folk songs, although he surely included many songs of recent vintage, and he definitely parted company with those ballad collectors who were interested only in Old World origins and connections.[7]

Along with Gordon's book, the National Service Bureau published a number of other ballad and folk song collections. Phillips Barry's early articles in the *Journal of American Folklore, Southern Folklore Quarterly,* and the *Bulletin of the Folk-Song Society of the Northeast* were brought together in *Folk Music in America* (1939). Two volumes of John Harrington Cox's *Traditional Ballads Mainly from West Virginia* also appeared in 1939, which were additions to his collection *Folk-Songs of the South* (1925). The National Play Bureau, another offshoot of the Federal Theatre Project, published Arthur Palmer Hudson's *Folk Tunes from Mississippi* in 1937, adding to his earlier *Folksongs of Mississippi and Their Background* (1936). These publications did not get wide circulation but indicated the government's commitment to promoting folk-song scholarship and circulation, part of the New Deal's grassroots cultural mission.

Phonograph records rapidly proliferated through the 1920s, including a large selection of ethnic recordings, appealing to a range of tastes, generations, and cultural groups (although the Great Depression of the 1930s resulted in the vast reduction of recordings and commercial labels). The record companies had refined their approach to the expanding markets through establishing separate race (African American) and hillbilly (white southern), as well as ethnic, lists. Race records officially started with Mamie Smith in 1920. In 1922 A. C. "Eck" Robinson and Henry Gilliland's Victor recording of "Sally Gooden" and "Arkansas Traveler" launched the hillbilly craze, quickly followed by Fiddlin' John Carson's Okeh recording of "The Little Old Log Cabin in the Lane" and "The Old Hen Cackled and the Rooster's Going to Crow." Brunswick, Gennett, Paramount, Columbia, and other companies quickly rushed to take advantage of the widening market of rural southern black and white record buyers (although some of them were moving to the urban centers of the South and North). Their records were marketed as "old familiar tunes," "old-time music," even "Popular Ballads and Mountaineer Tunes" and "Southern Melodies." As a Victor Records flyer stated in 1927: "Here's another set of 'Southern Specials'—the kind that have been getting more and more popular with each succeeding release. This is perhaps the most diversified list yet to appear. Ballads in 'mountaineer' style, on timely topics, such as Captain Lindberg's Paris flight, the Mississippi flood, sentimental songs, character songs with snappy bits of humor—and each one with a distinct appeal of its own." Some were traditional, others newly written event songs that captured the day's headlines, and many had been part of the minstrel repertoire dating to before the Civil War or produced by the Tin Pan Alley commercial tunesmiths.

While the record companies, based in the North, for various reasons targeted southern musicians and their audiences—although some of the hillbilly performers lived in the North, such as Vernon Dalhart, who was born in Texas but based in New York City—folk music collectors published collections, many issued by university presses, from throughout the country. For example, Louise Pound, an English professor at the University of Nebraska, compiled *Folk-Songs of Nebraska and the Central West* in 1914, which included songs of Indian, Irish, German, English, and African American background. Books from the Midwest continued to appear through the 1930s, such as Paul Brewster's *Ballads and Songs of Indiana* (1940), Charles Neely, *Tales and Songs of Southern Illinois* (1938), Emeyln Elizabeth Gardner and Geraldine Chickering, *Ballads and Songs of Southern Michigan* (1939), and Theodore Blegen, *Norwegian Immigrant Ballads and Songs* (1936).[8]

In New England, Fannie Hardy Eckstorm and Mary Winslow Smyth issued *The Minstrelsy of Maine: Folksongs and Ballads of the Woods and Coast* (1927). Two years later Eckstorm and Smyth, along with Phillips Barry, published *British Ballads from Maine* (1929). In neighboring Vermont, Helen Hartness Flanders and George Brown followed with *Vermont Folk-Songs and Ballads* (1932), the first of many publications by Flanders. Eckstorm, Barry, and others came together to form The Folk-Song Society of the Northeast and began publishing their *Bulletin* in 1930.

Some collectors had a geographical focus, while others specialized in specific genres. For example, George Korson's *Songs and Ballads of the Anthracite Miner* (1927) was based on his field collecting in Pennsylvania; he would quickly follow with numerous other compilations of miner's songs. Roland Palmer Gray, *Songs and Ballads of the Maine Lumberjacks* (1924), Franz Rickaby, *Ballads and Songs of the Shanty-Boy* (1926), Earl C. Beck, *Songs of the Michigan Lumberjacks* (1941), and Margaret Larkin, *Singing Cowboy* (1931), also focused on occupational songs.

While the record companies were scouring the South for white and black musicians with commercial potential, academic song collectors also kept busy with their southern regional publications. Examples include: Louis Chappell, *Folksongs of the Roanoke and the Albemarle* (1939), Josiah Combs, *Folk-Songs from the Kentucky Highlands* (1939), John Harrington Cox, *Folk-Songs of the South*, Arthur Kyle Davis, *Traditional Ballads of Virginia* (1929), Mellinger Henry, *Songs Sung in the Southern Appalachians* (1934), Arthur Palmer Hudson, *Folksongs of Mississippi and Their Background*, Jean Thomas, *Ballad Makin' in the Mountains of Kentucky* (1939), and Mary Wheeler, *Kentucky Mountain Folk-Songs* (1937). National nostalgia for the sunny South, captured by the book and film *Gone with the Wind* in the late 1930s, included both popular as well as folk melodies and pervaded national culture. There were also complex, indeed contrary, views of southern mountain people (hillbillies), both as destitute, rustic rubes with few social skills and prone to violence, but also as rugged individuals with Anglo-Saxon roots, protected from the corruptions of modern society by their apparent isolation and genetic superiority.[9]

Folk Festivals and Performers

There was also a proliferation of folk festivals that primarily featured regional performers. Ethnic music festivals, with performances of German and other European songs and dances, dated from the nineteenth century, and expanded into the twentieth. Fiddle contests began in the eighteenth century but were instituted in the modern era with the 1912 contest in Lawrenceville, Georgia, expanding the following year into the Georgia Old-Time Fiddler's Convention, which lasted into the 1930s. In 1928 Bascom Lamar Lunsford launched the popular Mountain Dance and Folk Festival in Asheville, North Carolina, which continues today. Jean Bell Thomas picked up the idea in 1932 for the American Folk Song Festival in Ashland, Kentucky, which also lasted for many decades. The White Top Folk Festival in Virginia began in 1931 and ended in 1939 after a slow death. Sarah Gertrude Knott launched the enthusiastic and eclectic National Folk Festival in 1934 in St. Louis, usually based in urban settings, and it, too, is still going strong. George Korson created the more focused Pennsylvania Folk Festival in 1935, but it only lasted until 1938. Often presenting a wide range of talents and styles, the festivals brought together performers and audiences to celebrate and appreciate folk music in local and regional settings.[10]

Numerous country music radio programs had appeared by the 1930s, offering and filtering a variety of songs to a national audience. Southern stations began programing country performers in the early 1920s, led by WSB in Atlanta, which featured Fiddlin' John Carson in September 1922. WBAP in Fort Worth, Texas, initiated an immediately popular hour-and-a-half square dance show on January 4, 1923. While country music was widely associated with southern musicians and musical styles, the most popular radio program existed in Chicago, which featured a variety of musical acts. WLS began with "The Aladdin Playparty" soon after its inauguration in April 1924, followed by the "Old Fiddlers' Hour" and finally the long-running *National Barn Dance* in 1926, which lasted for many decades. In late November 1925 the *WSM Barn Dance* began in Nashville, Tennessee, soon known as the *Grand Ole Opry*. Other programs followed in the 1930s, including the WHO (Des Moines, Iowa) *Iowa Barn Dance Frolic*, the *Boon County Jamboree* from WLW (Cincinnati), John Lair's Kentucky-based *Renfro Valley Barn Dance*, WBT's (Charlotte) *The Crazy Barn Dance*, and WWVA's *Wheeling Jamboree* from West Virginia. There were yet no programs with a blues format, although the African American harmonica player DeFord Bailey could be heard on the *Grand Old Opry*, and various hillbilly performers, such as Jimmie Rodgers, had incorporated blues guitar and vocal stylings. Moreover, hundreds of inexpensive country song folios (magazines with numerous song lyrics), with brightly colored covers, spread the music to a wide audience, while traveling tent shows and country music parks sprang up throughout the Northeast, Mid-Atlantic, and Midwest states by the late 1930s.[11]

Comprehensive folk song compilations also began to appear, beginning with Louise Pound, *American Ballads and Songs* (1922), quickly followed by Carl Sandburg's influential *The American Songbag* (1927). A few years later John and Alan Lomax, drawing heavily on their own fieldwork for the Library of Congress that continued into the early 1940s, issued the first of their influential songbooks, *American Ballads and Folk Songs* (1934), which would set the standard for such expansive collections.

In addition to the blues, hillbilly songs, Anglo-Saxon ballads, minstrel, and Tin Pan Alley tunes from the nineteenth century that entered the hillbilly repertoire, work and protest songs became part of the eclectic mix that would come together as folk music by the 1930s. The Industrial Workers of the World (IWW) began publishing *Songs of the Workers*, better known as the "Little Red Songbook," in 1909, which went through numerous printings through the century. Adopting radical lyrics to familiar tunes, Joe Hill, Ralph Chaplin, T-Bone Slim, and their colleagues stimulated a singing labor movement. Harry "Haywire Mac" McClintock added the jaunty "The Big Rock Candy Mountain" and "Hallelujah! I'm a Bum" early in the century—the latter was featured on the soundtrack for Charlie Chaplin's 1936 feature film

Modern Times—followed by Goebel Reeves, the hobo bard who seemingly penned "Hobo's Lullaby." By the 1920s various labor unions began publishing their own songbooks, which joined the academic labor song collections of George Korson and others. Textile workers, such as Dave McCarn, who wrote "Cotton Mill Colic," complained about work conditions, while Aunt Molly Jackson, for example, vividly expressed the hardships and sorrows of mining families. There were a few recordings of labor songs in the 1930s, but when Pete Seeger, Lee Hays, and Millard Lampell formed the Almanac Singers in New York in 1941, the labor movement had its first professional singing group. Soon joined by Bess Lomax, Butch Hawes, Sis Cunningham, Sonny Terry, Brownie McGhee, Josh White, and various others, the Almanacs recorded and performed a variety of left wing and traditional songs into 1942, serving as an important political and musical influence.

Beginning in the early 1940s folk music became more of a commercial enterprise, on the radio, in the press, and through the numerous song folios, recordings, and personal appearances. Alan Lomax hosted folk music radio shows for both children and adults over the CBS network early in the decade, which he would continue after World War II over the Mutual network, but he was not alone in using the airwaves to reach a national audience. As Pete Seeger explained around 1942, "What started thirty or forty years ago as a small trickle of professors going out to collect songs and ballads, write them down and publish them in expensive volumes, small editions, has grown now to an avalanche of 'Americana' phonograph albums, radio programs, popular collections of cowboy songs, sailor songs, ballads. Look through this newspaper any week and see the names of Huddie Ledbetter [Lead Belly], Joshua White, Tony Kraber, Burl Ives, Andrew Rowan Summers, Aunt Molly Jackson, Richard Dyer-Bennett [sic], Woody Guthrie, the Almanac Singers." *Tom Glazer's Ballad Box* aired over ABC from 1945 to 1947, while both Elaine Lambert Lewis and Oscar Brand had shows on WNYC in New York City following the war. Country performers and recordings—labeled as "folk" by the trade publications *Billboard* and *Cashbox*—became bestsellers, featuring artists such as Ernest Tubb and Tex Ritter. In late 1945 Seeger, fresh out of the military, formed People's Songs with a group of left-wing musicians, such as Woody Guthrie, which promoted a musical agenda supporting labor unions, civil rights, economic justice, and world peace. They were particularly active during the Henry Wallace presidential campaign on the Progressive Party ticket in 1948, and they were disheartened when Wallace came in a distant fourth in the election. There was an increasing number of popular folk singers, such as Ives, White, Dyer-Bennet, John Jacob Niles, and Susan Reed, who performed in nightclubs and on concert stages and recorded for Decca and other mainstream labels. In addition, Moses Asch kept up a steady stream of albums on his Asch, Disc, and finally Folkways labels beginning in the early 1940s.[12]

The Archive of American Folk Song at the Library of Congress continued to release albums of their field recordings, a project initiated by Alan Lomax. "This week the Library of Congress, a new entry in the record market, was selling, as fast as they could be processed, five unbreakable vinylite albums . . . of Lomax-collected blues, 'hollers,' Appalachian ballads and sacred songs," the mainstream *Time* explained in late November 1945. "As in the first six albums, released by the Library in February 1943, the voices had a native vitality that few nightclub singers could match, though some of the records had the noisy roughness of performances made far from recording studios." Lomax had already parted from the Library of Congress in October 1942, first to work for the Office of War Information. "Lomax, now a hefty Army private, disapproves of his own twangy Texas voice, uses it constantly to 'sell the Archive,'" *Time* continued. "When he gets out of the Army he hopes to take American folk songs to Russia, bring back Soviet ballads. The Russians, he says, use folk songs to make their minorities feel better and 'we should do that too.'" Once free from the military, however, Lomax produced Decca's American Folk Music series, including two albums of older commercial hillbilly recordings, *Listen to Our Story* and *Mountain Frolic*. "The two old-time albums are the real McCoy," *Newsweek* praised," for here, on disks, is a permanent record of the music pioneer America grew up with." While maintaining a left-wing tinge, folk music, however defined, remained a popular (as well as scholarly) musical form through the decade.[13]

Benjamin A. Botkin replaced Lomax as the Assistant In Charge of the Archive of American Folk Song in 1942 until he left in 1945. Born in 1901, he grew up in Boston, obtained his BA from Harvard in 1920, an MA from Columbia the following year, and later a Ph.D. from the University of Nebraska. He began teaching English at the University of Oklahoma, where he continued, off and on, until 1940. He initiated his folklore collecting in Oklahoma, then worked for the WPA in the late 1930s, partly as national folklore editor of the Federal Writers' Project before moving to the Archive of American Folk Song. His first major publication in the field, *A Treasury of American Folklore* (*TAF*) in 1944 (and still in print), became a bestseller and was quickly followed by many other such anthologies. *TAF* included a long section of folk songs, introducing a new audience to their geographical and topical range. "The folk basis of the blues and jazz in Negro blues, work songs, hollers, and reels points to the existence of an urban as well as a rural folk music and to the fact that folk music is not a pure but a hybrid activity, which is a fusion of 'folk,' 'art,' and 'popular' idioms and tastes," Botkin explained. "The exploitation of folk music and slickening up the product by means of hokum and 'corn.' But there is good 'corn' as well as bad 'corn,' and even 'hillbilly' has its place in the hierarchy of American folk styles." And he continued: "Almost every phase or period of American folk life has left its record in the form of folk songs that describe, reflect, or evoke the time and the place, their conditions, customs, and characters." In his many books Botkin spread his love for folk songs and their cultural significance.[14]

British Folk Music, Musicians, and Trans-Atlantic Musical Connections

Folk music had developed deep, tangled roots in the United States by the end of the 1940s, but such was not exactly the case in Great Britain. For a few centuries ballad collectors in the United Kingdom focused on traditional tunes, often without music, that had long been circulating, or so they thought. Beginning with Thomas D'Urfey's six volumes of *Wit and Mirth; or, Pills to Purge Melancholy* (1719–1720) and continuing through Frank Kidson's *Traditional Tunes: A Collection of Ballad Aires, Chiefly Obtained in Yorkshire and the South of Scotland* (1891), there were numerous published collections. Francis James Child established a new standard with the publication of *The English and Scottish Popular Ballads* in five volumes (1882–1898). Researching published and manuscript collections, but doing no fieldwork, Child included numerous variations of 305 ballads that would serve as the gold standard for future scholars on both sides of the Atlantic.[15]

Cecil Sharp, drawing on Child's work, was proud of his collecting in the United States, but it had little influence on the British folk scene, which remained quite insular through the 1930s. One exception was Paul Robeson, the African American actor and singer, who first moved to London in 1925 and quickly gained popularity for his role in *Othello* and extensive recordings and movie work. By the late 1930s his stage performances included not only black spirituals and songs such as "Water Boy," but also protest songs drawn partly from Lawrence Gellert's *Negro Songs of Protest* (1936), Spanish Civil War songs, and even Sharp's arrangement of "Oh No, John." Despite his immense popularity, Robeson moved back to the United States in 1939. Throughout the decade phonograph records sold in large numbers, mostly to the middle class because the discs were expensive, and about half featured dance bands. An occasional recording by a country artist, such as Jimmie Rodgers, Gene Autry, the hobo singer Goebel Reeves, even the cowboy performer John I. White ("Lone Star Ranger"), would be issued in the United States and in England. British vernacular music did occasionally appear on the British Broadcasting Corporation (BBC) but were primarily the features of glee clubs and BBC music department's musicians and singers. While the BBC generally avoided popular culture, believed to be too low class—BBC male announcers had to wear evening clothes while broadcasting—Alistair Cooke's programs proved to be an exception.[16]

Born in 1908, Alfred (later changed to Alistair) Cooke attended Cambridge University, then arrived in the United States in 1932, in the midst of the Great Depression, to study at Yale University and subsequently at Harvard. He soon returned to England to work for the BBC as their film critic and to launch *The American Half Hour*. In 1936 he aired *New York City to the Golden Gate*, a program on American hobo songs. In 1937 he returned to the United States, where he would live for the rest of his life, and launched his career as a freelance reporter. He soon landed a brief position at NBC with his own program, as well as the BBC show *I Hear America Singing* in 1938, which would stretch to thirteen programs.[17]

Cooke first met Alan Lomax in early 1938 through their mutual interest in Jelly Roll Morton, the legendary jazz musician who had fallen on hard times in Washington, D.C. "The British Broadcasting Company has asked for a large group of records to be used in a program on American folk music," Alan wrote to his father, John, in June, without mentioning Cooke's name. "As you know, BBC is not a commercial outfit; on the contrary, it is a state owned and state financed company and we have decided to loan them the records for that reason. . . . The producer [Cooke], with whom I had several long talks, is a very bright fellow and really knows more about American folk songs than nine-tenths of the folklorists." Cooke returned to England in the summer to produce his BBC shows, each half an hour, which began on July 5. He would begin writing the scripts at the last minute and continue to pull each show together while on the air. The shows exposed the British audience to a variety of southern field recordings and were quite popular. Unfortunately, Lomax missed them, as he informed D. G. Rowse at the BBC in December: "One of the disappointments of my summer in Michigan was that I failed to hear Mr. [Alistair] Cooke's programs on American folk songs and, in order that this will not happen again, I would appreciate your sending me the notices of future programs. I presume that these programs are broadcast by short wave or is that the case? Through some oversight, we have not received the recordings of the broadcasts of last summer and I take this opportunity to remind you of the promise that Mr. Cooke made the Library last summer in this regard."[18]

Cooke had returned to the United States in September, however, and his folk series was not repeated, nor were recordings ever made. On November 5, 1938, he narrated a jazz jam session from the St. Regis Hotel in Manhattan, aired live through a transatlantic relay, over the BBC. The large group of racially mixed musicians included Sidney Bechet, Tommy Dorsey, Lee Wiley, Bobby Hackett, and Mezz Messrow. A second live, although much smaller, session followed on January 20, 1939, from a CBS recording studio. The latter group included Jack Teagarden, Teddy Wilson, Harry James, and Chu Berry. In the late 1930s British fans had a large array of American jazz records available, as well as BBC programs of jazz and swing bands, but the live jam sessions were particularly welcomed. During World War II the BBC program *Radio Rhythm Club* aired British jazz musicians, further expanding the reach that would help fuel the skiffle movement of the 1950s.[19]

American music was popular in Great Britain during the war, often through the broadcasts of the American Forces Network and prewar records by swing bands and singers such as Bing Crosby. The BBC music programs also included Josh White recordings, who recorded new songs both for the domestic Office of War Information (OWI) and the BBC, as well as some spirituals and calypso music by other artists. Moreover, the singing cowboy Gene Autry had toured the country in 1939, performing in London, Liverpool, Glasgow, and Dublin. One exception to the general lack of American folk performances were a few BBC productions, beginning with *The Man Who Went to War*, a radio ballad-opera. Recorded in New York in 1943, from a text by the Harlem poet Langston Hughes and with the musical help of Alan Lomax, *The Man Who Went to War* was the story of an African American family in a war-torn city in England. It featured Paul Robeson, Sonny Terry, Brownie McGhee, and primarily Josh White and included the song "We're Gonna Move into Germany." The next year Lomax produced *The Martins and the Coys* from a text by his wife Elizabeth. The plot dealt with feuding southern families who came together for the war effort, with Burl Ives, Will Geer, Woody Guthrie, Pete Seeger, and others performing folk songs. Recorded in New York in May 1944, it was aired over the BBC on June 25 and again on August 17, to excellent reviews, promoting the release of a five-disc 78 RPM album. The show was never heard in the United States, however. The Lomaxes followed with another musical program for the BBC, *The Chisholm Trail*, broadcast in early 1945 and also not heard in the United States. Curiously, Guthrie did briefly appear on the BBC in early July 1944 while passing through London on his return to the United States from his duty in the merchant marine. Familiar from his appearance on *The Martins and the Coys*, he performed a few of his railroad songs on *The Children's Hour*.[20]

"In America, late in the Depression and early in the War years, traditional song and its topical imitations were coming into vogue, particularly among young radicals, as a consequence of the stresses of the time, and the rumble of newly-found or newly-made 'people's songs' was rolling towards us across the Atlantic," A. L. Lloyd would write. "The Workers' Music Association, that admirable but over-modest organization, sensed that similar enthusiasm might spread in England, and they were eager to help in the rediscovery of our own lower-class traditions." Formed in 1936, the Workers' Music Association (WMA) published Lloyd's first book, *The Singing Englishman*, in 1942. Another link between the British and American folk scenes was something of a tie to the Left, illustrated through a shared interest in songs of the labor movement and working-class experiences.[21]

Born in 1908 and working as a manual laborer in Australia during his youth, Lloyd returned to England in early 1930 and joined the emerging Communist Party. Basically self-taught and a natural singer, he joined the BBC in 1938 with a radio series, *The Voice of the Seamen*, introducing the audience to traditional folk music. In 1945 Lloyd published *Corn on the Cob: Popular and Traditional Poetry of the U.S.A.* Drawing upon a variety of musical sources, the sections included "The Old Songs from the Mountains," "The Songs of the Shifting Frontier," "Spirituals and Negro Protests," and much more. "Probably no country has such a great range of folksongs as America has nor such a variety of forms," he explained, without having yet visited the country. "The most of them—and this is the great characteristic of American folksongs—are songs of men at work." His brief booklet, published by a company connected with the Communist Party, had limited circulation, but for some it served as an introduction to folk songs from across the Atlantic. In 1947 he gave a lecture on American folk song at the Cecil Sharp House, the home of the traditional English Folk Dance and Song Society. Moreover, beginning in 1942 (until 1954) the BBC program *Country Magazine* presented folk culture through personal stories and folk songs. By decade's end folk music, native and American, had gradually crept into British life, and it was marginally connected with the popularity of square dancing. While Cecil Sharp had carried English Country Dance to the United States early in the century, Douglas and Helen Kennedy, who were active in the English Folk Dance and Song Society, imported American square dancing back to England in 1938. During the war the American military sponsored square dances for the soldiers, with local women as their partners, which continued after 1945 when callers and musicians were brought from the U.S.[22]

Contrary to the situation in the United States, there were no local or regional radio stations in Great Britain and fewer record companies. One exception was Topic Records, an offshoot of the WMA. Beginning in 1939 with Paddy Ryan's recording of "The Man That Waters the Workers Beer," the company continued to produce 78 RPM records until 1949, when long-playing vinyl albums appeared. The titles, which included "Young Comrade's Song" and "Soviet Airman's Song," were a mix of English and foreign songs and dances, with a pro-Soviet, anti-Axis flavor during the war There were a few more singles issued through the late 1940s until the first LP—the Centenary Choir performing "The Internationale" and the WMA Singers recording "England Arise!"—appeared in late 1949. The next year began with the release of "Paul Robeson's Message of Peace."[23]

By the end of the 1940s folk music in the United States and Great Britain had taken similar yet somewhat divergent paths, but they were also interconnected. In the United States, folk music was composed of three different strands—traditional, popular, and left wing—while across the Atlantic the focus was on the traditional and somewhat left wing aspects, with yet little indication of a popular component. Soon, however, all aspects of folk would began to flourish, and the transatlantic gap would narrow. In this regard Alan Lomax would continue to play an important role, having bolstered the careers of Burl Ives, Josh White, Richard Dyer-Bennet, Pete Seeger, Woody Guthrie, Lead Belly, and so many others, while becoming a major figure in the British Isles through the 1950s.

Carl Sandburg

Carl Sandburg had published *The American Songbag* in 1927 and later made some of his own commercial recordings, beginning with a Musicraft album in the late 1930s, *The American Songbag*, followed by the Decca album *Cowboy Songs and Negro Spirituals*. During the 1950s he would issue a series of spoken-word as well as musical albums, including *New Songs from the American Songbag* on the Lyricord label, which was partly drawn from the publication of *New American Songbag*, published by BMI (Broadcast Music, Inc.) in 1950. Sandburg had always included songs in his public poetry readings, and he continued to collect (sometimes obscure) folk songs.

"Here in the U.S.A. a phenomenon of the past generation or two is the tremendous upsurge of ballad and song research," Sandburg explained in the foreword to *New American Songbag*. "Now hundreds of groups from coast to coast, as in no former time in our history, foregather and give out with melody and words of the well-known old timers and with new songs dug up last year or just a week or two ago." Sandburg was well versed in the numerous songbooks published since the 1920s and had done much of his own collecting over the decades. "Into the night clubs and cafes have gone the deliverers of ballads and folk songs," he continued, "Burl Ives, Richard Dyer-Bennett [sic], Susan Reed, the Song Spinners, that notable quartet The Weavers, and other barnstormers. And we mustn't forget the latest arrival, radio's Disc Jockey." Bing Crosby was also induced to write a short note: "American Music lovers owe Carl Sandburg a great debt for the ceaseless research which has rediscovered so much authentic American music for their enjoyment. This here Songbag is just loaded with old goodies." Each song included an informative headnote.[24]

Carl Haverlin, who had become president of BMI in 1947 after a stint as vice president of the Mutual Broadcasting System, strongly encouraged Sandburg with the project. In 1945 Sandburg had moved from the Midwest to Flat Rock, North Carolina, where he continued his prolific writing and decided to update his earlier songbook. "It is our intent to put out a number of books, or folios, under the general title of 'Carl Sandburg's new Americana Song Book,'" Haverlin wrote to Eugene Reynal at Harcourt, Brace & Company in October 1949 with his expansive ideas in order to get the cooperation of Sandburg's first publisher. "We plan, with Mr. Sandburg's assistance, to include from 20 to 30 per cent new material in each of our publications so as to support the qualifications. As I told you, we do not intend to solicit book-store trade, but to concentrate our sales efforts on music stores." Reynal finally replied in early 1950 and pledged his cooperation. Haverlin approached Sandburg at the end of March: "We plan to issue folios, in accordance with the Harcourt, Brace agreement, and we should like approximately 20 per cent of the songs in each folio to be material which is not contained in THE AMERICAN SONGBAG and which is furnished by you, with whatever notes you feel appropriate, and with a preface written by you for each folio." Two weeks later Sandburg replied: "About the first week in June I expect to go to work actively on the New American Songbag. Materials for this have been laid aside and are awaiting the shaping up of manuscripts for BMI. My feeling now is that it will be a very genuine contribution."[25]

Sandburg did indeed take the project seriously and began to assemble songs from various sources, including former publications and his own fieldwork. He had an eclectic approach, with a broad definition of folk music; he even included "New York, O What A Charming City!" found in sheet music from 1831. A brief notice in *Billboard* in June announced: "The poet, renowned as a repository of American folk lore, works at the BMI offices here [New York] with BMI Prexy Carl Haverlin and director of writers relations Bob Sour several hours each day." Crosby submitted his short statement in early July. He had requested to see an advanced copy, which was sent in late November, with this note: "By the way, it may be that in looking over the material you will find something you would like to record and have Burke and Van Heusen publish in 'pop' version. Needless to say, it would please us to afford you first crack at anything you like. So far we have kept the contents of the book *sub rosa* for this purpose." Word had been already circulating, however, since Pete Cameron, the Weavers's manager, had requested recording rights from BMI for "Colorado Trail" and "The John B. Sails." Both had already appeared in *The American Songbag*—about 40 percent of the songs had previously been published there—so Harcourt, Brace referred him to BMI. At one point Haverlin suggested using a quote from Walter Savage Landor as part of an introduction, but it was withdrawn: "We often hear that such a thing 'is not worth an old song.' Alas, how few things are."[26]

New American Songbag appeared in December, and review copies circulated to numerous radio stations. Initially, there were twelve thousand paper copies and one thousand cloth-bound volumes. Those who received free copies were delighted, but retail sales were not great—fewer than five thousand in the first six months, and there was stiff competition from *The American Songbag*, which remained in print. Despite Haverlin's initial plans, no further folios were published, although *New American Songbag* did go through a couple of editions until fading away.[27]

While Sandburg's new book did not make a big splash, he was not alone in keeping up with the gathering interest in folk music. In 1950 Ben Gray Lumpkin, a folk song scholar at the University of Colorado, published the third edition of *Folksongs on Records* (the privately printed first two having come out a few years earlier). Like Sandburg, Lumpkin was most interested in traditional songs. Of the nearly four thousand record titles in his list, Lumpkin admitted that perhaps most of the 78 RPM records were unfortunately no longer available. "Folksongs yield their greatest pleasure to people who sing them or to those who hear good singers in person," he began in his "Comments on Traditional Folksong Records." "But recordings are necessary to demonstrate the amazing variety—the great range in ideas, words, tunes, settings, and singers from all parts of the world. Because of their folk quality, folksongs cannot be authentically sung by singers who are not native to the culture which produced the songs." He then went on to define his terms: "For two hundred years students and collectors of printed versions have used *folk songs* and *folk music* to mean songs in oral circulation as distinguished from art and popular songs. But during the last ten years, some of the makers of phonograph records have abandoned the terms 'Hill Billy' and 'Race Records' and have exploited the popularity of folksongs by classifying as 'folk songs' and 'folk music' popular songs sung in the mountains or country manner. . . . Frequently social protest songs with no traditional status but sung in the folk manner are called folksongs or folk music." The terms were confusing, but Lumpkin attempted in his listings to focus on recordings of traditional songs.[28]

Lumpkin and Sandburg depended on a large pool of folklorists, collectors, performers, and authors who had been promoting folk music for some decades and whose numbers would continue to grow. While many, such as Sandburg, Lumpkin, and their colleagues preferred tunes from venerable sources, there was no hard and fast line separating traditional and commercial songs. Indeed, there would soon be not only amazing success for the latter, but also increasing political pressure in the form of the escalating Red Scare.

2

The Weavers and the Resurgence
of Folk Music, 1950–1953

Peekskill

World War II ended in August 1945 after six years of bloody warfare, the
devastation of much of Europe and Asia, more than fifty million deaths and
injuries, with millions of civilians displaced and homeless. The Soviet Union
alone lost twenty-four million of its citizens. The United States, on the other
hand, emerged relatively physically unscathed, with roughly four hundred
thousand military deaths, and perhaps twice as many wounded. There was
practically no unemployment and a pent-up thirst for new houses and products. There was great optimism about the future, notwithstanding some lurk-
ing fears about the advent of a nuclear age following the devastation caused
by the two atomic bombs that quickly ended the war in Asia. With salaries
frozen during the war, workers were eager to make up for lost time, and a
rash of labor strikes broke out by year's end, trailing into 1946. There was also
some interest among African American activists and their progressive allies
in bringing home the fight against fascism through promoting a civil rights
agenda, although southern resistance quickly escalated. The labor strikes
and a rising conservative mood, fanned by the right-wing media, led to the
Republican Party's congressional victories in the fall election.[1]

Pete Seeger, Woody Guthrie, and many of their friends returned from war-
time service eager to resume their activist musical and political lives. At the
end of December 1945 a large group met at the home of Pete Seeger's in-laws
in Greenwich Village to organize People's Songs, an organization designed
to promote music with a progressive political agenda. For the next few years
People's Songs chapters throughout the country held concerts and worked

to promote peace, civil rights, labor unions, and a host of other causes. In early 1949, however, facing bankruptcy, People's Songs collapsed, although its offshoot, People's Artists, kept going. Seeger and his friends faced increasing political hostility as the international Cold War, spurred by the emergence of Communist governments throughout eastern Europe linked to the Soviet Union, escalated the internal hunt for anyone with perceived Communist ties, past and present, or even sympathies.

Following the Communist Party's rise to power in Russia in 1917 and the subsequent creation of the Soviet Union, Communist parties sprang up in the United States and Great Britain by the early 1920s. Repression of all radical groups was widespread in the United States following World War I, but less so in England, and it continued into the 1930s, when the Great Depression led many to seek alternatives to capitalism. The U.S. Congress created the House Un-American Activities Committee (HUAC) in 1938 to root out perceived subversives, including Communists and Nazis; HUAC was aligned with J. Edgar Hoover's Federal Bureau of Investigation (FBI) in these pursuits. Fears of Communism lagged during World War II, while the United States was allied with the Soviet Union, but quickly reappeared by 1947. The fear of spies and other subversives escalated, bolstered by creation of the Attorney General's List of Subversive Organizations in 1947, along with President Harry Truman's loyalty program for federal employees. In late 1950 HUAC was joined in its hunt for alleged subversives by the Senate Internal Security Subcommittee (SISS), initially chaired by Senator Pat McCarran of Nevada, designed to enforce the draconian Internal Security Act of 1950.

An increasing number of groups and individuals were now caught in the expanding anticommunist dragnet. Seeking an easy target, the HUAC held hearings in Hollywood in 1947 to expose perceived Communist influence in the film industry; at the same time three FBI agents organized American Business Consultants, which published *Counterattack*, a magazine designed to expose radicals in radio and television. The Catholic Church, the Chamber of Commerce, various business organizations, veterans groups, conservative newspapers and journalists, the Republican Party (and many Democrats, northern liberals as well as southern conservatives), the AFL as well as numerous CIO unions all hopped on the anticommunist bandwagon. The Communist Party's rise to power in China in 1949 and the Soviet Union's testing of an atomic bomb served to heighten political fears. Moreover, the nine-month federal trial at the Foley Square Courthouse in New York of the Communist Party's eleven top leaders, who were charged with violating the 1940 Smith Act (which made it a crime to advocate overthrowing the government through force and violence) focused attention on their apparent subversive ideas, based on what they read (but not on any overt acts of espionage). All eleven were convicted in October 1949 and given five-year prison sentences (except for a decorated World War II veteran, who got only three years). By the time Wisconsin Senator Joseph McCarthy gave his February 1950 speech warning of Communists in the State Department, the seeds of what would become known as McCarthyism—the heightened fear of internal Communist threats—had long been planted and would flourish through the decade and long after.[2]

One of the first displays of anticommunist physical rage occurred during the summer of 1949 in Peekskill, New York, a mostly blue-collar community located on the Hudson River, although also a summer vacation spot for Jewish workers from New York City. Paul Robeson, the prominent African American singer, actor, and left-wing activist, had previously given three concerts in the area when a fourth was announced for August 27, sponsored by the Harlem Chapter of the Civil Rights Congress and People's Artists. Fueled by right-wing propaganda, a "patriotic" mob prevented the concert from taking place, so another was scheduled for September 4. The second concert, also with Pete Seeger, did take place, but when the crowd was leaving they were attacked by a rock-throwing mob, protected by the police, with many injured. "So our concert went smoothly enough, and with all the difficulties there was good music there that day. The great voice of Paul Robeson echoed back from the hills . . . and Pete Seeger and his friends sang those fine old songs of a time when treason and hatred and tyranny were not the most admired virtues of Americans," the writer Howard Fast later commented. While under intense criticism in the United States, Robeson retained his popularity in England, where he had lived for so many years. In May 1950 he appeared at a World Peace Council meeting in London, where he performed for twenty thousand people at an outdoor rally. Soon after, however, the State Department, spurred by Robeson's outspoken criticisms of domestic racism and the Truman administration's hawkish foreign policies, cancelled his passport, which would not be restored until June 1958; a month later he was back in London to revive his singing and acting career, where he was welcomed by members of Parliament.[3]

The Weavers

In many respects the Peekskill riot seemed one low point (among many) in postwar political repression. However, at the same time a group was forming—led by the same Pete Seeger whose car was attacked when leaving Peekskill—that would quickly take the country by storm. In late 1948 Seeger,

no longer on the campaign trail performing with presidential candidate
Henry Wallace, joined with Lee Hays, his old colleague in the Almanac
Singers who sang bass, along with two younger People's Songs performers,
Ronnie Gilbert, a powerful soprano, and Fred Hellerman, a stellar rhythm
guitar player and baritone, in a fledging quartet. The idea was to have a
better-rehearsed group than the Almanacs, so they met in Seeger's Mac-
Dougal Street basement apartment in Greenwich Village each Wednesday
afternoon. They first appeared at a People's Songs Thanksgiving hootenanny
at Irving Plaza. Oscar Brand invited the quartet to perform on his WNYC
radio show, "Folk Song Festival," and they returned to Irving Plaza for a
Christmas Eve hootenanny. They soon adopted the name the Weavers,
suggested by Hellerman and based on a nineteenth-century German play
by Gerhardt Hauptman. They raised funds through a series of Sunday afternoon open houses in the basement of the Albert Hotel, accepting dona-
tions of twenty dollars or so. On March 7 they joined an amazing lineup
for Alan Lomax's lavish concert for People's Songs, "New York, A Musical
Tapestry," including jazz musicians Artie Shaw, Wild Bill Davidson, Pee
Wee Russell, as well as folk performers Harry Belafonte, Oscar Brand, and
Brownie McGhee.[4]

Through much of 1949, with the collapse of People's Songs in March due to
financial problems and the letdown after Henry Wallace's defeat, the Weavers rarely appeared together. While Hays and Seeger kept busy performing,
Gilbert worked in the typing pool of the Columbia Broadcasting System
(CBS), and Hellerman was completing his English degree at Brooklyn College and living with his parents in Queens. Gilbert and Hellerman performed
here and there, however, and were billed as "of the Weavers," while all four
would appear at a concert but be billed separately. "The first performance of
a new song, If I Had a Hammer ['The Hammer Song'], on the theme of the
Foley Square trial of the Communist leaders will be given at the testimonial
dinner for the '12' on Friday night at St. Nicholas Arena," the *Daily Worker*
announced in June. According to Seeger, however, he received the lyrics from
Hays in January and adopted the tune, but it "was simply written as a song
for liberation struggles in general." Laura Duncan, Betty Sanders, and Ernie
Lieberman joined Seeger and Hays in the concert. The Weavers would record
"The Hammer Song" for Boots Casetta's Charter Records in November 1949,
which remained unissued, one of their first recordings, and again for Irwin
Silber and Ernie Lieberman's Hootenanny label in December, which did ap-
pear on a 10" 78 RPM single. Charter released the Weavers' recording of Lee
Hays's "Wasn't That a Time," a powerful song about political repression. The
Weavers also recorded a two-sided single, "The Peekskill Story," along with

songs and narration by Paul Robeson and Howard Fast, for Charter in September, which was quickly advertised in the *Daily Worker* to spread word of that debacle. During the fall the Weavers appeared at a series of concerts at the Panel Room and the Penthouse on Astor Place. At year's end they joined others for a "Peace on Earth" hootenanny at Webster Hall, followed in January 1950 with the "We're on Our Way" hootenanny at the Penthouse.[5]

Having performed mostly for left-wing audiences through 1949, at year's end the Weavers opened at Max Gordon's Village Vanguard, a trendy nightspot that primarily featured jazz musicians, although both Lead Belly and Josh White had performed there in 1941. "In December '49 four of us, the Weavers, were about to go our separate ways. We wanted to sing for working folks, for the left-wing types. But McCarthyism [a term not yet in vogue] was coming in. We had no offers of jobs from unions," Seeger would later explain. "As a last resort (fate worse than death) we took a job at a tiny Greenwich Village nightclub the Village Vanguard. . . . For me the Village Vanguard was an education. Into it came a wider range of folks than I'd expected." The Weavers were initially paid two hundred dollars a week plus free hamburgers, but after Gordon discovered a hungry Pete using a half of a pound of meat, he revised the contract to stipulate two hundred and fifty a week, but no food. The *Daily Worker* soon announced "A THEATRE PARTY for civil rights. Presenting the Village Vanguard's new sensation 'The Weavers'" in late January. At the same, time they joined with Woody Guthrie, as well as folk and jazz stars, for a memorial concert organized by Alan Lomax at Town Hall in memory of Lead Belly, who had died in December. For a time the group continued with their political appearances, such as the "Walk Along Together" hootenanny in February, with Sonny Terry and Brownie McGhee for a tribute to Negro History Week at Irving Plaza, and the "Shoulder to Shoulder" concert to raise funds for a lawsuit against the Westchester County police for the "Peekskill victims" in March, joining with Paul Robeson. In April they appeared with the actress Judy Holliday, burlesque star Gypsy Rose Lee, and others at a performance at the Hotel Capitol to raise funds for the People's Drama Theatre. In early May they appeared at the Panel Room—"a rare concert appearance," the *Daily Worker* noted, as part of the series "Folksongs at 8."[6]

The Weavers' political involvements would fade as their fame spread, although Seeger would not completely curtail his musical commitments. Their commercial break came soon enough, as their Vanguard appearances began attracting larger crowds during their six-month stay. As early as January 4, Gordon Allison's column in the *Herald Tribune* broke the story: "While the Weavers avoid professional mannerism like the plague, there is something

beguiling about the simplicity with which they do things. . . . Their music is melodious and unspoiled and it emerges with a kind of spontaneity
that tears the place down." The following week Robert Dana's column in the
World-Telegram continued the praise: "The art of minstrelsy, deep rooted in
America customs and manners, continues to find a willing patron in Max
Gordon of the Village Vanguard. With the presentation of The Weavers, a
bizarre group of singers whose repertory includes blues ballads, hoe-downs,
folk tunes, work songs, prison songs and originals, he adds to the distinction
of his Greenwich Village basement club." Moreover, "Unlike most nightclub
acts, The Weavers have no set routine. There's no telling what songs they may
pick from their extensive portfolio. . . . 'Midnight Special' was one of Lead
Belly's most powerful songs. The Weavers do it in a rousing manner, with
plaintive undertones."[7]

As commercial success beckoned, the group obtained a manager and a
record company. Harold Leventhal, a song plugger for Irving Berlin in the
1930s, heard the Weavers at the Village Vanguard and immediately loved
both their music and their left-wing politics. His interest was shared by Pete
Kameron, who knew the record business and had contacts with radio disc
jockeys. He also had a connection with Howie Richmond and Al Brackman,
who owned TRO/Folkways Music, which would become the Weavers' publishing company, with Kameron getting his cut of any Weavers' publishing
royalties, which were soon hefty—any songs with no known author or with
the lyrics altered were attributed to "Paul Campbell." One night in April
Gordon Jenkins, the bandleader who worked for Decca Records, wandered
into the Village Vanguard and was smitten, becoming a regular, although
folk music was radically different from his standard pop fair.

Jenkins had developed a formula that proved very popular, working with
Decca's A&R (artist and repertoire) chief Milt Gabler. In the early 1950s the
creative Jenkins had three top-ten recordings, "I Wanna Be Loved," "Be-
witched," and "My Foolish Heart," with lush arrangements that were quite
foreign to the Weavers' acoustic instruments, folksy sound, and approach.
Jenkins also worked with Louis Armstrong, Peggy Lee, and a host of other
pop favorites. Other musical stars of the time included Bing Crosby, Doris
Day, Guy Mitchell, Teresa Brewer, Les Paul and Mary Ford, Ella Fitzgerald,
the Four Aces, Hank Williams, and Johnny Ray—essentially vocal stylists,
dance bands, and novelty numbers. There were a few folk-style recordings,
such as Jo Stafford's 1950 album *American Folk Songs* and Patti Page's "Mister
and Mississippi," but not many. In this mix the Weavers would definitely be an
oddity, which is why Decca head Dave Kapp walked out of their first audition,
muttering, "Oh, I know these people, they're not commercial." But Jenkins

persisted. Indeed, Kapp had hired Alan Lomax in late 1945 as the editor of Decca's Folk Music Series, which released albums by Josh White, Richard Dyer-Bennet, Burl Ives, Carl Sandburg, and many more for a couple of years, and even produced reissues of the Almanac Singers's *Sod Buster Ballads* and *Deep Sea Chanteys and Whaling Ballads*. There were also three albums of square dance music. Decca had soon abandoned the series, however, preferring to stick with the top-selling Bing Crosby and the Mills Brothers, as well as Sister Rosetta Tharpe and Louis Jordon. But in June Lomax brought Sandburg to the Village Vanguard to hear the group, and Sandburg "made a speech of praise from the floor for the folk-singing Weavers."[8]

Kapp held out for a while but agreed to hire the Weavers after Kameron approached the band leader Mitch Miller about signing them for Columbia Records. Their first Decca recording was in early May, an acoustic single, "Around the World" / "Tzena, Tzena, Tzena" (in Hebrew), followed a few weeks later by "Tzena, Tzena, Tzena" (in English) / "Goodnight Irene" backed by the Gordon Jenkins Orchestra. Amazingly, the English version of the Israeli dance tune "Tzena, Tzena, Tzena" shot up the pop charts in early summer, peaking at number 2 in July. Cover versions by Mitch Miller (Columbia), Vic Damon (Mercury), and Ralph Flanagan (RCA) quickly followed. Next, "Goodnight, Irene" skyrocketed to number 1 in midsummer. "In the never-ending race to dig out a new sparkle from the music hills, Decca just struck what looks like pay dirt," Bernie Asbell, one of the founders of People's Songs and an old friend of the group, explained in his music column in *Spin*, titled "Folk Songs Do It Again: Weavers Hit First Try": "Ear-catcher of The Weaver's [*sic*] fresh sound is the insistent tinkle of Pete Seeger's five-string banjo. It's the big-time debut for this strange instrument as well as for the gangling young man who plays it."[9]

Lead Belly, who composed "Goodnight Irene," had died less than a year earlier, but on August 14 *Time* ran a photo of him along with a column on the Weavers' hit: "Last week the old minstrel's old song, prettied up and cut in half, was in fifth place on the hit parade. A quartet called the Weavers, recording (for Decca) with Gordon Jenkins band, had used it as a filler to back *Tzena, Tzena*." Indeed, as *Time* pointed out, Lead Belly's closing verse "An' ef Irene turns her back on me, / I'm gonna take morphine an' die" was deleted. For Gilbert Millstein in the *New York Times*, "The most overpowering phenomenon in the music business these days is a lorn, whining ballad about a marriage gone sour, set in waltz tempo and called 'Goodnight, Irene.' . . . In one recent month 'Goodnight, Irene' was heard about 100,000 times over radio and TV, according to Broadcast Music, Inc., which monitored it. . . . Some people in the trade believe that no other song ever sold so fast in so short a time." It topped the pop charts for thirteen weeks, a record which held for over two decades. Cover versions quickly appeared by Frank Sinatra (Columbia, 175,000 sold, his most popular record for a few years), Dennis Day (Victor), the Alexander Brothers (Mercury), Jo Stafford (Capitol, which reached number 9 on the charts in September), and Red Foley (with Ernest Tubb and the Sunshine Trio, Decca). In early January Stafford had released her Capitol album *American Folk Songs*, which included the folk chestnuts "Shenandoah," "Old Joe Clark," "Barbara Allen," and "Cripple Creek" (but not "Goodnight, Irene").[10]

"Professional folk singing in the U.S. is mostly the province of a few long-haired purists who rarely get a hearing outside the clubs and recital halls where their small but fervent public gathers," *Time* explained in its breathless style in late September. "Last week a group of four high-spirited folksters known as the Weavers had succeeded in shouting, twanging and crooning folk singing out of its cloistered corner into the commercial big time." The article continued: "Last week, with 'Irene' standing first, both sides of the record were on the hit parade for the eleventh time. Sales had boomed to more than a million and a quarter. The Weavers had moved to Manhattan's Blue Angel nightclub, before the end of the month were scheduled to double into Broadway's Strand Theater for a total of $2,250 a week." They cut their next hit in October, "Lonesome Traveler" / "So Long (It's Been Good to Know You)," again backed by Gordon Jenkins Orchestra. Soon thereafter they entered Decca's studio in New York with the Larry Holmes Orchestra to record "The Wreck of the John B.," "Midnight Special"(another Lead Belly tune), "The Roving Kind," "Follow the Drinking Gourd," and four other songs. Both "The Roving Kind" and "So Long (It's Been Good to Know You)" did well, particularly the latter, which reached number 4 on the charts. Guy Mitchell also scored a hit in late 1950 with "The Roving Kind," the same time that the Weavers' version was popular.[11]

Besides the big-band backup on many of their recordings—but never when appearing in public—some of the songs, such as "Goodnight, Irene" and "So Long (It's Been to Know You)," had their lyrics smoothed out. Indeed, Kameron had asked Guthrie to rewrite "So Long (It's Been Good to Know You)," for which he received an advance of ten thousand dollars against royalties, a princely sum that went to Guthrie's six children, with his wife Marjorie as his business manager. According to Harold Leventhal, "Woody was at the recording studio in New York when the Weavers recorded his song. He stretched out on the floor and wrote new verses for the song on paper bags. . . . When Woody was in New York and not drifting out on the road, he would follow the Weavers wherever they performed." Guthrie appeared to approve of Decca's slick presentation of his song, as he informed Moe Asch at Folkways Records in October 1950: "I ran down via rollerwheels of all kinds and caught Pete Kameron over in the Decca Building helping the Weavers & Gordy Jenkins to record my very own 'So Long,' and a backside for it by the name of 'Lonesome Traveler.' All well done by a twenty piece choral chorus and a thirty piece orchestra of Jenkins's." Still, he applauded Asch for "putting out the stuff and the real life kind of stuff that is ten to one the best kind of stuff getting put down and spun around on records." Guthrie had the reputation as being unconcerned about money, but to Asch he noted his relief that he and Marjorie had found the original copyright for "So Long." Asch responded, "After all, you made those urgent calls to us here at Folkways, to be sure that we had copyrighted the SO LONG song before PETE KAMERON, the WEAVERS, DECCA, could as you put it 'swipe' it from you. All I did was to protect you."[12]

By early 1951 the Weavers were one of the most popular musical groups in the country. In February they moved from New York to Los Angeles for their next recordings, beginning with "Across the Wide Missouri" / "On Top of Old Smoky," with Vic Schoen leading a backup group that included Terry Gilkyson. The latter landed on the charts in April, reached number 2 for two months, and remained for a total of twenty-three weeks. Having employed Joe Glaser's powerful Associated Booking Corp, they were now appearing at the country's most lavish nightclubs, including Ciro's in Hollywood. "Ciro's had its most exciting night of the season with the L.A. debut of the Weavers this week," Paul Coates noted in the local press. "They're a brilliant vocal quartette. And they've renewed my faith in folk singers (which ebbed after I learned that Burl Ives has had annuities tucked in his brogans and a swimming pool in his backyard)." For the trade journal *Variety* the "Weavers pound over a half-hour of folksy balladeering that is infectious, succeeding in getting the audience to join in on familiar stuff." After Ciro's they appeared at the ultra-plush Shamrock Hotel in Houston, Texas. "There was plenty of shoutin' and singin' down in the Shamrock Tabernacle last night," according to a folksy article in the *Houston Press*. "The brethern and sistern listened to the word in song. The Weavers—three men and a gal—opened a two-week revival in the Emerald Room, and before it's over they'll have a lot of the local sinners hitting the trail." They next moved to the Minnesota Terrace at the Hotel Nicollet in Minneapolis, then to the Empire Room of the Palmer House in Chicago. In May they managed to squeeze in a series of recording sessions with Milt Gabler in New York, with little orchestra backing.[13]

During the Weavers' appearance at the fancy Shamrock Hotel, where they dressed in evening attire, Pete and Toshi Seeger, along with Fred Hellerman, took a side trip to the Ramsey and Retrieve (Texas) State Farms in February 1951 to record African American prisoners. "Worksongs are basically a participative art form, rather than a performance form, such as narrative ballads," Pete wrote in the liner notes to the album *Negro Prison Camp Work Songs*, released by Folkways Records in 1956, drawn from their field recordings: "Today, in mechanized North America one can only rarely hear such music. Certain scattered ethnic groups, such as the Gaelic-speaking Cape Breton Islander of eastern Canada, still preserve some worksongs. But among the Negro people of southern United States there is still a relatively strong tradition of worksong. . . . In the Negro prisons of the south, where older prisoners pass on songs to younger men, some of the oldest and most traditional are still sung." John and Alan Lomax had done extensive recording of traditional songs among southern black prisoners in the 1930s, and Pete Seeger (as well as other folklorists) continued to follow in their footsteps. Despite the Weavers' stunning commercial success, Seeger and Hellerman could not abandon their commitment to grassroots music.[14]

During August 1951 the Weavers appeared at Café Society Downtown in New York for a month, before another national tour. According to a piece in *Newsweek*, "The folk-singing quartet can now look back at a career as brief as it has been spectacular." "The Weavers are still starry-eyed with their sudden rise to fame but they all agree that their most thrilling moments are when an audience will spontaneously join them, singing both words and melody," *The Compass* noted in its glowing article. The Weavers attracted positive notices for the most part, but there were stirrings of political problems that would soon emerge full blown. The four members were certainly aware of anticommunist hostilities, having been political activists during the 1940s, but for a brief time their commercial success might have seemed to counter such fears. The euphoria did not last long.[15]

The three ex-FBI agents who had launched *Counterattack*—John C. Keenan, Kenneth M. Bierly, and Theodore C. Kirkpatrick—were joined by the radio writer and former naval intelligence officer Vincent Harnett in publishing *Red Channels: The Report of Communist Influence in Radio and Television* in June 1950, a widely distributed book with a listing of 151 suspected subversives. According to the introduction, "In indoctrinating the masses of the people with Communist ideology and the pro-Soviet interpretation of current events, the Communist Party, with set purpose, uses not only Party members, but also fellow-travelers and members of Communist adjuncts and periphery organizations." The list included many with folk music connections, including Pete Seeger, Oscar Brand, Richard Dyer-Bennet, Tom Glazer, Burl Ives, Earl Robinson, Millard Lampell, Alan Lomax, and Josh

White. The editors did admit, however, "It must be remembered that the Red Fascists and their sympathizers, for all their numbers and influence, are still in the minority." Indeed, party membership had dwindled to perhaps a few thousand, but they were still to be feared because of their past organizational activities.[16]

Drawing upon extensive files of left-wing publications, secret FBI records, and much other information, *Counterattack* launched its attack in its June 9, 1950, issue: "This folk-singing quartet . . . is well known in Communist circles. The folk songs they sang for 'Broadway Open House' [NBC-TV] are not the 'folk songs' they sing for the subversive groups they frequently entertain. On such occasions they usually sing fighting songs of the Lincoln Brigade (which fought for Stalin in the Spanish Civil War) and other Communist song favorites." This initial attack led to Van Camp Beans canceling a Weavers summer TV show. Pete Kameron rushed to *Counterattack*'s office to complain, as the newsletter noted in late September: "He explained that he didn't know anything about Communism, or much about the Weavers' past. Since some facts had been brought to his attention, he had spoken to the 'boys' about the problem and felt that they were just gullible and well-meaning. He said that he would try to persuade them to cease their pro-Communist activity as individuals and, as their manager, would refuse engagements for any Communist front groups." *Counterattack*'s editor assured Kameron that the newsletter was "eager to cooperate and help people break with the Communist Party and its fronts." The next paragraph, however, mentioned the Weavers' appearance on the Art Ford show on WPIX in New York City, and that Seeger, a member of the "Communist entertainment front" People's Artists, performed the peace song "Old Man Atom" at a National Council of the Arts meeting. So much for cooperation. On his part, Kameron ordered the group not to perform at political events, including the funeral of Communist Party stalwart Mother Bloor, and not to commercially record "The Hammer Song."[17]

The *Counterattack* and *Red Channels* charges did not initially derail the Weavers' popularity; they continued on track through 1951, but others were not so fortunate. "In the past week, two incidents [the firing of Jean Muir from the "Aldrich Family" TV show and the political troubles of Josh White] occurred which have clearly demonstrated the effectiveness of *Counterattack*, the anti-Communist newsletter, on the destinies of showbiz personalities who have become involved in the Commie issue," *Billboard* explained in early September 1950. Numerous issues of the show business weekly documented the mounting hysteria, various attempts to fight back, and the weakening spine of the show business establishment. Jerry Wexler, a music writer for *Billboard* and close friend of Howie Richmond, would recall his editor asking him in 1951 "to get a dossier on a folk group called the Weavers." "The dark days of Joe McCarthy and blacklisting were upon us," he said, "and I wasn't about to do that kind of dirty work. I refused." He soon moved to Atlantic Records.[18]

Decca issued the Weavers' records through 1951, with Milt Gabler continuing as their producer. In May, without a backing orchestra, they recorded "The Frozen Logger," "Follow the Drinking Gourd," "Darling Corey," and "Easy Rider Blues," soon followed by "When the Saints Go Marching In" / "Kisses Sweeter Than Wine" (with the Lew Diamond Orchestra), which charted for a few weeks. They soon recorded eight holiday songs, which would appear on their 10" LP *We Wish You a Merry Christmas*. Their other Decca album, *Folk Songs of America and Other Lands*, explained their dedication: "When they sing folk songs, The Weavers know what they are singing about. They have sung and lived with folk songs for many years and they share a combined knowledge which gives them authority in their field. Their repertory of songs has never been counted; they claim to sing more kinds of music than any other singing group." In late October, again backed by the Gordon Jenkins Orchestra, they did "Old Paint" and "Wimoweh." The latter climbed to number 14 on the charts, starting in February 1952, where it remained for fourteen weeks and would become one of their most influential songs.[19]

While their popularity held through 1951 and into 1952, the reactions in the press were decidedly mixed, with ongoing political repercussions. Frederick Woltman, in his red-baiting column in the *New-York World Telegram*, kept up the attack. "From 'People's Artist' for the Communist party to a smash commercial success in television, the record industry and swank night clubs throughout the country may seem like an insuperable jump. Especially when accomplished in almost no time flat," he wrote, with much disgust, in late August 1951. "Not so for Pete Seeger, founder, director and member of the Weavers, that folk-singing quartette which has practically revolutionized music publishing by popularizing such hits as 'Good Night Irene,' 'Sweet Violets' and 'On Top of Old Smoky.' Pete has a long record of singing for the revolution—the Communist revolution, that is." During the summer the Dave Garroway TV show canceled their appearance, the FBI stepped up its surveillance, and Pat McCarren's Senate Internal Security Subcommittee, believing the Weavers' rendition of "Rock Island Line" had a "red taint," launched its own investigation of possible subversive activities. The Weavers' shows with Horace Heidt's band at the Ohio State Fair were canceled "because of complaints charging that they had performed for left-wing organizations," based on *Counterattack*'s allegations. In response, according to *Variety*, "Members of the group say they are primarily interested in songs and singing and not in politics." On the other hand, Bill Coss had a glowing review in *Metronome*, the music publication: "Their repertoire of over 700 songs from Indonesian ballads, to African chants, Tennessee hoedowns, Israeli horas, and Negro blues will seldom, I fear, be dented by recordings. But this is a magnificent group whose ideas and purpose far exceed a first glance." While the Weavers did abandon their overt political commitments, in their choosing music from around the world they demonstrated their search for world peace and understanding, deftly countering Cold War xenophobia. Their international repertoire would serve, in a muted way, to represent their left wing politics, as it would for a variety of other folk performers by mid-decade.[20]

"Folk music has taken over the juke boxes this season and has completely disrupted the entire popular music publishing and recording field," Virginia Wicks explained in her *Compass* review of the Weavers in August 1951. Folk music didn't quite usurp the field, since there was much else to listen to that summer and fall, such as Les Paul and Mary Ford's "How High the Moon," Perry Como's "If," Patti Page's country-influenced "The Tennessee Waltz," Frankie Laine's powerful "Jezebel," and Bing Crosby's "In the Cool, Cool, Cool of the Evening." Since a commercial youth culture was just emerging, most pop tunes would appeal to various ages, as did the Weavers' recordings, although their public appearances were pretty much limited to nightclubs with an adult audience. The same was true in 1952: hits from the year included Johnnie Ray's emotional "Cry," Kay Starr's "Wheel of Fortune," the Mills Brothers' "Glow Worm," Frankie Laine's "High Noon," and Jimmy Boyd's novelty "I Saw Mommy Kissing Santa Claus."[21]

The Weavers kept going into 1952, while facing increasing hostility. "A GLUM DELEGATION of American Legion officials sat in an Akron night club Monday night while the Weavers sang 'On Top of Old Smoky' despite Legion effort to stop the show [at the Yankee Inn]," according to the *Akron Beacon Journal* in early February. "THE FOLK-SINGING Weavers— three men and a girl—are riding the crest of a popularity wave that has sold 5,000,000 of their recordings and brought appearance from Ciro's in Los Angeles to the Blue Angel in New York." The article also mentioned that the "group caused a small furor in Cleveland Saturday night when some public officials declined to appear with them on a Heart Society TV benefit show after pressure from Knights of Columbus and American Legion officials." That same week the *York* [Pennsylvania] *Journal-American* regaled its readers with the article "Singers at Cafe Here Called Reds by Tipster in Ohio; They Deny It": "A folk-song quartet known as the Weavers, now appearing in

Philadelphia, is composed of three Communists and a former Communist, a tipster charged yesterday. Harvey M. Matusow, who was associated with the Communist Party as an undercover agent, testified to that effect before the Ohio Un-American Activities Commission which is investigating subversive activities in Ohio."[22]

Harvey Matusow did not launch the attack on the Weavers—far from it— but he had a knack for grabbing headlines and scaring the public, thereby fanning the anticommunist flames. His origins were modest enough. Born in 1926 to a middle-class Bronx, New York, Jewish family, he joined the Army in 1944 and served in Europe. Retuning home and with little to do, he joined the Communist Party and soon found a congenial political home. By decade's end he was working for People's Songs and Henry Wallace's 1948 presidential campaign, and he fancied himself a budding actor. For a variety of reasons, in March 1950, soon after Senator McCarthy's Wheeling, West Virginia, inflammatory speech, Matusow contacted the FBI and volunteered to be an informant. He supplied names and other information to the FBI until the Communist Party kicked him out. No longer undercover, he began testifying before HUAC in November 1951, launching a public career that would take him to the heights of the anticommunist movement for a few years. On February 6 and 7, 1952, he testified in public before HUAC's hearings on *Communist Activities among Youth Groups*, based on his supposed expertise, then for the Ohio Un-American Activities Commission, and in March before the SISS's hearings titled *Communist Tactics in Controlling Youth Organizations*. He began to name the Weavers, whom he had known in People's Songs, first before HUAC and then in Ohio. The group's popularity "was used to attract many young people to the movement because they respected the Weavers and thought they were good singers and entertainers," Matusow claimed. "The bobbysoxers go for that. Once the young people were at the affair, the Communist Party organizer took over. He had a good chance to recruit many of the young people." When asked by the Ohio interrogators, "You are not testifying, or want to give the impression that there is anything subversive or un-American about folk singing or square dancing," he readily agreed. Matusow would go on to work for Senator McCarthy and remain in the center of the anticommunist crusade until 1955, when he recanted all of his testimony and wound up going to prison on a perjury charge. While he would long be blamed for leading to the Weavers' blacklisting, he was only one aspect of their demise.[23]

While Matusow was testifying and some of the Weavers' shows were being cancelled, the group continued to record for Decca. In February they were joined by Gordon Jenkins Orchestra for "The Gandy Dancer's Ball" and

"Around the Corner (Beneath the Berry Tree)." "Wimoweh" hit the charts in February and remained for eleven weeks; "Around the Corner" followed for one week in April, "Midnight Special" for another week in September. In May the quartet waxed Woody Guthrie's "Hard, Ain't It Hard" and followed in September with "Bay of Mexico," "True Love," "Clementine," and "Down In the Valley." Their final session in February 1953, backed by the Larry Clinton Orchestra in New York, produced "Rock Island Line," "Benoni," Guthrie's "Taking It Easy," and Lead Belly's "Sylvie," which would finally make the charts for two weeks in January 1954. Their final concert was a sold out affair at Town Hall in December 1952, although their Decca contract ran until July 30, 1953. All the while they were shadowed by the FBI and its informants. Pete summed up what happened next: "Ronnie decided to have a baby and she and her husband did have a baby. Fred thought he'd try doing some arranging and songwriting, Lee went to writing short stories, and I took off singing by myself." Actually, Pete got a part-time teaching job in New York City while issuing a stream of albums for Folkways; the family continued to work on their house in Beacon, up the Hudson from the city. Pete also launched his tour of college campuses, beginning with Oberlin in Ohio in early 1954, where he returned each year for increasing fees, soon amounting to $1,000. "Actually, this is probably the most important job I ever did in my life," he would recall years later. "Before that only John Jacob Niles had tried to sing college concerts and he'd dress up in a tuxedo, and things were very formal. I made things as informal as I could and went from one college to another and made a good living out of it." As for Decca, despite the Weavers' amazing popularity, their records were soon deleted from the catalog. They would soon be back, however, with their delightful, infectious sound, a mix of extraordinary voices and musical abilities, along with an ethnically and racially mixed repertoire that would become most influential.[24]

Lomax in England

When the Weavers' career skyrocketed, their patron and friend Alan Lomax, also listed in *Red Channels*, had decided to move to England. In late January 1950 he organized the memorial concert for Lead Belly, then published *Mister Jelly Roll: The Fortunes of Jelly Roll Morton, New Orleans Creole and 'Inventor of Jazz,'* based on his extensive interviews in 1938. Later in the summer he met with Goddard Lieberson, president of Columbia Records, and persuaded him to issue in the new LP format a series of albums of the world's music, to be known as the *Columbia World Library of Folk and Primitive Music*, produced by Lomax. Moreover, increasingly worried by the new McCarran Act in the

Senate, which required the registration and fingerprinting of all suspected subversives, he took off for Europe on September 24 and landed in Belgium. "My sudden departure for Europe apparently left a very bad impression," he confided to the actress and singer Robin Roberts. "It was foolish, but I was afraid that the MacCarran [*sic*] act would keep me from seeing you again and from traveling round the world the way I'd always wanted to. But I don't feel like coming home until my World Library really gets into publication."[25]

He quickly traveled to Rome and then to Paris, accompanied by Robin Roberts. In December 1950 they moved to London, which would remain his base for much of the decade. "Perhaps you have heard this or that about my departure [from the United States]," he quickly wrote to friends. "Fact is, I just couldn't stand the possibility of being cut off from Robin by the worsening political atmosphere." His reasons were certainly more complex, while his future remained unclear: "I'm buying a car . . . and I'm going to see as much of the world as I can. London before Xmas, Scotland for New Year, Ireland for 2 weeks—then South for a long time—Africa, Egypt—. Then home to starve." Lomax immediately connected with Douglas Kennedy at Cecil Sharp House, the home for the English Folk Dance and Song Society (EFDSS), formed early in the century, the bastion of traditional songs. He also met with Geoffrey Bridson and others at Broadcasting House, the BBC's headquarters (he had worked with Bridson in New York during the war). "Robin & I just saw *Bartholomew Fair* at the Old Vic," he soon wrote. "We are going on BBC together & then go to Ireland to record folk songs & fairy tales." Although he had come to collect vernacular music throughout Great Britain (and on the Continent), his connections with the BBC quickly landed him a radio program, *Adventure in Folksong*.[26]

In England Lomax initiated an energetic broadcasting, collecting, performing, and traveling career. Coming from an affluent country, unscathed (indeed energized) by the recent war, he arrived in a London, where, as recalled by the historian Tony Judt, "everything was in short supply. . . . Clothes were rationed until 1949, cheap and simple 'utility furniture' until 1952, food until 1954. The rules were briefly suspended for the coronation of Elizabeth, in June 1953: everyone was allowed one extra pound of sugar and four ounces of margarine. But this exercise in supererogatory generosity served only to underscore the dreary regime of daily life." As for the folk music scene, it held some promise. The EFDSS remained active, along with the Communist Party's continuing interest through the Workers' Music Association (WMA), formed in the 1930s, and its Topic Records label. American performers and songs garnered much popularity, such as Perry Como, Guy Mitchell, Doris

Day, Frank Sinatra, and Frankie Laine, with Burl Ives scoring in 1949 with the folk-style "Big Rock Candy Mountain." The BBC had earlier blacklisted Bert Lloyd because of his Communist affiliations but allowed him to present hymns from the Sacred Harp Singing Convention in Alabama, and he worked his way into numerous other programs by the mid-1950s.[27]

Lomax obtained a temporary work permit based on his arrangement with the BBC, but soon enough the Special Branch, a unit of London's Metropolitan Police in charge of national security, began inquiring about his status, prodded into action by the ever-vigilant American embassy. "It appears from the papers that he was brought to this country on Ministry of Labour Permit to take part in several programmes based on his specialised knowledge of international folk music and songs," N. E. Wadsley of the BBC informed Miss N. Dabell in late December 1951. "He has not been on the staff but has been given a separate contract for each programme of which there have been about twelve." Dabell quickly responded: "LOMAX has recently been in touch with the Hungarian Press Attache in the United Kingdom. In view of LOMAX's interest in international folk dancing, however, this may have no sinister significance, but I thought you would like to have this information for record purposes." Soon after, in March 1952, J. Philip O'Brien, administrative legal attaché of the American embassy, reported that Elizabeth Harold (Lomax), who had divorced Alan Lomax in January 1950, was traveling to London with their daughter Anna to meet him: "Information has been received to the effect that Alan LOMAX may be a member of the Communist Party." During his time in England he was continually shadowed and reported on by both U.S. and British officials, his comings and goings to Europe especially noted, even his mail inspected. A Special Branch report from August 1953 is particularly revealing: "LOMAX is a single man and from the nature of some of the programmes of folk song which he has chosen to broadcast as representative of America there is no doubt that he has been interested in current as well as historical extremist groups in various parts of the U.S., at least in so far as is shown by their particular brand of folk music. While his political opinions are not clear, there would appear to be some sympathy towards the 'extreme left wing' generally in his choice of material."[28]

Lomax eagerly plunged into his BBC show, *Adventure in Folksong*, with four broadcasts beginning on February 13, 1951, and continuing in late May. Drawing from his Library of Congress collections, he and Roberts mixed traditional English, Scottish, and Irish ballads with American (mostly African American) folk songs. For example, Roberts performed "Who Killed Cock Robin," "Molly Bawn," and "Matty Groves," while Lomax put on "Sam

Bass," "Pretty Polly," "Po' Lazarus," and "Take This Hammer." Lomax, always the educator, was particularly interested in introducing a British audience to mostly unfamiliar American folk songs. As an example of his style and thinking, he discussed "On Top of Old Smokey" this way: "By now most of you must have heard this American folk song, recently twisted into a popular song hit, a few too many times. But still there may be some of you who wonder if there is any such thing as American folk music. . . . Yes, there is an American folk song in precisely the same sense as there is an English or a French folk song—only Americans have more varieties than most countries." He not only spread his love for American ballads and folk songs, but also made an intellectual argument that they were as legitimate for scholarly study as British ballads, which he also cherished. For example, he introduced "Who Killed Cock Robin": "This California version of the old English rhyme suitably introduces the subject of this second recital of American ballads . . . the bad man ballads. I suppose if there is any taste that links the British Isles with the United States it is our fondness for tales, novels, films, radio programmes and folk ballads dealing with mayhem and bloody murder."[29]

The *London Times* correspondent was intrigued by Lomax's radio programs, but somewhat less than enthusiastic:

> Most of our popular music is based ultimately on American folk songs, many of them Negro songs, and when we hear the originals we often find we like them better than the commercialised versions Tin Pan Alley turns out. The chief source of genuine American songs is the Lomax collection in Washington, and veteran listeners like me remember with pleasure the series of broadcasts of them that Alistair Cooke gave before the war. Now we have Alan Lomax here in person, giving us gems from his discoveries on Tuesdays in the Home Service. I found his first broadcast disappointing. His dialogue with his girl singer, Robin Roberts, was as wooden as the worst in "In Town Tonight," and used as we are to American accents on our air, his Texan seemed to me very hard to understand.

Yet despite Lomax's failings as a singer, the *Times* reviewer concluded, "This week's installment conquered me. The mixed white-and-Negro songs of the chain gangs, steel gangs, and dynamite gangs did something to the singers, and Robin Roberts sang the blues like one inspired."[30]

Lomax's next BBC series, *The Art of the Negro*, which aired in October and November 1951, was strictly concerned with American music, with programs entitled "Mr. Jelly Roll [Morton] from New Orleans," "Trumpets of the Lord," and "Blues in the Mississippi Night." He drew upon his original recordings of Jelly Roll Morton, Vera Hall, Big Bill Broonzy, as well as the African American performers Robert Johnson, Sleepy John Estes, and Muddy Waters (although a recording of Woody Guthrie singing "Talking Columbia Blues" appeared during "Blues in the Mississippi Night"). This was among the last of Lomax's radio programs for the next four years that dealt with the Western Hemisphere, since he would subsequently focus on "World Folk Songs," "Spanish Folk Music," and "Folk Music of Italy."

Having burned his broadcasting bridges in the United States, Lomax appreciated the BBC's initial welcoming tolerance. As he later wrote: "In the days before the hostility of the tabloid press and the Conservative Party had combined to denature the BBC's *Third Programme*, it was probably the freest and most influential cultural forum in the Western world. If you had something interesting to say, if the music you had composed or discovered was fresh and original, you got a hearing on the 'Third.' . . . My broadcast audience in Britain was around a million, not large by American buckshot standards, but one really worth talking to."[31]

By the early 1950s Lomax was not alone in introducing a British audience to American folk music and musicians. Josh White arrived in January 1951 to a generally positive reception, toured until April, then returned later in the year. Paul Oliver, the blues scholar, was not particularly impressed, however. "His visit was anticipated with enthusiasm by those who knew his records on the ARC labels, like Melotone and Perfect," Oliver would recall. "He played the Kingsway Hall in London in 1951, but Josh has been playing too long for American urban 'folk club' audiences," and he had lost his authentic touch. Charles Chilton featured White in a series of BBC programs titled *The Glory Road*. His second trip overlapped with the popular appearance of Big Bill Broonzy in the summer of 1951 (he would return to London twice in 1952 and again in 1955, before making his final visit in 1957). As the emcee for Broonzy's first two concerts in Kingsway Hall, Lomax spent some time with his introduction and intimate questioning of the famed bluesman, whom he had met a few years earlier. Oliver complained about Lomax's windy remarks, yet he admitted, "[W]hen Bill stepped in and began to play, the relatively small audience was captivated. . . . I learned a lot from Big Bill; if our collecting and research had enabled us to take the measure of the blues in its diversity and distribution, it was Broonzy who gave an insight of its depth." Burl Ives, the popular performer and actor, and Jean Ritchie, a traditional musician from the South, also arrived in London and soon had their own temporary BBC shows. In late 1952 Ives's "Historical America in Song" was aired, and in 1953 "Jean Ritchie in Kentucky" was heard on the BBC Third

Programme. Ives was in England in 1952, traveled to Australia and New Zealand, then returned in 1953.[32]

Lomax also met Ewan MacColl in early February 1951 at the BBC, igniting a lasting friendship, since they had a musical and political affinity. "He is big, but not gigantic," MacColl later enthused. "The illusion of size is the result of his expansiveness and of the warmth he generates. . . . Everything in his world is big. Words like 'English,' 'French,' 'Italian,' 'American,' don't come readily to his tongue. He sees human beings in anthropological categories, as groups and sub-groups, as representatives of this or that culture or sub-culture, this or that linguistic area. His one conversational lack is small talk." MacColl had much to learn from Lomax: "In the course of the next year or so I spent more and more time listening to Alan's enormous collection of tapes, to songs from the Americas, Africa, India, Italy, Spain and Britain, arguing, discussing, learning and trying to acquire Alan's world-view of this extraordinary corpus of songs and stories." "Alan has amazing energy," he continued. "Everything is done at breakneck speed. No sooner is a task completed than he is hurrying to begin the next one."[33]

Born Jimmy Miller in Lancashire, MacColl (1915–1989) had an active career as an actor and playwright before turning to folk music in the late 1940s. His left-wing political commitments began as a teenager, when he joined the Young Communist League, and he maintained a firm commitment to the Communist Party throughout much of his life. He began to popularize older folk songs, particularly sea shanties and industrial songs, as well as the ballads collected by Francis James Child. His early recordings for Topic, starting in 1950 with "Collier Laddie" / "Johnny Lad," included "Moses of the Mail," "The Ballad of Stalin," and soon the album *Sailors Songs and Shanties* (with Bert Lloyd and Harry Corbett). In 1953, MacColl initiated the BBC radio series *Ballads and Blues*, which "consisted of six half-hour programmes, each dealing with a different theme such as war and peace, love, the sea, railways, work, the city. Each of the programmes featured seven or eight British and American songs about these subjects, sung by American singers Big Bill Broonzy, Jean Ritchie, Ma Rainey and Alan Lomax," MacColl explained. "Bert Lloyd, Isla Cameron and Ewan MacColl sang the British songs. . . . The main objective of the series was to demonstrate that Britain possessed a body of songs that were found in the United States." Mixing both live and recorded performances, the programs resembled in style and substance Lomax's earlier radio shows in the United States. "At that time, the only singers we could really draw upon, that could handle scripted material, were Bert [Lloyd] and myself and Isla Cameron, and that was about it on the English side," MacColl would recall to Fred Woods. "On the American side we brought in Jean Ritchie, Big Bill Broonzy, [Alan] Lomax himself and one or two other American traditional singers who were known and who happened to be in England or Europe at the time." A loose coalition of performers, also under the name "Ballads and Blues," soon emerged, including MacColl, Lloyd, and Cameron, which raised funds for the *Daily Worker*. In December 1953, Lomax shared the stage with MacColl, Lloyd, and others as part of the Ballads and Blues "Songs of the Iron Road" program at St. Pancras Town Hall.[34]

While Lomax became acquainted with Lloyd, MacColl, and their colleagues, he also began his ballad collecting, setting off for Ireland with Robin Roberts in January 1951. Near Dublin he met with Seamus Ennis, the master singer and piper. A few months later Lomax traveled with Jean Ritchie and her husband George Pickow through England; soon after, he conducted his own field trip to Scotland. In March 1952 he moved to Paris for further work on his *World Library of Folk and Primitive Music* and did not return to London until April 1953. Lomax did not remain cut off from contacts in the United States, however. In March 1952, while in Paris, he corresponded with Ruby Pickens Tartt in Alabama, demonstrating his interest in southern field recordings, which would continue after his return to the United States in 1958. A white woman who had worked for the Federal Writers Project during the Depression, Tartt had introduced John Lomax to the African American musicians Dock Reed and Vera Hall in 1937. Later she would assist Harold Courlander in his blues collecting. A folklorist, Courlander had begun his fieldwork in Haiti in the 1930s and connected with Moses Asch soon after World War II, producing a series of ethnic recordings for the Disc label, which soon became the Ethnic Folkways Library. He also turned his attention to southern blues field recordings in the early 1950s and connected with the elderly Ruby Tartt, who introduced him to the guitar player Red Willie (Willie Turner). Some of his Alabama recordings would appear in his Ethnic Folkways series. Tartt complained of some unfortunate treatment from Courlander, however, and Lomax responded from Paris: "I feel responsible for your unpleasant experience with Courlander. I have known him slightly for years and have always believed he was a very sweet and honorable person. What he has done to you is neither one." He encouraged her to write a book and issue recordings from her collections, rather than let others get the credit. "About the records—Folk Ways [Folkways] Company hardly pays expenses," he continued. "It does publish good records. It is the only house that does, and although this is no excuse, its business methods are almost by necessity not what they should be."[35]

Revival Stirrings in the United States

While Lomax and others worked on expanding the interest in folk music in Great Britain and the Weavers' career ground to a halt, there was much else happening in the United States. The *Saturday Review of Literature* certainly had a premature celebration in late 1951: "Back in the days of Federal Works projects, folk singing was a wholesome, inexpensive way for people to entertain themselves and each other. One group of citizens even decided to emulate the old minstrels, traveling about, echoing the workers' plaints, but eventually camped out for long runs in small Greenwich Village night spots. For Pete Seeger, Burl Ives, Cisco Houston, Tom Glazer, Woody Guthrie, and others of this hard core the struggle is over—they have arrived." The piece reviewed albums by the Weavers, Glazer, Houston, Guthrie, and others. The Weavers would eventually collapse, but something was stirring beyond them.[36]

People's Songs had folded in 1949, along with their bulletin, having gone broke, but People's Artists, its booking agency, continued to function, keeping the progressive musical flame alive. People's Artists launched *Sing Out!*, a small monthly magazine in May 1950, with Robert Wolfe as the editor. Contributors included Paul Robeson, Alan Lomax, Earl Robinson, and Pete Seeger. Devoted to "people's music," each issue would "include union songs . . . songs of the Negro people . . . songs of other nations . . . articles of musicological and theoretical interest, articles on organizing choruses, song writing, etc., reviews of records, books, concerts." Irwin Silber would soon emerge as the editor, yet he began as the executive director, having previously served in the same capacity for People's Songs along with his membership in the Communist Party. Silber had little patience with commercial music, as he expressed in a disparate review of his friends the Weavers. "Surely, SING OUT readers need have no illusions that the 'success' of The Weavers signifies a new concern on the part of the entertainment industry monopolies with providing mass outlets for genuine expressions of people's culture," he argued. "Doubtless many people's singers will have more of an opportunity to make a living at their craft as a result of the sudden commercial popularity of the 'folk idiom.' But the achievements here can only be of a limited nature and it would be completely near-sighted to have any illusions on this score." As for the Weavers, they "would have sounded far better in the more vital and vibrant Hootenanny setting than they did in their formal evening attire on the Town Hall stage. But if they are not able to be an integral part of the growing people's cultural movement, which is what I am sure they would prefer, they are still maintaining high standards of performance and artistic integrity in their work."[37]

If the Weavers had strayed from performing the people's music (at least according to Silber), others stepped forward to take their place. People's Artists presented a "One World Hootenanny and Dance" in June 1950, for example, with Pete Seeger, Betty Sanders, and Edith Allaire. In July the "Festival of Song" week at Schroon Crest, organized by Milt Okun at the summer resort in the Adirondacks in Pennsylvania owned by his parents, featured Seeger, Oscar Brand, and the composer Elmer Bernstein. "There were several other camps in the area that catered to progressive people and had live music," Okun would later write. "But we were the first one that really concentrated on folk music. Each summer we had a folk song festival and invited well-known singers—the Weavers, Pete Seeger, Woody Guthrie, Cisco Houston, some lesser-known people. That was the forties—before, during, and after World War II." Although Seeger would began to devote most of his time to the Weavers, others stepped into his place. For example, the "Chicago Bound Hootenanny and Dance" in June 1951 featured members of the People's Artists integrated quartet—Ernie Lieberman, Betty Sanders, and Osborne Smith (the fourth was Laura Duncan). The quartet joined with Earl Robinson, the calypso singer Duke of Iron, and the blacklisted actor Howard DaSilva in a "Freedom Festival," part of the United Electrical, Radio, and Machine Workers of America (UE) convention. The UE had recently been booted out of the CIO for its left-wing politics. Despite the mounting anticommunist scare, People Artists hootenannies continued into 1953. Moreover, Seeger began to reappear at these events, such as the "Hootenanny and Dance" in September 1953. That summer Seeger also organized the Fourth Adirondack Folk Song and Dance Festival at Schroon Crest: "Well known folk artists will again be invited but a significant and exciting new feature will be the presentation of Adirondack residents who are preserving and creating a folk heritage. Mr. Seeger will personally conduct the research for this material and talent."[38]

People's Songs had an active chapter in Los Angeles, which included the newspaper reporter Vern Partlow. On assignment from the *Los Angeles Daily News*, he began covering atomic scientists, which promoted him to write "Old Man Atom" (also known as "Talking Atomic Blues") in late 1945, soon after the final bombings of Japan. Although published in the *People's Songs* bulletin in January 1947, it was not recorded until 1950 by Sam Hinton. A marine biologist at the Scripps Institute in LaJolla, as well as talented folk performer, Hinton first recorded "Old Man Atom" for the small California ABC-Eagle label, but when it received an unexpectedly favorable reception, Columbia Records picked it up for national distribution. A surprising hit, with rave reviews in *Billboard*, *Cash Box*, and other music trade publications, cover versions quickly emerged by the seemingly conservative Sons of the Pioneers for RCA Victor and others.[39]

"Sam Hinton's disking of 'Old Man Atom' ('The Talking Atomic Blues') may zoom into national prominence as the most controversial record of the year," *Movie Stars Parade* announced in August. "Its enthusiastic reception is indicated by its prompt rise to number 2 on the 'Hillbilly Hit Parade,'" noted *Sing Out!* "Old Man Atom" was Hinton's first commercial recording, which he completed at the prompting of the music publisher Irving Bibo. "Four nickels of every five deposited in tavern jukeboxes produce Hinton's dolorous ditty, it is reported," according to the *San Diego Union Leader*, Hinton's local paper. Considering the escalating fear of Communism, heightened by the outbreak of the Korean War in 1950, the song's popularity was surprising, but it also generated a vehement, conservative backlash. When Columbia quickly withdrew the records, *Life* magazine initially opposed the censorship. Although admitting that it "is not in line with the latest military views of the atom bomb's effectiveness," it argued "that's no reason why any private group of censors should be allowed to keep the rest of the U.S. people from buying or refusing to buy a recording of 'Old Man Atom' as they choose." The *Saturday Evening Post* and the *New York Times* also agreed, but this was not enough to rescue the song from commercial oblivion. Partlow quickly followed it onto the blacklist, while Hinton had his own political problems, although not so severe, and he began recording folk albums for Decca.[40]

Along with "Passing Through," Ed McCurdy's "(Last Night I Had) The Strangest Dream" would become a perennial peace song favorite and gain worldwide popularity. Born in Willow Hill, Pennsylvania, in 1919, McCurdy left home in 1937 to become a singer and disc jockey at a gospel radio station in Oklahoma, and within a few years he had become a popular performer in nightclubs throughout the country. In 1948 McCurdy moved with his Canadian wife to Vancouver, where he launched a radio show for the Canadian Broadcasting Corporation (CBC) that moved to Toronto. He featured Pete Seeger, Lena Horne, and Josh White on his show and soon released his first folk music album. He and his family moved to New York in 1950, where he became one of the most popular of the emerging crowd of folk singers, as well as a television performer; he was soon recording dozens of albums for Elektra and other labels. He wrote "The Strangest Dream" just before arriving in New York, and its grassroots popularity spread rapidly.

"In 1950 Ed McCurdy came up to the hotel room of the Weavers, who were working in the vaudeville show at the Strand Theater on Broadway at the time," Pete Seeger later explained. "He sang to us 'Last Night I Had the Strangest Dream' which he'd just made up. The song has never been on the top forty, but has gradually spread throughout much of the world, and has been translated into several languages." Although the Weavers did not initially record "Strangest Dream," it would be included on later Vanguard Records releases of their performances. *Sing Out!* published the lyrics in July 1951. Seeger included it in his own concerts at the time, and his performance of the song at Reed College in Oregon in 1950 was quickly released in a bootleg album.[41]

In the public mind, fanned by the plethora of anticommunist groups and the mass media, peace had become associated with the Communist Party and surrender to the Soviet Union, but others did not agree. *Sing Out!* posted a call for peace songs in early 1951: "The Peace Crusade competition will culminate in a national cultural festival for peace in Chicago at the end of June. Among the prizes being offered by the Peace Crusade are: a fifty dollar cash award against royalties; a guarantee of commercial publication in sheet-music form of the prize-winning song; a guarantee of recording (on the Hootenanny label) of the two best songs by some of the nation's leading performers." In a letter in the September issue, Woody Guthrie praised *Sing Out!*: "I believe in peace and SING OUT believes in peace; I do my best to fight against war and SING OUT fights just as hard to stop wars as I do."[42]

"Through public peace concerts, recordings and its monthly magazine, SING OUT, People's Artists is bringing its musical message for peace to hundreds of thousands of people throughout the USA," Bob Claiborne explained, with much optimism. But the going was rough. In early 1952 *Sing Out!* editor Irwin Silber and Betty Sanders were called to testify before HUAC. "This investigation comes at a time when America's cultural workers are growing more and more aware of the need to express the peace sentiments of the American people," ran a statement from People's Artists executive board. "Betty Sanders and Irwin Silber have been identified with the peace movement, both organizationally and individually as creative artists." The committee soon cancelled the summons, but Silber did testify in 1958, when his peace activities continued to be an issue. Asked about his promotion of Communist peace petitions a few years earlier and his authorship of "Put My Name Down," Silber admitted writing the song but denied he knew anything about peace petitions.[43]

Sing Out! supported the Progressive Party's presidential ticket of Vincent Hallinan and Charlotta Bass in 1952. "We, the readers of and editors of SING OUT, can help make this a singing campaign," Silber declared. "With songs that reach into the hearts of the people we can help bring a message of peace and brotherhood to the millions who will go to the polls in November." Betty Sanders, Laura Duncan, and Ernie Lieberman performed at the party's national convention in July, although the candidates received a miniscule 140,000 votes in November.[44]

There were few recordings of progressive songs except for those from the small Hootenanny label, founded by Irwin Silber and Ernie Lieberman in 1949. Within three years they issued nine records, beginning with the Weavers singing "The Hammer Song" and "Banks of Marble," followed by Lieberman and Hope Foye, the Jewish Young Folksingers with "We Shall Overcome," Martha Schlamme, and a few others. The 12" album *Hootenanny Tonight* appeared in 1954, recorded at two earlier shows with Pete Seeger, Sonny Terry, Leon Bibb, and Earl Robinson. Joseph Starobin reviewed one hootenanny at the Pythian Temple in September 1953 in the *Daily Worker*, similar to the two recorded for *Hootenanny Tonight*: "It is something to see 1,500 young fellows and girls having a wonderful time, singing for an hour or two, led by Pete Seeger with his magic banjo and Leon Bibb with his magnetic voice, and Al Moss, who makes the piano sing with him and Martha Schlamme, like a young willow tree, and all the others of the goodly company which People's Artists brings together." Following a detailed rundown of the songs, he concluded: "I was struck by the wholesomeness of the Hoot, by its straight-forward solidarity and simple comradeship and one of the many strong-points is the goodly number of Negro young people." In the depths of the Red Scare, folk music kept alive the progressive hopes for peace as well as racial and social equality, at least for some.[45]

3

Blacklisting and Folk Developments, 1953–1954

Harry Smith's *Anthology*

"Around 1953 Folkways Records put out a six-LP set called the *Anthology of American Folk Music*, culled from commercial recordings of traditional rural musicians that had been made in the South during the 1920s and '30s," the Greenwich Village musician Dave Van Ronk would explain.[1] "The *Anthology* was created by a man named Harry Smith, who was a beatnik eccentric artist, and experimental filmmaker, and a disciple of Aleister Crowley. . . . Harry had a fantastic collection of 78s, and his idea was to provide an overview of the range of styles being played in rural America at the dawn of recording. That set became our bible. . . . Without the Harry Smith *Anthology* we could not have existed, because there was no other way for us to get hold of that material." The *Anthology*'s influence on Van Ronk, a budding blues performer, was not unique.[2]

Harry Smith (1923–1991) was born in Portland, Oregon, and as a teenager began recording the songs of local Native Americans. He briefly studied anthropology at the University of Washington during World War II but soon became involved with the bohemian community in the San Francisco Bay Area. He became part of a loose, tiny network of blues and hillbilly record collectors scattered around the country. Smith scoured the used record and Salvation Army stores to save the old shellac records before they were recycled for military use, and after the war he continued his passionate pursuit of these artifacts. When Luis Kemnitzer, an anthropologist and political radical, visited Smith in 1948 in Berkeley, California, he found a house crowded with records, books, and much else, and they immediately connected. As Kemnitzer later recalled, "Now we could talk about record collecting, blues, jazz, hillbilly music, gospel music. We shared a love for the records themselves as well as the music that was encoded in them. The labels, the record jackets, the catalogs, and the announcements from the early thirties and before were sensual tokens of the eras, and we felt, saw, and smelled what the music was expressing."[3]

By the early 1950s the collectors community included Bob Pinson in Northern California, Joe Bussard in Maryland, Archie Green in San Francisco, Dick Spottswood in Maryland, James McCune and Pete Whelan in New York, and even the young John Edwards in Australia. The insular world of record collectors had few academic connections, with their focus on objects rather than scholarly studies, although D. K. Wilgus of Bowling Green State University in Kentucky was an exception. In early 1951 Joseph Nicholas, in Palmer, Michigan, launched *Disc Collector: Organ of National Hillbilly Record Collectors Exchange*, a quarterly publication "for the sole purpose of helping record collectors secure old records which they are looking for." The third issue, with an article and discography on Burl Ives, included a column by Wilgus explaining the listing of current records:

> We will be concerned basically with three types of records—or styles of performance: folk (f), Hillbilly (hb), and citybilly (cb). Most of the records now being issued fall into the citybilly class: sweet or hot, accompaniment with emphasis on electrified instruments; slick arrangements; either sweet or burlesque-hillbilly vocals. . . . The distinction between folk and hillbilly is finer; folk will be used to distinguish either ethnic recordings or those presenting the traditional rendition without vocal tricks or dramatic expression. The present interest of this reviewer (and I believe of most of the membership) is in the folk and hillbilly styles, which still persist and for which there is more of a market than the issues of the major record companies would suggest.[4]

Smith's *Anthology*, appearing in 1952, was not the first reissue of early hillbilly and blues recordings, since John Lomax had produced *Smoky Mountain Ballads* (Victor 1941), followed by Alan Lomax's two compilations, *Listen to Our Story* and *Mountain Frolic* (Brunswick 1947), but it was certainly the most influential in introducing a younger audience to such music. Moreover, *Anthology*'s six LP albums with eighty-four selections included a wide range of styles and performers, organized into three categories: "Ballads," "Social Music," and "Songs." Black musicians and white musicians were mixed together, an unusual combination, with Memphis bluesman Furry Lewis following the

Carter Family, Charlie Poole and the North Carolina Ramblers preceding Mississippi John Hurt, and the Texas bluesman Blind Lemon Jefferson linked to Cleoma Breaux and Joseph Falcon's Cajun recording of "C'est Si Triste Sans Lui." Smith was interested in content rather than musical style, and in the process he introduced a new audience to a plethora of fascinating blues, hillbilly, cowboy, and Cajun recordings. In an accompanying booklet there were numerous illustrations, and most of the songs had a pithy, humorous summary, in the form of a headline, such as the Carolina Tar Heels' "Got the Farm Land Blues": "Discouraging acts of god and man convince farmer of positive benefits in urban life." For the Masked Marvel's (Charley Patton) "Mississippi Boweavil Blues": "Bollweevil survives physical attack after cleverly answering farmers questions [sic]." As for the Bently Boys's "Down on Penny's Farm": "Renters caught by poverty on George Penny's farm picture landlord as miser, thief, and liar." A few of the performers, long since forgotten but still alive, would be rediscovered in the early 1960s.[5]

While Folkways Records usually had limited circulation because of their high prices and scarcity in record stores, and the six-record set was certainly not cheap—although owner Asch pretended the recordings were in the public domain and thereby avoided paying for any copyright permissions—the anthology was widely appreciated, perhaps because it could be found in many public libraries. The *New York Times* welcomed its release: "Thus Harry Smith's collection of early phonograph records has become both valuable in the monetary sense and interesting in what it reveals about American popular music before it became so standardized by coast-to-coast radio programs, nationally distributed talking pictures, and phonograph releases that blanket the country."[6]

In addition to both old and new recordings, those anxious for traditional music could visit the various folk festivals and string band contests dotting the landscape. Dating from the nineteenth century, such events mushroomed by the 1930s. These included the Georgia Old-Time Fiddler's Convention in Atlanta; the Old-Time Fiddler's Convention in Union Grove, North Carolina; Bascom Lamar Lunsford's Mountain Dance and Folk Festival in Asheville, North Carolina; Jean Bell Thomas's American Folk Song Festival in Ashland, Kentucky; Annabel Morris Buchanan's White Top Festival in southwest Virginia; and the long-running (into the twenty-first century) National Folk Festival, launched by Sarah Gertrude Knott in 1934. "The folk festival movement has contributed greatly to the awakening of interest in the folksong heritage of America," Knott wrote in 1953. "In addition, the recordings of folk festival activities have made available a body of folksong materials that have . . . enriched the archives of American folk music." Unlike many festival promoters, Knott always featured a variety of ethnic and racial performers, representing a range of cultures. For the Indiana University folklorist Stith Thompson, "At their best, the folk festivals serve the function of continually bringing this revival back into first-hand contact with the genuine surviving tradition."[7]

Besides the Asheville festival, Lunsford launched the Carolina Folk Festival in Chapel Hill in 1948, which lasted until 1956. "This festival is sponsored by the FOLKLORE COUNCIL of the University of North Carolina," the flyer for the 1950 event announced.

> It draws 600 or more folk participants from various parts of the state and some of other groups from Kentucky, Virginia, Tennessee, South Carolina, and Texas. Its purpose is to recapture the cultural values in our traditional American music, dancing and balladry, and to present them in their unspoiled best in a fast-moving, three-evening event, free from caricature mockery or ridicule. The festival is a presentation of the ballads, songs and dances which the people of our region and their forebears have transmitted orally for centuries, and our audiences as of previous years have found these programs highly entertaining and instructive; the dances beautiful and moving.

Banjo player George Pegram appeared at many of the festivals. Lunsford also initiated a folk festival for the North Carolina State Fair in Raleigh in 1948, which existed for decades, but his Virginia Folk Festival appeared only in 1950. University of Virginia students Paul Clayton and Bill Clifton participated, long before the start of their careers as musicians. The annual National Hillbilly Music Contest near Warrenton, Virginia, starting in 1951, would feature such professionals as fiddlers Chubby Wise and Scott Stoneman.[8]

Knott also kept busy with the three-day All-Florida Folk Festival in May 1953. "Opening with Indian songs and dances, the program moved on to American square dances, British ballads and folksongs, Negro games, spirituals and other songs and tales; fiddle, harmonica, guitar, and banjo tunes," folk music historian Ray Lawless explained. This one also included Spanish, Irish, Mexican, Scandinavian, and Israeli performances. "The very branches of the giant pines and moss-draped oaks trembled to traditional melodies handed down through generations of Spanish, Greek, Czech, Jew and Negro and blended into a democratic pattern of musical culture," Gladys Henley raved in *Etude*, the music magazine. With the name changed to the Florida Folk Festival, it would continue for many years. Other local festivals sprang up, such as the Arkansas Folklore Society's event on the Fayetteville campus of the University of Arkansas beginning in 1947 and the Ozark Folk Festival in Eureka Springs, Arkansas, which featured local performers and where the folklorist Vance Randolph long remained active.[9] There were fewer festivals in the North. The New England Folk Festival, launched in Boston in 1944, traveled around Massachusetts for a few decades and featured a variety of ethnic performers. Swarthmore College in Pennsylvania initiated its annual festival in 1945 and early featured such mainstream singers as Richard Dyer-Bennet, Susan Reed, and even Lead Belly. Woody Guthrie appeared there with John Jacob Niles in 1949, and Pete Seeger arrived in 1953, followed by Sonny Terry and Brownie McGhee the next year, when the festival was attracting thousands of college students. In 1950 three professors from Franklin and Marshall College in Lancaster, Pennsylvania, created the Kutztown, Pennsylvania, Festival, with the focus on Dutch music and crafts. The Berkshire Folk Music Festival in Lenox, Massachusetts, launched in 1954, presented an array of ethnic performances. The variety of folk festivals seemed to offer something for everyone, with most presenting few, if any, of the popular commercial performers. Such eclectic festivals, personified by the National Folk Festival, would expand in subsequent decades.

By mid-decade an increasing number of commercial folk recordings managed to satisfy the expanding audience. One problem, however, was how to define folk music for the commercial market. In the 1940s the term "folk" was used to sell a wide range of country music recordings and performers. The *Billboard Music Year Book* for 1944–1946 had a section titled "American Folk Music," with a long list of country and western stars, such as Red Foley, Bill Boyd, Burl Ives, Roy Acuff, and Spade Cooley, as well as numerous country music radio programs. "Folk records added still more followers last year as servicemen in the South and West took their tastes with them and as servicemen from the North became acquainted with this type of music for the first time in mountain music territory," explained the article "Disks Spread Folk Fame to Every Corner of Country." The caption for a photo of Burl Ives read: "Burl Ives's albums and single records have zoomed to new popularity heights in the past year. Part of the continuing trend toward more music that is truly representative of American folkways." By 1953, however, *Billboard* had dropped "folk" and used only "country" as the designation for the commercial music of the (rural) South and West. The anticommunist assault seems to have given "folk" a negative, radical taint. Still, Columbia Records issued a "Folk Music Catalog" for 1952/53, beginning with "American Folk and Sacred Selections" by Gene Autry, The Chuck Wagon Gang, Molly O'Day, Roy Acuff, and others. A concluding short list of "Traditional

Folk Music" included Burl Ives, Bob Atcher, the Carter Sisters with Mother Maybelle, as well as Roy Acuff and his Smoky Mountain Boys.[10]

If there was some lingering confusion in the commercial marketplace over what constituted folk music, with its political overtones, this did not seem to be a problem for those searching for acoustic recordings of traditional or political songs with a hillbilly or blues accent. Before mid-decade they were rather scarce, however, apart from the Decca catalog of Burl Ives, Josh White, Josef Marais and His Bushveld Band, as well as additional albums by Marais and Miranda. Both Stinson and Folkways had the largest number of LP selections, with the former featuring Ives, Richard Dyer-Bennet, Pete Seeger, Hally Wood, Josh White, Duke of Iron, and the four earlier volumes of Folksay with Seeger, Lead Belly, Woody Guthrie, Bess Lomax, Sonny Terry, and Josh White. Folkways had an expanding folk catalog. Seeger recorded *Darling Corey* in 1950, then returned in 1953 after his recording hiatus with the Weavers, with *American Folksongs for Children* and a steady steam of albums thereafter, such as *Goofin' Off Suite*; *Birds, Beasts, Bugs, and Little Fishes*; *Frontier Ballads*; and *The Pete Seeger Sampler* in 1954. There was little from Woody Guthrie, however, except the 1950 album *Talking Dust Bowl*, as well as Lead Belly, although the two-disc set *Lead Belly's Last Sessions*, based on 1948 interviews by Frederick Ramsey, appeared in 1953. There were also albums by Brownie McGhee and numerous foreign recordings.[11]

Other companies had more limited, but still interesting, selections as the folk boom slowly accelerated. For example, the California jazz label Fantasy issued *Odetta and Larry*, recorded mostly at the Tin Angel in San Francisco, in 1953 and 1954. Odetta Holmes, born in Birmingham, Alabama, grew up in Los Angeles and relocated to San Francisco in the early 1950s. An African American with a classically trained voice, she soon moved into folk music and in San Francisco connected with the banjo-playing Larry Mohr. Having grown up in Detroit, with a Jewish background, Mohr visited the folk music scene in New York and learned the banjo from Pete Seeger's banjo instruction booklet before moving to California in 1953. Mohr was one of the few five-string banjo players in New York, including Tom Paley, Roger Sprung, Joe Jaffe, and Erik Darling. He met Odetta in San Francisco, and they performed at the small local club the Tin Angel. *Odetta and Larry* included a rich selection, mostly African American tunes, such as "Rock Island Line," "I've Been Buked and I've Been Scorned," "No More Cane on the Brazos," and "John Henry," but also Woody Guthrie's "Car Car." Odetta and Larry would continue to perform together for a short while, although he would not record again. But Odetta had launched a stellar career, and she would become highly influential through the century.

Maynard and Seymour Solomon started Vanguard Records in 1947, with a concentration on classical recordings, but they quickly branched out to jazz and folk with *Folk Songs of Spain* in 1953 and Martha Schlamme's *Folk Songs of Many Lands* the next year. Also in 1954 Brother John Sellers, a blues and gospel performer, released *Blues and Folk Songs*, followed in 1955 with *Blues and Folk Songs, Volume 2* as well as *Jack of Diamonds* and other folk songs and blues selections. Vanguard's major breakthrough would come in 1957, however, with the influential album *Weavers at Carnegie Hall*. Jac Holzman launched Elektra Records in 1950, connected with his New York store the Record Loft; two years later *Jean Ritchie Singing the Traditional Songs of Her Kentucky Mountain Family* appeared, quickly followed by Frank Warner's *American Folk Songs and Ballads*, Shep Ginandes's *British Traditional Ballads in America*, and others by Cynthia Gooding, Tom Paley, Frank Warner, and Oscar Brand. Paley's 1953 *Songs from the Southern Appalachians* would become particularly influential, introducing a northern audience to southern banjo tunes. Ed McCurdy's *Sin Songs—Pro and Con* would soon launch a popular string of bawdy albums. "In 1954, with seven or eight records released, I decided to close the Record Loft and move Elektra around the corner to larger offices at 361 Bleeker Street," Holzman recalled. "Financing expansion was a continuing problem. New releases were paying for themselves out of moderate sales but not much more. Elektra needed cash to grow. I talked . . . Leonard Ripley into buying a piece of the company" for $10,000. By decade's end Elektra would be a thriving company, having recorded many of the key folk performers. "My upbringing and my own sentiments were liberal," Holzman later explained. "The witch hunt would have no effect on my musical judgment," such as recording Josh White. He was certainly not alone in bucking the conservative tide.[12]

Two other performers continued in popularity, Richard Dyer-Bennet and John Jacob Niles, although they would be somewhat out of the folk mainstream. Born in 1892 in Kentucky, Niles began to collect and perform rural folk songs early on, and he emerged as a professional musician in the 1920s. He also published songbooks, beginning with *Seven Kentucky Mountain Songs* (1929) and *The Anglo-America Ballad Study Book* (1945). With a large, stylized ballad presentation, Niles appeared in numerous concert halls. While not known for having a political agenda, he did appear with Pete Seeger, Woody Guthrie, Lead Belly, and even Carl Sandburg in a Carnegie Hall "Concert of American Folk Music" as a benefit for the Greater New York Committee for Russian Relief in 1946. His prolific recording career included RCA Victor's issuing a few prewar albums, such as *Early American Ballads* (1939), then three Disc albums following the war; RCA reissued the earlier albums on their Camden label in the 1950s. "The weird, hoarse falsetto of John Jacob Niles adds a strange power to some of his renditions," the performer and promoter Oscar Brand explained in the *Saturday Review* in 1955. Brand particularly liked his popular compositions "Go Away from My Window," "I Wonder as I Wander," and "Black Is the Color of My True Love's Hair." In 1957 Niles switched to the folk-friendly Tradition label.[13]

Richard Dyer-Bennet joined Niles as a traditional performer with an Old World minstrel style that did not appeal to everyone. Born in England in 1913, he grew up in California and first lived in New York in 1938. Within a few years he had met Pete Seeger, Woody Guthrie, and Burl Ives, who got him into the Village Vanguard in 1942, where he performed throughout the war, along with concerts at Town Hall and Carnegie Hall. His recording career began in 1941 for Keynote, with albums flowing from Stinson, Decca, and other labels until 1955, when he began his own Dyer-Bennet Records label. His brief listing in *Red Channels* had served to sideline his career, which led to making his own recordings, and he found a growing audience. He had tried to clear his name with the blacklisters but refused the suggestion that he write an apology to be published in the *Saturday Evening Post* or *Colliers*.[14]

While Dyer-Bennet did not cave to the political pressure and as a result suffered some of the consequences, both Burl Ives and Josh White bent, although the latter did not break. Following his listing in *Red Channels*, Ives felt some political heat. On May 20, 1952, he voluntarily appeared before the Senate Internal Security Subcommittee to clear his name, particularly now that his film career was in high gear. He readily admitted appearing before progressive groups in the 1930s and then agreed to name four people with left-wing ties, including Dyer-Bennet, along with Ives's former publicity agent Allen Meltzer: "I am very sorry that I have to bring up names in this manner, because I would like to be able to not mention other names, but I can't [avoid it]." As for White, also listed in *Red Channels*, in June 1950 he quickly returned from London to meet with the publishers of *Counterattack*. On September 1 he appeared before HUAC and denied any knowing involvement in subversive organizations, but he said, "I did on many occasions appear at benefits and rallies which I was led to believe were for worthwhile causes." He refused to name names, in particular Paul Robeson, despite pressure to do so. White next published his testimony under the title "I Was a Sucker for the Communist Party" in the December 1950 issue of *Negro Digest*. White salvaged his career, partly by appearing more in England and Western Europe. Others, such as Tom Glazer and Oscar Brand, faced a semi-blacklist, although they managed to continue their careers through the decade. Jac

Holzman was happy to record Josh White for Elektra, with *The Story of John Henry & Ballads, Blues and Other Songs* appearing in 1955, closely followed by *Josh At Midnight*. Holzman recalled: "Josh was nearing the twenty-fifth anniversary of his first recording in 1931 and he had this notion to create an assemblage of railroad songs, tied together with a short narrative which we called 'The Story of John Henry.' It sold close to twenty thousand, a big hit for us."[15]

Along with such older musicians as Ives, Dyer-Bennet, and Niles, whose recording careers continued through the decade, there was a budding generation of enthusiasts who would soon make their commercial mark and who remained essentially untouched by the anticommunist scare. There was a burgeoning folk community in New York, and also in Chicago, Los Angeles, the Bay Area, and other locales, a network spanning the country. During the summer of 1953 three musicians—Frank Hamilton, Guy Carawan, and Jack Elliott—launched their careers by touring the South. Hamilton and Carawan had grown up in Los Angeles in the 1940s, which soon hosted a thriving, left-wing folk community, including Dave Arkin (father of Alan Arkin, the folksinger and later actor), Rich Dehr, Frank Miller, Bill Oliver, Vern Partlow, Will and Herta Geer, Ray Glaser, Wally Hille, and Ernie Lieberman, as well as Bess and Butch Hawes. Some of them formed the Songmakers Workshop in June 1953 to promote topical songs.

The Geers had first met Woody Guthrie in Los Angeles in the late 1930s and kept in touch over the years as Geer's acting career took off. They moved back to Los Angeles in 1948, where Geer soon faced the movie blacklist, and they were forced to sell their Santa Monica house and moved north to the scenic but remote Topanga Canyon. As for Guthrie, due to his increasingly erratic behavior caused by Huntington's disease, in October 1952 he moved from his family in New York to the Geers' house in Topanga Canyon, which became one center of the local folk community.

As they developed their musical skills, Hamilton and Carawan often visited with the Geers, where they met Guthrie. They performed locally and appeared in concerts with the Sierra Folk Singers. In the summer of 1953 they decided to meet in New York and then embark on a folk tour of the South. While attending a Brownie McGhee concert, Hamilton and Carawan met Jack Elliott, and the three decided to travel together. Elliott had been born Elliott Adnopoz in Brooklyn in 1931, the son of a doctor, and at an early age he became captivated by cowboys and all things western. Having developed into a decent singer and guitar player, with his name now changed to Jack Elliott, he first met Woody Guthrie through his friend Tom Paley in early

1951 and quickly became his loyal student and friend. For the next two years they were seldom apart, until Woody's health became increasingly fragile by the summer of 1953—he would spend the rest of his life in hospitals until his death in 1967—when Elliott connected with Carawan and Hamilton. They visited with Bascom Lamar Lunsford at the Mountain Dance and Folk Festival in Asheville, North Carolina, where they were impressed by the local performers. They next stopped at the John C. Campbell Folk School in Brasstown, North Carolina, then the Highlander Folk School in Monteagle, Tennessee, followed by the Grand Ole Opry in Nashville, where they heard Roy Acuff, Hank Snow, and Grandpa Jones. After six weeks on the road they wound up in New Orleans, there to meet Billy Faier.

Born in Brooklyn in 1930, but mostly growing up in Woodstock, Faier moved back to New York in 1947 and found himself among the folk singers in Washington Square on Sunday afternoons. Developing as one of the adept, and scarce, banjo players, he arrived in San Francisco in the early 1950s and joined the local folk music community of Jo Mapes, Barbara Dane, Rolf Cahn, and Odetta, before briefly landing in New Orleans. As for Carawan, Hamilton, and Elliott, as well as Faier, they quickly returned to New York. Carawan and Hamilton were soon back in Los Angeles, where they performed with many of the local musicians for the next few years, while Elliott would give his first professional concert at the Cherry Lane Theater in Greenwich Village in the early winter of 1954.

In April 1953 folk music appeared to have enough commercial appeal to encourage Gordon Burdage to publish the magazine *American Folk Music*, with the budding collector and record producer Kenneth Goldstein listed as "Manager Editor." Its sixteen pages included articles, ads, songs, book and record reviews, and illustrations. Under the heading "U.N. Folk Ballad Jubilee Success," the editor made this comment: "The persistent practice of lumping 'folk' music and 'country and western' in the same category by publishers, recording companies and periodicals, is the source of much confusion to the public. Collectors, folklorists and fans alike are united in an effort to achieve the acceptance of a standard definition of 'folk' music by organizations commercially interested in the subject." A hodgepodge of information included an article on Jac Holzman's Record Loft. This first issue was not followed by a second, however, since the market proved too slim.[16]

Sing Out! had been optimistically launched as a monthly in 1950, but was forced to skip a few issues from May until the fall of 1954. "I'm going to have to change my schedule though," Editor Silber announced. "Instead of getting out once a month (no laughs now), I'm going to come out four times a year. . . . I get out to about 1,000 people every month—and according to the experts who are supposed to know about such things, that's not enough to warrant a monthly visit." The first quarterly appeared as the Winter 1955 issue, which would long remain the format: "This issue is a good idea of what we hope to keep going—sixteen songs, two major articles, reviews of books and important new music, and our three new regular features: Record Reviews, Johnny Appleseed Jr., and The Folk Process." Pete Seeger's column, "Johnny Appleseed, Jr." would become a staple of all future issues through the decade and long after.[17]

American Folk Music did include reviews of John Greenway's American Folk Songs of Protest along with Margaret Boni's updated Fireside Book of Favorite American Songs (1952), and a notice of the forthcoming Ballads Migrant in New England (1953) by Helen Hartness Flanders and Marguerite Olney. There were now numerous books of lyrics readily available. Boni had first published the popular and colorful Fireside Book of Folksongs in 1947, the same year of Tom Scott's Sing of America and John and Alan Lomax's Folk Song U*S*A*: The 111 Best American Ballads. The next year Ruth Crawford Seeger, wife of Charles Seeger, issued American Folk Songs for Children; also in 1948 Sylvia and John Kolb produced A Treasury of Folk Songs in an inexpensive Bantam Books edition, which long remained in print. In 1950 Beatrice Landeck followed with Songs to Grow On, and four years later More Songs to Grow On. By mid-decade folk songs, in books old and new, were readily at hand, including Burl Ives's Sea Songs (1956).

Great Britain and the Emerging Folk Revival

The folk revival also burgeoned in Great Britain by mid-decade, although the scope was not as broad. On the traditional side, the English Folk Dance and Song Society continued to promote what they perceived as vintage musical and dance styles. The traditionalists were getting increasing opposition from the growing ranks of the left-wing folk musicians, however, as well as those influenced by American jazz and blues. Topic Records continued to release songs by Ewan MacColl and Patrick Galvin, and the Workers' Music Association backed the London Youth Choir in launching the bimonthly Sing in May 1954. Edited by Eric Winter, with John Hasted as the music editor, Sing long served as the link between the Communist Party and the promotion of folk music.

While Communist Party members represented one group contributing to the growing popularity of folk music and drew inspiration from the American performers such as the Almanac Singers, People's Songs, and the Weavers, at the same time there developed a parallel, popular folk movement. Anthony James (later Lonnie) Donegan was born in Glasgow, Scotland, in 1931, but he grew up in East London. Donegan began playing the guitar in 1946 but then switched to the banjo in 1948 when he joined the Chris Barber jazz band, which was playing the New Orleans-style jazz then becoming popular among younger fans. Donegan remembered being influenced by the jazz he heard on the BBC, as well as by "Josh White, who happened to have a record issued in England" in 1946 by Brunswick. Donegan was drafted for national service in 1949, and upon returning two years later he formed the Tony Donegan Jazz Band. He began to borrow records from the library at the American Embassy and for the first time heard Woody Guthrie, Lead Belly, and many of the Library of Congress recordings by John and Alan Lomax. "I did discover one or two very nice Blues records there and I stole them—I didn't see what harm there was in that as no one else was listening to them and I must have been the only one in the library for ten years," Donegan explained. "I got this guy, a fabulous Blues player and his name was McKinley Morganfield—he later came to light as Muddy Waters, but when I knew him he was McKinley Morganfield." He also bought records at the left-wing Collet's Bookshop, where jazz trumpeter Ken Colyer worked, and where the manager, Ken Lindsay, corresponded with Woody Guthrie. Lindsay "used to show me these letters which were superb, like poetry, Woody used to paint on the letters."[18]

The Donegan Jazz band first appeared at a concert at Royal Albert Hall on June 28, 1952, which included the American blues artist Lonnie Johnson; the announcer mistakenly announced the "Lonnie" Donegan band, and the new name stuck. In 1953 he rejoined Barber's band, soon known as Ken Colyer's Jazzmen; they made the first skiffle recordings, which were released on the Storyville and Decca labels. Skiffle bands originally emerged from small African American (and occasionally white) ensembles in the United States, both North and South, in the 1920s, often using homemade instruments (hence the name washboard or jug bands). Recordings such as "Hometown Skiffle" and Lil Johnson's "House Rent Scuffle" appeared, a mixture of jazz, folk, and blues. According to Donegan, "Our egos were devoted to playing New Orleans Jazz, there was no division of interest in any way, shape or form—we all wanted to do the same thing. Ken had his ego on the trumpet, I had mine on the banjo, Chris on the trombone but we all wanted to play exactly the same thing in exactly same way."[19]

By early June 1954 Colyer had left the group, and Chris Barber's Jazz Band opened at the 100 Club in London. A month later, on July 13, the trio of

Donegan, Barber, and washboard player Beryl Bryden—she was a friend who happened to be in the studio—made their first skiffle recordings for Decca, "Rock Island Line," "John Henry," "Nobody's Child," and "Wabash Cannonball," with the last two never issued. "Rock Island Line" and "John Henry" were initially part of the 10″ LP *New Orleans Joys*, with the remaining six tracks only instrumentals, and appeared as 78 RPM singles in 1955, quickly gaining popularity. The album sold sixty thousand copies. In early 1956 the traditional blues and jazz scholar Paul H. Oliver covered "Hometown Skiffle" in *Music Mirror*, summing up what he saw as the situation: "The skiffle bands are attempting a difficult undertaking in trying to create a folk music divorced from a folk tradition. In doing so they have inspired in many jazz enthusiasts an interest and an appetite for the more primitive but most authentic of American musical forms. It is up to the record companies now to meet this interest and potential market to the benefit of themselves, the collectors—and the skiffle groups."[20]

While skiffle was just beginning to emerge, Alan Lomax had taken himself out of the picture, but only for a while. In December 1953 Lomax shared the stage with MacColl, Lloyd and others as part of the Ballads and Blues "Song of the Iron Road" program at St. Pancras Town Hall, featuring railway songs and ballads. In late 1953 and early 1954 Lomax also had an eight-part BBC television series, *Song Hunter*, and one show featured Theodore Bikel. Born in Austria, Bikel had relocated to Palestine at the outbreak of World War II; a budding actor, he moved to London in 1946 to study at the Royal Academy of Dramatic Art. Within a few years he also began to sing and play the guitar, learning American folk songs while becoming involved in the expatriate community, until he moved permanently to the United States in 1954. Bikel recalled, "[I remember] the time Lomax brought Margaret Barry [Barrie] to my apartment. She was an Irish Gypsy with swarthy, leathery skin and a mouth that seemed lopsided because quite a few of her teeth were missing." A Special Branch report commented on Lomax's *Song Hunter*'s shows, "in which he introduced examples of folk music he had discovered during visits to the coal mining areas of the Clyde Valley, Tyneside and South Wales. The general trend of the songs, several of which were sung by A. L. LLOYD . . . accompanied by Bob HOLLAND, a Scots miner, was to portray the bad conditions and general oppression of the mining industry during the earlier part of the century." The report further stated: "It has recently been learnt that Burl IVES, the well-known broadcaster of hill-billy music, was first given his chance to broadcast on the American radio by LOMAX who also assisted Josh WHITE another American singer to gain public approval." The Special Branch considered Bikel someone to watch.[21]

Lomax specialized in making introductions and stimulating musical exchanges. As he wrote to his sister Shirley in early 1954, "Here I've become sort of the American singer in England. Without wanting to, you know. . . . All very silly because I don't sing particularly well, or even like to very much." And he continued, "I've always hated radio performing and concerts, and I suddenly found myself liking TV. . . . Most of the time I had no prepared script but just worked out what I had to say on the air." The TV series proved to be a success.[22]

Lomax's work with the BBC impressed and influenced Ewan MacColl. As MacColl later wrote,

> Both Bert [Lloyd] and I, quite independently, were writing scripts dealing with various aspects of folk-song for the BBC Home Service and the Third Programme. Alan, much more perceptive than either of us about the future of television, presented three one-hour programmes on the BBC, in which singers and instrumentalists from all over the British Isles demonstrated the magnificent riches of our traditional music and song. The programmes were produced by David Attenborough and, though they delighted the hearts of the small band of folk enthusiasts who witnessed them, they were not popular with the general public.

As they influenced each other, Lomax, MacColl, Lloyd, and their friends were walking a fine line by the mid-1950s between traditional and commercial, American and British music, but always with some sort of left-wing tilt. While the British Communist Party was wary of foreign cultural influences, particularly from the United States—the party even supported a ban on comic books from across the Atlantic—it seemed to have no problem with Lomax's promotion of American folk songs, since they were perceived as having working-class and African American origins. Lomax spent seven months recording in Spain in 1952–53, and after playing excerpts from this field trip, the BBC sent him off to Italy for more field recordings during 1954–55. Upon his return he plunged back into a thriving folk scene.[23]

MacColl, Lloyd, and the Workers' Music Association (WMA) took center stage in promoting the activist role of folk music. With Alan Bush as president, the WMA had an impressive list of vice presidents, including Paul Robeson and the American composers Aaron Copland, Morton Gould, Wallingford Rieger, and Elie Siegmeister. In 1952 the organization published A. L. Lloyd's *Coaldust Ballads*, a selection of songs from his larger collection *Come All Ye Bold Miners: Ballads and Songs of the Coalfields*. "Some of the songs chosen are for performance by men, others by women, and, in most cases, optional parts are added to enable singing by choirs as well as—or in place of—solo voices," according to the introduction.[24]

With the bimonthly publication of *Sing* beginning in May 1954, organized by Eric Winter, John Hasted, and Johnny Ambrose, the WMA began to reach a broader audience and maintained relations with the left-wing movement in the United States. Winter became the editor, remaining for thirty years. "We have just received the first issue of your new publication, SING. Please accept our heartiest congratulations and best wishes for a long and fruitful life on this new venture," *Sing Out!* editor Irwin Silber wrote. "Needless to say, we are honored to be referred to as SING's 'big brother.' You must know, of course, that much of our work has been inspired by the fine work done by singers and writers in the Workers Music Association for many years." The second issue's editorial focused on the Ban the Bomb movement, heightened by the recent hydrogen bomb tests by the United States. "Readers will remember that the 'ban the atom-bomb' petition was launched to the music of 'Put My Name Down,' and already in the new petition campaign singing is playing its part." "Put My Name Down," first published in *Sing Out!* in 1950, was based on Woody Guthrie's "Hard Traveling," with updated lyrics by Irwin Silber. The same issue of *Sing* also included "The Rosenbergs Were Murdered," with words by Eric Winter and music by John Hasted, referring to the execution in the United States of Julius and Ethel Rosenberg in June 1953 for alleged atomic espionage.[25]

Usually filled with critical accounts, *Sing's* third issue began with "Peace Hath Her Victories: ANOTHER war is ended and peace has come to the plains and hills of Vietnam. We make no apology for the 'Far Eastern' flavour of much of this issue of SING. The victory won at Geneva for the forces of peace must surely be a spur to all SINGers and lovers of song and the good things of life, to end the slaughter which is still going on, in our name to our shame, in Malaya and Kenya." The first song in the issue, "Ghost Soldier," was attributed to "AN AMERICAN NEGRO SOLDIER." The Geneva Accords, signed in July 1954, appeared to divide Vietnam into two parts temporarily, ending the French colonization, but the future would prove that peace was a false hope. The issue also included Hasted's "When Asia Came to Geneva" and MacColl's "Ballad of Ho Chi Minh," praising the leader of North Vietnam. While British authorities had some suspicion of Communism, there was nothing like the inquisition in the United States. Britain had MI5, its domestic intelligence agency, as well as the Special Branch of London's Metropolitan Police, but nothing resembling the intense pressure put on suspected Communists in the United States by the numerous local, state, and federal governmental investigating bodies. Indeed, there was ethnic, racial, class, religious, political, and economic paranoia, all of which had deep historical roots in the United States. Britain had religious conflicts centuries earlier and economic clashes more recently, but the country was ethnically and racially rather homogenous and secure in its national identity. The Communist Party in Great Britain continued through the decade as a viable political entity, although one's party membership could be interpreted as suspect; various party members, such as Bert Lloyd, continually faced semi-blacklisting.[26]

John Hasted, *Sing's* music editor, was one example of an active Communist who maintained his political and as well as musical activities while influenced by American folk music. Born in 1921, Hasted attended Oxford University, soon became attracted to workers' songs, joined the Communist Party, and emerged as a college physics teacher in 1948. He was already familiar with the Almanac Singers, as he would explain: "Bob Hinds, a merchant seaman, had brought the Almanacs 78 RPM record 'Talking Union' for me to hear in 1946. I at once wanted to make music like this. But it was years before I could even got [sic] hold of a folk guitar, let alone find other people with similar aspirations. Eventually I found folklorist Bert Lloyd, and asked him if he wanted to start an Almanac group in England. To my astonishment his voice dropped about an octave, and he said very quietly, 'Passionately.'" Around 1952 they formed the Ramblers, along with Neste Revald and Jean Butler, an American now living in London who had visited Almanac House in New York in the early 1940s. "The name for the group came directly from Woody's song ['I Ain't Got No Home'] which Jean sang for us." "The Ramblers lasted only a couple of years as a group," Hasted continued, "but the sound we made was solid, since Bert had a high-up voice and I was bass-baritone." They performed both British and American folk songs, mostly before trade unions, beginning with the Clerical Workers' Union. Hasted later recalled a key challenge: "How much emphasis was there to be on British material, and how much on American? Some favoured a purely ethnic approach, unaccompanied English songs in local dialects and style. Others wanted no more than to sing the Blues, with a few unconscious concessions to the English idiom. Folklorist Alan Lomax was on hand to help us with detailed analysis and advice."[27]

In July 1954, MacColl organized a Ballads and Blues concert at the Royal Festival Hall, advertised as "Work Songs of Britain and American, Calypsos, Blues, Folk Jazz." The stellar lineup included the British performers Margaret Barrie (Irish), Isla Cameron, Alf Edwards (concertina), A. L. Lloyd, MacColl, and the Ken Colyer Skiffle Group (Colyer, Alexis Korner, Bill Colyer, Micky

Ashman), but no Americans. Lloyd performed "The Commissions Report" (Trinidad Calypso), "Pay Day at Coal Creek" (American labor song), "Cosher Baily's Engine" (Welsh railway song), and some shanties with MacColl. Mac-Coll also joined Colyer in "Another Man Done Gone," while his skiffle group did a half-dozen songs. The review in *Sing* particularly praised the Lloyd-MacColl duet "Go Down, You Blood-Red Roses": "This is certainly the way to sing sea shanties, not with the salt-tang of the concert hall but with the solidity of a dock-side crane. We doubt Mr. Lloyd and Mr. MacColl have better things to do but if they will take to the pubs and take their shanties with them it is beyond peradventure that they will never buy a drink." The previous March, MacColl had issued his own collection of workers' songs, *The Shuttle and Cage: Industrial Folk-Ballads*, published by the WMA. He explained in the preface: "There are no nightingales in these songs, no flowers—and the sun is rarely mentioned; their themes are work, poverty, hunger and exploitation. They should be sung to the accompaniment of pneumatic drills and swinging hammers, they should be bawled above the hum of turbines and the clatter of looms for they are songs of toil, anthems of the industrial age." Collected by MacColl, they underscored his emphasis on authentic industrial songs.[28]

Clubs with folk music were just making their appearance in 1954, beginning with The Good Earth, located near Piccadilly. "It is the first venue of this sort to be started in England," Hasted reported, "and SING wishes it every success." It soon moved to Mac's in Piccadilly and hosted music three nights a week. About the same time, Hasted opened the 44 Club on Gerard Street. Clubs would quickly proliferate, providing welcome performance space for the emerging skiffle movement. Eager to reach a broader audience, in 1955 MacColl and Lloyd continued the "Ballads and Blues" concerts at St. Pancras Town Hall. They were joined by a skiffle group and others, under the new name British Folk Song and Dance Ensemble, as folk music began reaching a wider audience through the clubs, concert halls, and recording studios.[29]

Back in the United States

The Weavers' career ground to a halt by January 1953, just as Senator Joe Mc-Carthy became the chair of the Permanent Subcommittee on Investigations of the Senate Committee on Government Operations, following the Republican Party's congressional and presidential victories in the fall 1952 elections. From this prominent position of power McCarthy coordinated a relentless campaign against alleged subversives, even some connected with President Dwight Eisenhower. Quickly tainted by scandals, McCarthy's fall was relatively swift.

In January 1955 the Democrats regained control of Congress, following their victories in the fall election, but McCarthy's Senate Republican colleagues had censured him prior to this for his outrageous conduct, in particular for attacking the Eisenhower administration. His power base now gone, he continued to drink heavily and would be dead within two years. Although McCarthy the senator was no longer a threat, McCarthyism—the broad-based fear of and attack on alleged subversives, former or current Communist Party members, their liberal allies, and anyone else considered subversive—would long endure. This included those engaged in folk music (as well as the arts in general, including Hollywood films), although many managed to survive and perhaps thrive in such a lingering, still harsh, political climate. Even Harvey Matusow, who had helped dig the Weavers' grave, abandoned the McCarthy ship. By late 1954 Matusow began to recant his extensive earlier testimony against the Weavers and so many others, and he published his full-blown confession in book form, titled *False Witness*, in March 1955. For his troubles he was convicted of perjury and later spent some months in federal prison.[30]

Despite the lingering political miasma, popular folk music remained in the news. *Sing Out!* editor Irwin Silber continued his promotional efforts, while attacking anticommunism:

> Perhaps some historian of the future, when he writes about the U.S.A. of the 1950s, will call today 'the time of the lists.' It is the time of shame when a whole new profession has developed composed of people who earn their '30 pieces of silver' by compiling lists of organizations and individuals who are alleged to be 'subversive.' . . . The reason for the existence of SING OUT and People's Artists is to try to break through the morass of anti-human culture—and its very life depends upon hitting back at the philosophy of guilt by association.

Silber also took a strong civil rights position and criticized Burl Ives for not including more African American songs in *The Burl Ives Song Book* as well as in the performer's repertoire. The February 1954 issue of *Sing Out!* was dedicated to Negro History Week, with an article on Sonny Terry along with two South African folk songs discussed by Pete Seeger, "Somagwaza" and "Oonomathotholo." Taking a strong internationalist position, which countered Cold War nationalism, future issues included songs from Australia, Romania, Trinidad, South America, China, and much else. The Weavers had earlier promoted world folk music in their records and concerts, which would soon capture much of the developing folk market. *Sing Out!* also included the words and music to many protest, labor, and traditional songs.[31]

The *New York Times* reviewed a few "Folk Music on Disks" in early 1954, including the two-volume Folkways release *Lead Belly's Last Sessions*, recorded a few months before his death in late 1949. The reviewer noted that 'Elektra is another firm that has made some good folk records and it has two new ten-inch disks that increase the store of musical Americana,' including Hally Wood's *O Lovely Appearance of Death* and Tom Paley's *Folk Songs from the Southern Appalachian Mountains*. The stage was set for the upsurge of folk music in 1955, drawing upon a wide range of cultural and political influences, in particular led by Harry Belafonte and a variety of fledgling performers. Woody Guthrie, on the other hand, was now completely out of the public spotlight, mostly confined to his hospital bed at the Brooklyn State Hospital since September 1954, but his songs and fame would become increasingly popular over the coming decade, on both sides of the Atlantic.[32]

4

Popular Folk Music Comes
of Age, 1955–1956

Hillbilly Collectors and the British Revival

The British interest in American folk and country music stretched to a small group of record collectors who formed the Hillbilly-Folk Record Collectors' Club and launched the quarterly *Hillbilly-Folk Record Journal* in early 1954, which lasted until 1957, when the name changed to *Folk Style*. The first issue was dedicated to Jimmie Rodgers, the second to Hank Williams. Each issue included a variety of feature articles, discographies, news items, and record company information. A drawing of Lead Belly graced the cover of issue number 3, followed by a short biography. While all the issues would focus on Americans, with a primary emphasis on popular country performers and their recordings, British singers such as Ewan MacColl were not neglected: "No one will deny the revival of interest in genuine folk songs which has taken place during the past few years. The enjoyment of folk songs has ceased to be the right of a small select group of students and has been brought to the listener by singers such as Burl Ives from the United States, and Ewan MacColl in England. . . . He has been associated with a number of excellent folk song programmes on the third wavelength, but to my mind his most enjoyable radio series was the 'Ballads and Blues' show, which ran to six programmes on the B.B.C. North Region last spring."[1]

The late 1954 issue of *The Hillbilly-Folk Record Journal* featured an article on Big Bill Broonzy, and a few months later the editors happily announced that "the folk singer—BURL IVES has accepted the designation of Honourary President of the Hillbilly-Folk Record Collectors' Club." The issue included Ives's article "What Is a Folk Song and Why It Is Important": "Folk Music is made up by just anybody who can; it is music used by people as their own personal musical expression. This is especially true of folk songs, that part of folk music which has interested me. . . . The folk songs of America, present and past, are everybody's heritage." The issue also included features on Jean Ritchie and Josh White, followed in mid-1955 with a short biography of Ives, as well as a review of A. L. Lloyd and Ewan McColl's album on the Topic label, *The Singing Sailor*. Indeed, the left-wing Topic company received good coverage in most issues.[2]

The mid-1956 issue featured country singer Carl Smith on the cover, while there was a notice for "Admirers of Woody Guthrie (and I know there are many among our readers), [who] will be sorry to learn of his recent spell in Brooklyn State Hospital. . . . One solitary Melodisc 78 RPM disc is our only reminder of Woody Guthrie's recorded work, to be found in the English catalogues. But we are pleased to hear that the American folk singer (and friend of Woody) Jack Elliott has recorded an album of Woody Guthrie for the Topic label." The column also noted the recent Topic releases of Margaret Barry (Barrie), Ewan MacColl, and Bert Lloyd, the Riverside series of *Child Ballads*, and the Weavers' recent Carnegie Hall reunion concert. The early 1957 issue featured a readers' poll of the most popular performers. Hank Williams headed the country and western list, while Burl Ives was the top folk performer, followed by Josh White, Lonnie Donegan, Big Bill Broonzy, Huddie Leadbetter (Lead Belly), Woody Guthrie, and Mahalia Jackson. This proved the last issue under the original name, replaced by *Folk Style* in December 1957. This issue included a discography of Jack Elliott's Topic records, and John Edwards's biographical essay of Buell Kazee; Edwards was their Australian representative.[3]

While the *Hillbilly-Folk Record Journal* focused on the various styles of (white) country music, the blues scholar (and architecture expert) Paul Oliver covered African American performers. In the May 1954 issue of *Music Mirror* he discussed "the influence of the railroad on the religious music of the Negro." He referred to "John Henry," "Rock Island Line," "Honky-Tonk Train Blues," and others. He followed with "The Folk Blues of Sonny Terry" in late 1955: "A devil he is, a wild singer, a playing fool—and a great folk artist; one of whom both his mother, and his Mother Race have good reason to be proud." Then in mid-1958 he wrote about "Odetta" as well as "Brownie McGhee and Sonny Terry" in the *Music Mirror*. [4]

The April 1955 issue of *Cosmopolitan*, a popular American magazine, featured the article "Greenwich Village—1955," with a photo (taken by George Pickow, husband of Jean Ritchie) of Ramblin' Jack Elliott. According to the

caption, "Balladier Jack Elliot [sic] makes money putting on folk-song concerts from the enormous repertoire of melodies he has collected in years of
walking, hitchhiking, range riding and itinerant listening. He often sings at
impromptu socials held Sunday afternoons around the Square's fountain,
where the entertainment may include anything from acrobatics to authentic Indian dancers." Curiously, there is no mention of Elliott working with
Woody Guthrie, probably because Guthrie was now an obscure figure in a
local hospital. The article also included a photo of Susan Reed, a popular
ballad singer, who now owned an antique shop.[5]

Erik Darling was another musician appearing in Washington Square at the
time. Born in 1933 in Baltimore, Maryland, by the early 1950s he found himself
living with his mother on New York's Upper West Side and visiting Washington
Square on summer Sunday afternoons. He became part of the developing folk
community and began a friendship with Elliott, who, according to Darling,
"imitated Woody Guthrie but never came out of that role." A talented player of
banjo and guitar, Darling would soon be a member of various influential folk
groups, including the Song Swappers, the Tarriers, and the Weavers (replacing
Pete Seeger). His friend Jack Elliott would take another path with his move
with his wife June in late 1955 to England, where he would be a cultural sensation and cement closer ties between folk songs and their communities across
the Atlantic. The American Slim Whitman, dressed in western costumes and
yodeling cowboy songs, had already introduced a British audience to country-
pop music and long remained popular; in 1955 his recording of "Rose Marie"
remained on the U.K. singles chart for 11 weeks.[6]

Elliott arrived in London just as skiffle was emerging as a pop phenom-
enon, a mixture of British and American styles. Chris Barber's Jazz Band had
a busy recording schedule—their Decca album *New Orleans Joys* appeared in
January 1955, with two Lonnie Donegan skiffle cuts, "Rock Island Line" and
"John Henry"—as well as various club dates. The skiffle scene had to com-
pete with some American imports, including "Ain't That a Shame" by Fats
Domino and "Rock Around the Clock" by Bill Haley and the Comets; "Rock
Around the Clock" climbed to number one on the hit parade and remained
there through late 1955. Both Big Bill Broonzy and Josh White were touring
in England in late 1955 (Broonzy for the fourth time), giving an authentic
flair to the African American musical sound and style that underlay skiffle.
"[Broonzy] sang at concerts and at private parties, showing all the time what
a fine guitarist he was," the skiffle player and blues enthusiast Alexis Korner
wrote in 1955. "He had all that was of the Mississippi in his singing and playing and this was our information for he was not a talkative man from whom

collectors could glean untold gems. . . . At approximately the same time a flying visit from Lonnie Johnson permitted us, at the Festival Hall, to hear another singer whose records we had cherished." While in England White also published *The Josh White Guitar Method*, a pioneering book on the blues guitar. Within the year Donegan's singles would be major hits, with "Rock Island Line" reaching number 10 on the U.S. pop charts by mid-1956; soon after it reached the top of the charts in England.[7]

Paul Robeson appeared on the cover of *Sing* in mid-1955, along with his published letter to the magazine: "Deeply cherished is my long association with the Labor and Peace groups in Great Britain, and it's good to know the youth are carrying on, and especially in the field of People's music." Still a hero in England, he could not travel there because the State Department had canceled his passport in 1950 (not to be restored until 1958), while the blacklist crippled his domestic career. Although Alan Lomax was not directly involved with *Sing*, he nonetheless appreciated its politics when he returned to London from his collecting trip to Italy in November 1955. His illustrated children's book, *Harriet and Her Harmonium*, had recently been published in England and garnered a positive review in *Sing* by "Uncle Sing": "Tell your Dad that it's got lots of social history and commendable ideas about freedom and tolerance too." The story traced the travels of an English girl visiting her father in San Francisco in the mid-nineteenth century and was filled with songs such as "Paddy Doyle," "Springfield Mountain," and "The Chisholm Trail."[8]

"The Italian trip was extremely fruitful in every way," Lomax informed his brother John in November 1955. "Most of the voyage was paid for by BBC broadcasts, and my welcome back to London has been very warm." He thought he might return to the United States in a year. "This period of being abroad and completely dependent on my own efforts and my own name has been awfully good for me," he continued. "I've at last almost emerged completely from father's shadow, which I now realize always hung over me in America." In January he requested a year's extension on his work permit from the Home Office, which quickly checked with the Special Branch. The latter responded that while he was in contact with a known Communist and had long been suspect of left-wing sympathies, they had no objection.[9]

Lomax's return to London was celebrated at a party at Ewan MacColl's apartment, where he met Shirley Collins, a young singer from Hastings who had been in London since 1953. "I already knew of Alan through his series of folk music, radio programmes for the BBC—*Adventures of a Ballad Hunter*. . . . I remembered how enthralled I was by both the music and Alan's accent," Collins would later write. "I fell in love, and he seemed to like me too. . . .

Reader, I didn't marry him, but after a short courtship, I went to live with him in Highgate." They worked closely together for the next three years.[10]

Collins would play an important part in Lomax's life, connecting British and American musical styles. So too did Jack Elliott and his wife June, who arrived in London in September 1955, having shared the ocean voyage from New York to Le Havre, France, with Peggy Seeger, the half-sister of Pete, who would also turn up in London. Elliott quickly plunged into the local folk scene, a popular figure with his Stetson hat and guitar, who had a list of contacts provided by Pete Seeger, including Lomax, Bert Lloyd, and MacColl. Through the Lomax connection he quickly released an album for Topic Records, *Woody Guthrie's Blues*, which was recorded in MacColl's mother's house and served to mark his distinctive role in the expanding British folk scene. The six songs on the small LP included "Talking Columbia Blues," " Hard Traveling," and "Talking Dust Bowl Blues." "We found, to our great pleasure, that the audience in Britain knew all about Woody Guthrie and other American folk and country singers, and seemed to understand everything Ramblin' Jack was talking about," June Elliott would explain. Jack also performed as a surprise guest at a concert at Festival Hall sponsored by the National Jazz Federation, alongside the head-liners Chris Barber and Lonnie Donegan.[11]

Both Jack and June Elliott also appeared in the musical *The Big Rock Candy Mountain*, produced by MacColl's former wife, Joan Littlewood, who explained the situation: "We were putting on *The Big Rock Candy Mountain*, [written] by Alan Lomax, for Christmas and he came along to join in the fun . . . with a sackfull of catchy tunes and 'Rambling Jack Elliott, the Singing Cowboy' in tow. Mind you, Rambling Jack had never seen a cow in his life, being born and bred in New York. All the same, his cowboy hat and boots caused a sensation in Angel Lane [London's East End] and brought the kids in. In fact, they fol-lowed him wherever he went." The two-week run generated positive reviews and further introduced the audience to a smattering of American folk tunes, such as the title song, Guthrie's "So Long, It's Been Good to Know Yuh," "Take This Hammer," and "Fireball Mail." With only a three-month tourist visa, Jack did not stay long—the Elliotts were soon off on a trip to the continent—but he managed to meet such traditional performers as Seamus Ennis in London and Margaret Barrie in Dublin. Meanwhile, *Woody Guthrie's Blues* began to garner avid fans and reviews. As June would comment, "Jack didn't have a lot of ambition. He was content to keep drifting. All he wanted to do was sing his songs[,] dream of sailing on old ships and hitchhike in lorries."[12]

While Elliott and Lomax were spreading the gospel of American folk songs, skiffle, the musical hybrid, began its rise in popularity. Donegan's

"Rock Island Line" hit the charts in early 1956 and remained for weeks, along with the American songs "The Ballad of Davy Crockett" and "Sixteen Tons" by Tennessee Ernie Ford, joining such English fare as "Never Do a Tango With an Eskimo" by Alma Cogan, and "Pickin' a Chicken" by Eve Boswell. The Chris Barber Band with Donegan continued to tour provincial town halls, although Donegan would break off on his own by early May, when he was recording for the Nixa label; his version of "Lost John" quickly become a hit. During the summer he toured in the United States, where "Rock Island Line" had already reached number 10 on the charts. Meanwhile, in September 1955 London's first skiffle club had opened at the Roundhouse in Soho (Jack Elliott was an early attraction, with later appearances by Big Bill Broonzy, Sonny Terry and Brownie McGhee, and Muddy Waters, when its managers Alexis Korner and Cyril Davies had shifted the focus to blues), followed in April 1956 by the Forty-Four Skiffle & Folksong Club at 44 Gerrard Street, then a third at the Princess Louise on High Holborn (in late 1957 it became the home of MacColl's "Ballads and Blues" club).

The Forty-Four Skiffle & Folksong Club launched the John Hasted Skiffle and Folksong Group, with Shirley Collins. While Hasted had a strong political bent, he welcomed skiffle, with no overt political message, as a fresh folk sound. "Most SING readers will have heard a skiffle group, but fewer will have been to a skiffle *club*," Hasted wrote in *Sing* at the end of 1956. "There aren't so many yet where this kind of music is played in the evening. How can you start a skiffle and folksong club in your part of the world? This is certainly the time to start one." Hasted would later explain, "Very seldom was there any complaint that our folk revival was part of a Communist plot, despite the strong political convictions of so many of the prominent singers. Only one country singer actually declined to appear at my London Skiffle and Folk Club on political grounds." And he would conclude: "We had three years of real excitement and inspiration with Skiffle music. And when in due course the craze was superseded, the washboards returned to the cupboard under the sink and the tea-chests to the dump, those of us who had started it at least felt the satisfaction of having changed the face of British popular music, with a public revival of harmony, rhythm, counterpoint, and a celebration of laughter, love, drama, fame and money."[13]

Alan Lomax and Ewan MacColl were quick to hop on the developing skiffle bandwagon while busy with their other commitments. "I am pooped at the moment, having just finished revising a huge new American ballad book which Doubleday will now publish," Lomax informed his sister Shirley in April 1956. "*Westminster* records have just published the first four of 11 Spanish albums of mine they will issue this year." The book, *The Folk Songs of North America*, would appear in 1960, and the remainder of the Spanish albums would be released by 1959. While still being shadowed by the Special Branch (and back home the FBI queried the CIA about Alan's politics), he yet embarked on new ventures. Lomax had earlier worked for the BBC, but in 1956 he switched to Granada Television, where he produced *The Ramblers*, fourteen one-hour music programs. "Alan planned to have a small resident group which would be supplemented from time to time by Bert [Lloyd], Fitzroy Coleman, Alf Edwards, Bruce Turner, Seamus Ennis, Michael Gorman and others," MacColl would explain.[14]

A new skiffle group, Alan Lomax and the Ramblers, now emerged, with MacColl, Coleman, Shirley Collins, Turner, and the newcomer Peggy Seeger. "I was staying in a Danish youth hostel when the folklorist Alan Lomax put a call through from England," Seeger later wrote. "Granada Television needed a female singer-cum-banjo player for a production of *Dark of the Moon*. So at the age of nearly twenty-one, on March 25, 1956, at 10:30 in the morning I entered a basement room in Chelsea, London, and sealed my fate. Ewan MacColl was sitting on the other side of the room." Not yet, but soon enough, they would launch a relationship that only ended with MacColl's death in 1989. Decca released a few of their skiffle recordings—one 45 with MacColl's compositions "Dirty Old Town"/"Hard Case" and an EP with four songs in 1956 under the title *Alan Lomax and the Ramblers*—to no apparent popularity, and the Granada programs, filmed in Manchester and aired during the summer, had scant reception as well. Lomax also joined the Ramblers, Lonnie Donegan, and Ken Colyer in the 1957 Decca album *Kings of Skiffle*. "The group never took off—its goal was the Top Ten but it had no artistic destination," Seeger explained. "It was a stew made of good ingredients but impossible to cook. We didn't deserve to succeed—and we didn't." A few of their songs were published in *The Skiffle Album, featuring Skiffle and Folk Songs Popularised by Alan Lomax and the Ramblers*, including MacColl's "Dirty Old Town." The introduction read: "Alan Lomax and Ewan MacColl, both of whom were raised in their youth with ballads and folk songs, hope that skiffle and folk singers everywhere will find these songs as exciting as they have. They hope too that British skifflers will find more of their songs on their home ground and that is one of the reasons for the publication of this book."[15]

Alan Lomax and the Ramblers represented an early attempt to make commercial use of skiffle. Jack Elliott, the incarnation of Woody Guthrie, a skiffle muse, also tried his hand with the City Ramblers. They were a rag-tag ensemble, formed by Russell Quaye, and including Hylda Sims, who usually performed at the Princess Louise. They released a Topic single, "Round and

Round the Picket Line"/"Nine Hundred Miles." Jack and June were busking in Europe during the summer when they heard about the City Ramblers' decision to tour Germany and Scandinavia, so they returned to London. "Before the big trip we took some time to travel round Wales and Ireland," June would write, "getting as far as the Aran Islands." The City Ramblers' tour was more or less a bust, although they did record an album in Copenhagen in September, later released on Storyville Records. Jack seldom performed with others, appearing only on one song on the EP, "Midnight Special." Jack and June would not return to England until early 1957.[16]

By year's end skiffle bands were proliferating, while rock 'n' roll groups also formed, stimulated by the opening of Alan Freed's film *Rock around The Clock* in July; soon, Tony Crombie and the Rockets would hit the charts with "Teach You To Rock." Lonnie Donegan returned from the United States in August and continued his skyrocketing career. The Avon Cities Skiffle Group from Bristol, the Railroaders Skiffle Group from Newscastle, and the Delta Skiffle Group from Glasgow were among thousands of skiffle groups that began springing up around the country, most located in decent-sized towns. Leeds would host the world skiffle competition in 1957. "This month's paradox: they are trying to kill skiffle off," Hasted explained in mid-1957. "The kings of entertainment and publicity are seeking to make it nothing more than a fashionable craze. . . . The real music is being strangled in a welter of skiffle clothes, skiffle outfits (with specially designed washboards) and skiffle toilet rolls. Old music is being recomposed and the people who first made it (Leadbelly [*sic*], Uncle Dave Macon, [Ken] Colyer) quietly forgotten. But the music behind the ballyhoo will survive." In June 1957 the BBC launched the *Saturday Skiffle Club*, a weekly radio program; regular performers included Chas McDevitt, Vipers Skiffle Group, Johnny Duncan and his Bluegrass Boys, and George Melly and his Bubbling Over Four. With skiffle's demise, the name was changed to the *Saturday Club* in October 1958. In early 1958 Bert Lloyd gave talks on "English Folk Song and Skiffle" and "Jazz, Blues and Skiffle."[17]

"My own fortunes this year have been most peculiar," Alan Lomax informed his family as Christmas approached, with no word of his skiffle career. "I wrote a play last Christmas which had a successful run. . . . Then I spent the spring and part of the summer producing a TV show for one of the commercial networks." He mentioned composing a book with Peggy Seeger, *American Folk Guitar: A Book of Instruction* (1957), and returning to the United States, but this was still a ways off. Along with the numerous transatlantic musical connections, Kenneth Goldstein, a producer at Riverside Records, arranged to issue eight albums a year that would appear on the Topic label.[18]

Back in Greenwich Village

While skiffle provided a dramatic boost to the popularity of folk-style music in Great Britain, a different musical hybrid, calypso, shot up the charts and captured the public's imagination for a relatively short time in the United States. It was promoted as a counter to the scruffy, bad-boy image of rock 'n' roll, particularly as exemplified by Elvis Presley. But calypso was not the only aspect of folk music that received some commercial recognition. Overall record sales increased by 43 percent from 1955 to 1956, the equivalent of an additional $100 million in revenue. The baby-boom generation (born after 1945) was just entering its teen years, but an emerging youth culture, made up of an accelerating number of college students, fueled much of the expanding record market. For 1955 the bestselling records included a hodgepodge of styles and performers, such songs as "Cherry Pink and Apple Blossom White," "Rock around the Clock," "Yellow Rose of Texas," "Autumn Leaves," and "Ballad of Davy Crockett." The mix of popular country-western, rhythm and blues, and pop artists included Chuck Berry, Teresa Brewer, Pat Boone, Little Walter, Eddy Arnold, and the Drifters. Elvis Presley was just beginning his rocket-like rise to pop stardom, signing his first three-year contract with RCA in November. Within this eclectic mix, folk music had to discover its own audience.[19]

Although Senator Joe McCarthy's reign was over, the Red Scare continued to send a chill through popular culture, with the blacklist remaining strong in Hollywood and on network television. Pete Seeger would finally appear before the HUAC in August 1955, but he refused to discuss his views, citing the First Amendment: "I am not going to answer any questions as to my association, my philosophical or religious beliefs or any political beliefs, or how I voted in any election, or any of these private affairs. I think these are very improper questions for any American to be asked, especially under such compulsion as this." He did admit, however, "I have sung for Americans of every political persuasion, and I am proud that I never refuse to sing to an audience, no matter what religion or color of their skin or situation in life. I have sung in hobo jungles, and I have sung for the Rockefellers, and I am proud that I have never refused to sing for anybody."[20]

Almost two years later a federal grand jury cited Seeger for contempt of Congress (although he would not go to trial until 1961). Folk singers Lee Hays and Tony Kraber, an actor and singer with strong left-wing ties, had been called by HUAC at the same time, with a similar result. "The House Committee on Un-American Activities, which seems bent on making our country a sorry spectacle in the eyes of the world, spent four days this summer 'questioning' a group of actors, writers and singers about 'subversion' in the entertainment field," Irwin Silber wrote in *Sing Out!* "Millions of Americans applauded the gallant stand made by these entertainers in defying the un-American inquisition into the arts." While Silber might have overestimated the popular response, his optimistic thoughts resonated with a growing audience. Deep in the shadows, however, J. Edgar Hoover continued the FBI's fervent pursuit of "communists," a broad designation referring to anyone he didn't like, such as civil rights advocates, student activists, and those working for peace. He launched the Counter Intelligence Program (COINTELPRO) in 1956, an array of covert operations designed to "disrupt" and "neutralize" any groups deemed subversive. The FBI also continued its close relationship with HUAC.[21]

Sing Out!, a small quarterly under Irwin Silber as editor, now shied away somewhat from overt politics. Each issue had an international flavor in song and story, representing the movement to counter the polarizing chill of the Cold War. The summer issue featured a review of Ernie Lieberman's *Goodbye, Mr. War* album on the Amerecord label. An early supporter of the British *Sing*, the spring 1955 issue included a flattering review by Pete Seeger of Ewan MacColl's recent Stinson recording *Fourpence a Day, and Other British Industrial Folk Songs*, as well as his two songbooks, *Personal Choice, 50 Scottish and English Folksongs* and *The Shuttle and the Cage*. The article included two of his recorded worker songs, "The Blantyre Explosion" and "The Work of the Weavers." Riverside's arrangement with Topic would also result in issuing numerous MacColl records, initially including a series of *English and Scottish Popular Ballads*.

The 1950s Counterculture

While folk music struggled to survive commercially in mid-decade, in many ways it was linked with the developing countercultural movement—poetry, films, novels, comic books, jazz, comedy—spreading across the country at the time. On the one hand, the decade has been depicted as one of domestic prosperity, fueling the brisk move to suburbia and increasing consumer spending. Still, there were disturbing elements: the Cold War abroad and the deadening influence of the domestic Red Scare, leading to widespread blacklisting and paranoia; heightened fears of youth's corruptibility, even delinquency; an unfolding civil rights movement; and straight-jacketed corporate jobs tied to middle class conformity and the proliferating suburban communities. Resulting from this queasy intermingling of serenity and trepidation, the various countercultural movements emerged.

Rock 'n' roll apparently served as one challenge to the status quo, marked by Elvis Presley's vibrating torso and songs drawn from rockabilly and the repertoire of African American performers. The establishment reacted in predictable, frightened ways, through economic pressures, repressive laws, public demonstrations of record breaking, and heightened rhetoric. Fears went way beyond potential internal and external communist threats, including an atomic holocaust, and now included the apparent rash of juvenile delinquency, violent comic books, vulgar literature, and so much more.

Repression appeared in various forms—the Comics Code of 1954 which censored sex and violence, even titles that included *horror* and *terror*, from the colorful kids' magazines; concerns about the spate of delinquency films; and the backlash against rock 'n' roll, fueled by fears of race mixing and sexual promiscuity. Anticommunist propaganda masqueraded in the plentiful horror films or perhaps the numerous westerns and Biblical/religious movies; there were, oddly, only a paltry few, low-budget Hollywood films or television shows specifically about the Red Menace, including the Korean War. Society seemed to be flying apart in the midst of the prevailing *Ozzie and Harriet / Leave It to Beaver* TV culture.[22]

By mid-decade the Beat movement appeared as another challenge to the perceived cultural and social blandness, which had dark, rather anarchistic undertones. Folk and Beat bohemian communities emerged in Greenwich Village, San Francisco's North Beach, as well as selected neighborhoods in Chicago, Denver, and other urban centers. Folk music possessed a somewhat renegade image, partly from its connection with Communism, real or imagined, partly from its counter to accepted musical standards. On the other hand, the Beats championed creativity, independence, and freedom, as they dropped out physically and spiritually, aided by alcohol and a variety of other drugs. They also dropped out artistically, preferring modern jazz with its pulsating beat and African American overtones to Tin Pan Alley tunes. They were joined by Lenny Bruce and the other "sick" comedians, who tackled a range of offbeat subjects through their political, religious, and cultural jokes.[23]

Folk music represented another alternative milieu, even if essentially aural, and began to attract those searching for something different, particularly in Greenwich Village, New York's bohemian heart. Joyce Johnson, for example, found herself hanging around Washington Square a few years before plunging into the Beat scene. "Here is the arch, as described by the Trotskyite girls, and there is the fountain, the circle in the square, where, according to them, people gather every Sunday to sing folk songs," she would recall. "I'd imagined hordes of people, a whole guitar-and-banjo-strumming population, their music ringing through the park." She was not disappointed. The budding journalist and novelist Dan Wakefield arrived in the Village from Indianapolis in 1952 and quickly discovered the White Horse Tavern: "There the talk continued over pints of ale or beer, or the favored combination of arf 'n' arf, and soon everyone broke into songs of Irish rebellion, or love, or protest, folk songs joined and swelled by the Clancy Brothers or long-haired, blond Mary Travers, who also hung out in the back room of the Horse."[24]

San Francisco's North Beach spawned clubs that attracted both Beat poets and folk singers. The former gathered at Six Gallery, where Alan Ginsburg presented his groundbreaking poem "Howl" in 1955, as well as the Cellar, the Iron Pot, Vesuvio's bar, and Fugazi Hall. Enrico Banducci opened the hungry i (the i standing for id) at 149 Columbus in 1949 and introduced folk music with the African American singer Stan Wilson in 1952. Banducci launched the Purple Onion across the street in 1953, and when he moved the hungry i to larger quarters at 599 Jackson in 1954, it became the city's top spot for folk performers and topical comics, including Lenny Bruce and Maya Angelou. By mid-decade the city hosted a lively folk community, including Wilson, Odetta, Jo Mapes, Larry Mohr, Lou Gottlieb and the interracial Gateway Singers, and soon the Kingston Trio.

Chicago had no exact match for Greenwich Village or North Beach, but the city possessed a vibrant music, literary, and theatrical scene split between the Northside and the Hyde Park/University of Chicago neighborhood. Myron Reed "Slim" Brundage was the noted founder and janitor of the College of Complexes, a bar opened in 1951 that served as the heart of bohemian culture through the decade. Mixing poetry, jazz, blues, plays, old movies, ethnic dance, the College became a magnet for the politically and artistically disillusioned. A most unusual group was "I Come for to Sing," a quartet made up of Studs Terkel, Big Bill Broonzy, Win Stracke, and Larry Lane, which debuted at the University of Chicago's Mandel Hall in 1947. Broonzy performed blues songs, Stracke played folk songs of the American West, and Lane sang Elizabethan ballads, with Terkel serving as the narrator for each show. In 1952 they landed a regular Monday night slot at the Blue Note, a jazz club; Stan Kenton, Buddy Rich, and even Duke Ellington often caught their show, whose residency lasted for several years, although they also performed in other locations. Albert Grossman and Les Brown opened the first regular folk club, the Gate of Horn, in 1956, which featured not only a range of folk performers but also many of the growing number of irreverent comics. Chicago, along with other urban centers, served as a hotbed of poetry, jazz, comedy, and folk music, which were often linked together, part of the counterculture that challenged the status quo.[25]

Sing Out!

"It is hard to believe that SING OUT has completed its first five years—and is actually embarking on its next five with this anniversary issue," Silber began the winter 1956 issue. "Hardly a year of those five was not accompanied with grave crises which periodically threatened to mark the end of our publishing venture." But survive it did, having published almost four hundred songs. Two individuals were particularly praised, staff member Jerry Silverman and Pete Seeger, with Aaron Kramer's "Blues for Emmett Till" leading off the issue, about the young African American boy who was brutally murdered in Mississippi for supposedly whistling at a white woman. Pete Seeger introduced two songs from the Georgia Sea Islands, "Michael, Row the Boat Ashore" and "Pay Me My Money Down," which would soon be folk hits. The issue also included "Black and White," with words by Dave Arkin (the father of Alan) and music by Earl Robinson, celebrating the recent *Brown v. Board of Education* Supreme Court decision outlawing school segregation ("Black and White" would become a hit for the rock group Three Dog Night in 1975).[26]

In the same issue Silber welcomed the return of the Weavers to Carnegie Hall on Christmas Eve 1955, which served as their resurrection after three years of blacklisting: "That our country should not be able to enjoy its own musical riches through the voices of The Weavers is the price we pay for our tolerance of the war fever and its necessary partner, the contemporary Inquisition." Their manager Harold Leventhal was unable to rent Town Hall due to the ongoing blacklist, but Carnegie Hall became available because the management was unaware of their political problems. Fortunately, Leventhal had the concert recorded, then convinced Vanguard Records, which had a small folk catalog, to issue the album. *The Weavers at Carnegie Hall*, appearing in 1957, quickly became a major spur to folk music's developing popularity, with the group's presentation unadulterated by the orchestral arrangements that Decca had previously demanded. "Here's a peculiar situation: with the American folksong revival on in full force, with 500,000 guitars sold last year, and millions more having fun singing folk songs together, why is it that still there are comparatively few choruses in the country, and such as there are find themselves hard pressed to keep up their membership?" Seeger wrote in his column. Seemingly unimpressed by the Weavers' newfound popularity—Vanguard would issue additional albums through the decade, as the group continued to give concerts—he was more concerned about the lack of attention to grassroots singing groups. *Sing Out!*'s spring 1956 issue began by announcing, "Folk songs are making the Tin Pan Alley cash registers ring again. Since the fabulous popularity of [Tennessee Ernie Ford's] 'Sixteen Tons,' the pop publishers are scouring the hills and libraries once again in search of American folk songs which can be turned into coin of the realm. Among the latest releases making their 'hit parade' bid are 'Rock Island Line,' 'John Henry,' and 'This Land Is Your Land.'"[27]

Harry Belafonte and Calypso

While the Weavers and other folk groups, such as the Gateway Singers and the Easy Riders, were gaining popularity, the most interesting development was the emergence of Harry Belafonte and calypso music. As much a surprise as skiffle in England, calypso first appeared in Port of Spain, Trinidad, part of the Carnival celebrations in the late nineteenth century. A particular form emerged before World War II: it told stories, conveyed news, and was led by chantwells, or singers, such as Atilla the Hun, Lord Invader, and the Roaring Lion. Some calypso artists arrived in New York City in the 1930s, developing a following and producing numerous recordings. In 1944 the Andrews Sisters had a hit with "Rum and Coca-Cola," written by Lord Invader. In the early 1950s the Duke of Iron and Sir Lancelot gained a following in New York and Miami, and they influenced Stan Wilson in San Francisco and especially Belafonte.[28]

Born in New York in 1927, Belafonte grew up in Harlem and in Jamaica, living with relatives, experiencing poverty until he joined the segregated Navy in March 1944 following his seventeenth birthday. He began to develop a political awareness about society's inequalities and the possible alternatives. "My eighteen-month hitch ended December 3, 1945," he recalled in his autobiography. "I could have reenlisted—I had no better prospects—but I'd had enough of military service; not just the numbing routine and the mortal risks with munitions, but the all-too-frequent incidents of prejudice that kept me in an almost constant state of simmering rage." Back in Harlem, he soon became involved with the city's black left-wing theater, American Negro Theater (ANT), and met Paul Robeson and other activists. Belafonte recalled, "What I remember more than anything Robeson said was the love he radiated, and the profound responsibility he felt, as an actor, to use his platform as a bully pulpit. I had no expectation that my acting on a basement stage in Harlem would lead me anywhere. But I knew I'd found my role model." As his dramatic and political connections expanded, Belafonte became active in People's Songs and Henry Wallace's presidential campaign in 1948 while also hanging around the city's jazz clubs, which featured bebop.[29]

He recorded for two small labels in 1949 and 1950, Roost and Jubilee, and even cut a few sides for Capitol, but with little success. He opened a small restaurant in Greenwich Village, the short-lived Sage, and began to study folk songs while continuing his political activism. His career picked up in October 1951 when he began a three-month stay at the famed Village Vanguard; he then moved uptown to the Blue Angel, where he remained until April 1952. Max Gordon, the owner of both clubs, originally had his doubts. During his audition "Harry went into his first number, 'Take This Hammer,' a Leadbelly [*sic*] song. (Leadbelly used to do it at the Vanguard every night.)," Gordon would later explain. "So Jack's [Jack Rollins, Harry's manager] making a folk singer out of this guy. I thought Harry's no Leadbelly, no prisoner swinging a hammer on a chain gang down in Georgia. But he made me listen anyway." Gordon was not even impressed by "The Banana Boat Song"—"I hate a phony Caribbean accent. I've had the real thing at the Vanguard—Calypso singers from Trinidad: the Lion, Attila the Hun, King Radio, MacBeth the Great. What the hell am I going to do with a phony Caribbean accent?" Belafonte had his own doubts, but his voice and sexy looks made up for any deficiencies, and his career took off: "What I suspected was that audiences liked not only my voice and my presence, but also the global range of the materials from the American chain-gang songs like 'Tol' My Captain,' 'Jerry,' 'Another Man Done Gone' to 'Oh No, John,' an English ballad, to 'Merci Bon Dieu,' a Haitian folk song, to the American ballad 'Shenandoah,' and back to 'Mo Mary,' an Irish standard, even 'Hava Nagila,' the Hebrew anthem."[30]

When he finished at the Blue Angel, Belafonte cut his first singles for RCA, beginning with "A Rovin'"/"Chimney Smoke," then the calypso "Man Smart (Woman Smarter)." In late 1953 he starred in *John Murray Anderson's Almanac*, a Broadway show that ran for 229 performances. While mostly unscathed by the McCarthy witch hunts, Belafonte's activist background did not go unnoticed: "But in January 1954, with *Almanac* packing the house every night, the editors of *Counterattack* accused me of being a 'Communist fronter.' . . . With that, columnists Walter Winchell and Dorothy Kilgallen took up the cry. Suddenly my whole career seemed to hang in the balance." With the backing of Michael Grace, *Almanac*'s producer, Belafonte survived the attack. "When he sings 'Mark Twain,' he makes you feel the weight of the Mississippi riverman's labor as well as the struggle of the human personality to dominate it," Howard Taubman explained in his review of *Almanac* in the *New York Times*. It was not until his first album, "*Mark Twain" and Other Folk Favorites*, that Belafonte's popularity soared. During the spring of 1954, and backed by a small ensemble, Belafonte had recorded a number of eclectic songs, some credited to "Paul Campbell," a pseudonym of the Weavers, as well as his own composition "Mark Twain." It would reach number 3 on the album charts by early 1956.[31]

Belafonte continued to pack them into his nightclub act; he also starred in the touring show *Three for Tonight* with the dancers Marge and Gower Champion, which appeared on CBS television on June 23, 1955. His next album, *Belafonte,* reached *Billboard*'s number 2 position in May 1956 and was another eclectic collection drawn from *Three for Tonight*: "Scarlet Ribbons," "In That Great Gettin' Up Mornin,'" "Noah," and the calypso "Matilda." *Belafonte* appeared just as Elvis Presley's first album topped the charts. "I could see that in one way, at least, we were on parallel tracks," Belafonte would explain. "Elvis was interpreting one kind of black music—rhythm and blues—while I found my inspiration in black folk songs, spirituals, and calypso, and also in African music." Popular magazines would soon feature them in a staged musical duel. *Ebony*, the popular African American magazine, was naturally proud of Belafonte's success in "playing chi-chi night clubs where Negroes had never performed before," and that "he fights hate with song." At the same time he began his relationship with Martin Luther King Jr., supporting his fundraising campaign in New York for the Montgomery, Alabama, bus boycott, which challenged segregation on the city's buses. Belafonte would become one of King's key financial supporters and closest advisors until King's death in 1968. He also backed Adlai Stevenson as the Democratic Party candidate for president in 1956, performing an updated version of the Earl Robinson/Lewis Allen Popular Front song "The House I Live In" for a television broadcast; moreover, he recorded "Adlai is de Man," a calypso-style song, to be played on sound trucks during the campaign.[32]

Belafonte's third album, *Calypso*, released in May 1956, reached number one on the charts by early September, where it remained for thirty-one weeks and altogether for ninety-nine weeks; it became the first million-selling album. His idea to have a complete album of calypso songs met with initial skepticism from RCA executives, who believed it would be "too ethnic, too black, too out of the mainstream." As for Belafonte, "I myself didn't want to be typecast as a calypso singer." He won out, although the album would not include traditional calypsos but calypso-style songs. "Bill Attaway, my good friend, former Sage [restaurant] partner, and resident musicologist became one of my two co-writers for the album," Belafonte later wrote. "He, in turn, told me about Lord Burgess."[33]

Irving Burgie, with the calypso name "Lord Burgess," had grown up in Brooklyn but was of West Indian heritage, served in the Army during World

War II, then attended the famed Juilliard music school in New York. After Juilliard he began playing the guitar and learning about folk music while attending the University of Arizona. By the early 1950s he had become a calypso singer, and through Attaway he was introduced to Belafonte, for whom he wrote songs for the *Colgate Comedy Hour* television show, including "Day-O." "The 'Banana Boat Song' was how islanders knew it," Belafonte would explain. "We called our version 'Day-O,' and made it the album's opening track, but none of us had any idea, when we recorded it, that it would be spun off as a single, much less rocket up the charts." Originating as a Jamaican work song and first recorded by the Trinidadian group Edric Connor and the Caribbeans in their 1952 album *Songs from Jamaica* (under the title "Day Dah Light"), Burgie's version rocketed to number 5 on the charts. Indeed, Burgie had a hand in writing most of the album's songs, including "Jamaica Farewell." "The song was also unusual in that the title does not appear in the song," Burgie wrote. "We discussed this and decided to keep the name as it was. Belafonte recorded it on the *Calypso* album, and it became a tremendous singles hit afterwards. Belafonte made it his theme song."[34]

Belafonte's success stimulated a calypso craze that would last through 1957 before quickly collapsing. Belafonte's "Day-O" single joined a crowded field, including covers by the Fontane Sisters, Steve Lawrence, Sarah Vaughan, and even Stan Freberg's satire recording. One of the most successful was the Tarriers' version on the tiny Glory label, named "The Banana Boat Song," which reached number 4. The interracial trio—composed of Alan Arkin, Erik Darling, Bob Carey—first had a hit with "Cindy, Oh Cindy," written by Bob Nemiroff, husband of playwright Lorraine Hansberry, and Burt D'Lugoff, brother of Art D'Lugoff, the concert promoter who connected the Tarriers with Glory's owner Phil Rose and became their manager. Glory didn't release "The Banana Boat Song" (which included the chorus from the Jamaican folk song "Hill and Gully Rider") until "Cindy, Oh Cindy" had quickly peaked at number 9 (Eddie Fisher's version was not far behind at number 10). "We had begun the calypso craze . . . and would be typecast as a calypso group, not as singers of folk songs," Darling would later explain. "The T.V. show 'Your Hit Parade' had production numbers of the song for eight weeks with dancers in costumes and sets suggesting bananas and Bahaman vacations. Except for the Ed Sullivan Show, every T.V. show we did had us sitting or standing in stage sets of dock pilings, barrels, netting, bananas, or palm trees. . . . We were booked into the Apollo Theater in Harlem, with steel drum bands and the Duke of Iron, a calypsonian from Trinidad. This guy was for real, although a bit hard to understand because of his West Indies accent."[35]

The passing calypso fad, often with a slight nod to authenticity, knew no commercial bounds. Along with the various cover recordings of "The Banana Boat Song," authentic calypsonians were snapped up by the record companies: Duke of Iron and Zebra on RCA, Lord Christo on Mercury, Lord Flea on Capitol, and the Massie Patterson calypso troupe on Columbia, for example. Terry Gilkyson and the Easy Riders had a hit with "Marianne" in early 1956, followed by versions from the Hilltoppers, the Lane Brothers, and even Burl Ives. Maya Angelou (later the famed poet and author) began as a singer and recorded *Calypso Lady* in 1957. Louis Eugene Wolcott (later known as the Nation of Islam leader Louis Farrakhan), a classically trained musician, began his professional career early in the decade as the calypso singer "The Charmer." Backed by Johnny McCleverty's Calypso Boys, he recorded on the Monogram label, although by 1956 he had abandoned this career.

"At the end of that landmark year [1956], generally conceded to be the birth year of rock 'n' roll, the bestselling album wasn't *Elvis Presley* or *Elvis*," Belafonte would explain in his autobiography. "It was *Calypso*. Critics took bets on which kind of music would prevail, rock 'n' roll or calypso. Even well into 1957, many critics predicted calypso would win . . . By the end of that next year, of course, the raw power of Presley's rhythm-and-blues rock 'n' roll would dominate the charts, and calypso as a trend would peter out." Various magazines appeared in 1957, aimed at teenagers, some with such outlandish titles as *Tommy Sands vs. Belafonte and Elvis*, and *Elvis vs. Belafonte: The Big Battle of 1957—Rock 'n' Roll vs. Calypso!*, an edition of *16* magazine. There was a rash of more specific titles: *Calypso Stars* (The Tarriers, Duke of Iron, William Attaway), *Calypso Album!*, *Harry Belafonte: His Complete Life Story*, *Calypso: The Belafonte Story*, *Calypso Songs: Lyrics of All the Great Record Hits*, *Calypso Song Craze*; and *'TEEN: The Magazine for Young Americans* featured "The Belafonte Secret": "The musical world has gone Calypso crazy! Spearheaded by Harry Belafonte, the rhythmical beat of the West Indies has captured the imagination and opened the pocketbooks of millions of Americans, especially the teenagers."[36] Since calypso existed mostly on long-playing records, it generally appealed to an adult market, however, with young people continuing to prefer rock 'n' roll and other popular styles with danceable rhythms, music available on the smaller, more portable 45 RPM records.

Three calypso films were quickly rushed into production in 1957, and soon flopped. *Calypso Joe* appeared first, starring Angie Dickinson and featuring the Easy Riders, Lord Flea, Herb Jeffries and His Calypsomaniacs, and the Duke of Iron. Columbia Pictures released *Calypso Heat Wave* in June, with Johnny Desmond, Joel Grey, Maya Angelou, and the Tarriers. *Bop Girl Goes*

Calypso followed in July, starring Lord Flea, with the bandleader Les Baxter composing most of the songs. There were many more rock 'n' roll teen films, although *Untamed Youth*, with the rock 'n' roller Eddie Cochran, curiously ended with Mamie Van Doren singing the Les Baxter composition "Go, Go Calypso." Besides Belafonte and Presley, popular performers of the year included the varied grouping of Pat Boone, Debbie Reynolds, Sam Cooke, Perry Como, the Everly Brothers, Paul Anka, and the Diamonds.[37]

While the commercial side of calypso flashed through 1957, there were local promoters who focused on the traditional performers. Art D'Lugoff in New York, for example, staged a series of concerts as well as representing Lord Burgess, who appeared on the NBC *Tonight* show in October 1956. D'Lugoff planned various events, including "Calypso War Declared" at the Brooklyn Academy of Music in May 1956, featuring Duke of Iron, Trinidad Steel Band, Lord Carleton vs. King Rudolph, Lady Calypso vs. Princess La Doll. The series "Calypso at Carnegie" in August headlined the Trinidad Steel Band, Duke of Iron, Lord Burgess, Massie Patterson, and Lloyd Thomas. In September there was the "Calypso Steel Band Clash: Trinidad Panamonic versus Virgin Isles Merry Makers," with Duke of Iron and Lord Burgess. D'Lugoff did not wait for calypso's peak of popularity in 1957 but rather was quick to take advantage of the interest he anticipated would increase in New York.

As the calypso fad, part of the developing folk scene, waned, RCA released *Belafonte Sings of the Caribbean* in 1958, with many of the songs again written by Irving Burgie. But Belafonte was working hard to move beyond his vibrant calypso image, as the craze was visibly slowing by mid-1957. "The present hysterical type of fervor for any melodies that even remotely resemble Calypso will wear out and drive it to premature obscurity," he wrote to the *New York Mirror* in May 1957. "I wish to be accepted strictly on my merits as an artist who sings songs of all the world, rather than be representative of any specific area—and certainly not as a symbol of a contrived craze." Years later, in his autobiography, he expressed his relief: "If I had any doubts I'd survive the passing calypso trend, they were put to rest that July and August of 1957 at the Greek Theater in L.A., where I played the longest run for any individual artist in its nearly thirty-year history." In addition to increasing bookings and major news stories, Belafonte noted, "I was immersed in the civil rights movement." His album *An Evening with Harry Belafonte* was drawn from the stage show *Sing, Man, Sing*, which flopped but featured an array of international songs: "Danny Boy," "Hava Nagila," "The Drummer and the Cook," and "Merci Bon Dieu." Skiffle in Great Britain, which had longer staying power, served as the stimulus for numerous performers who would use it as their entry into popular music. Calypso had its fleeting moment in the sun, although the Tarriers, Stan Wilson, Belafonte, and the Easy Riders got a commercial boost from calypso, and even the fledgling Kingston Trio benefitted from its brief popularity.[38]

International and Bawdy Songs

The Weavers and Harry Belafonte were not alone in promoting an international repertoire by mid-decade that transcended calypso. While Alan Lomax worked on the *Columbia World Library of Folk and Primitive Music* during his time in England, drawing upon his extensive recording in Great Britain, Spain, and Italy, international music found a popular audience in the United States. Much of the interest came from a search for international understanding and world peace during the harsh years of the Cold War. Jim Morse published *Folk Songs of the Caribbean* in 1958, with the subtitle "Fifty Favorite Love Songs, Work Songs, Game Songs, Ballads and Calypsos from the Exotic Islands and Countries of the Caribbean." "This community of spirit exists in all good folksongs," Tom Glazer explained in the book's introduction, "and of course in this excellent collection of Caribbean songs. It will do for Americans what all good songs do: It will bring us closer to the people who made the songs and who sing them, and that is good, because it is impossible to hate someone whose songs you love."[39]

Record companies issued a wide range of international albums, led by Moses Asch's Folkways with dozens of albums of music recorded from around the world. There were also many domestic recordings of music from outside the United States by artists such as Theo Bikel, Cynthia Gooding, Oranim Zabar, Marais and Miranda, and numerous others. Jac Holzman at Elektra issued a steady stream of such albums: Bikel, *Folksongs of Israel*; Bikel and Gooding, *A Young Man and a Maid (Love Songs of Many Lands)*; Gooding, *Turkish, Spanish and Mexican Folk Songs*; and Bikel, *Songs of a Russian Gypsy*, to name a few. The Clancy Brothers launched Tradition Records in New York in 1956, which specialized in Irish songs, although they also issued Hillel and Aviva, *Songs of Israel and Many Lands*. Kenneth Goldstein had done research for Fairchild Publications and began producing albums for Stinson in 1951. In 1956 he increased his output to about one per week for Folkways, Elektra, Vanguard, and Tradition into the 1960s, with a particular emphasis on music from the British Isles. For example, he issued four volumes of *The English and Scottish Popular Ballads (The Child Ballads)*, followed by one album of *Great British Balllads*, all recorded for Riverside by Ewan MacColl and A. L. Lloyd.[40]

Irwin Silber, *Sing Out!*'s editor, included international songs as part of his struggle against the Cold War. The Spring 1956 issue included a review of the book *Irish Songs of Resistance* by Patrick Galvin, published by Goldstein's Folklore Press, followed by Galvin's article "From the Famine to the Fenians." The issue also featured an article on "People's Songs of India," two Indian songs, and Silber's review of Pete Seeger and the Song Swappers's Folkways album *Bantu Choral Folk Songs*. The Song Swappers (Mary Travers, Erik Darling, and Tom Gerasi) recorded two other albums with Seeger for Folkways in 1955, *Camp Songs* and *Folksongs of Four Continents*. Indeed, during this period Folkways produced numerous Seeger albums, keeping him visible and busy despite the commercial blacklist; they also revealed his deep interest in world music. *Sing Out!* paid slight attention to the calypso fad, although it did publish a few songs: Malvina Reynolds and Cal Grigsby's (aka Lou Gottlieb) calypso-style "Monaco" and Blind Blake's more authentic "Love Alone." While Silber did publish John Hasted's article "Don't Scoff at Skiffle," there was nothing comparable about calypso.[41]

In addition to international songs, recordings of bawdy songs and ballads temporarily captured the interest of a popular folk audience. Ed McCurdy, a Canadian who had moved to New York in 1954, issued a string of bawdy Elektra albums, with McCurdy on the guitar and Darling on the banjo: *Barroom Ballads, Blood, Booze 'n' Bones*, and *Sin Songs, Pro and Con*. Most successful was a four-volume series of double-entendre Elizabethan ballads titled *When Dalliance Was in Flower and Maidens Lost Their Heads*. "The [first] album was an instant smash in college dorms, not six years after the birth of Elektra in a similar dorm," Elektra owner Jac Holzman recalled. "The original cover was line drawings of buxom maidens. After the album took off I decided to switch to a color photo. We shot photos of saucy wenches, featuring some nubile Playmates of the Month and some horny dallying dudes." The four albums eventually sold more than one hundred thousand copies.[42]

In a different vein, Oscar Brand produced a number of more contemporary bawdy albums, starting in 1955 with four volumes of *Bawdy Songs and Backroom Ballads*, then *Bawdy Songs Goes to College, Bawdy Hootenanny*, and *Bawdy Sea Chanties* on the Audio Fidelity label. Similar to the McCurdy albums, these also became popular in college dorms and teenage bedrooms, offering a salty contrast to the usual pop songs, even rock 'n' roll, which was considered racy enough by parents and ministers. Folk music had a broad range of contents and styles by mid-decade.

Woody Guthrie

"One of the most unusual evenings of folk music that I ever participated in was the program of songs of Woody Guthrie called *Bound for Glory* put on in New York over a year ago," Pete Seeger wrote in *Sing Out!* in late 1957. "When we first proposed such an evening, some friends said, 'Won't all the songs sound alike? Will there be enough variety? Well, there was plenty of variety." Pete was referring to the concert at the Pythian Hall on March 17, 1956, featuring not only Seeger, but also Ed McCurdy, Robin Roberts, Rev. Gary Davis, as well as Marjorie Mazia (Woody's ex-wife) and her dance group. Woody was living in the Brooklyn State Hospital at the time but would soon move to the Greystone Park Psychiatric Hospital in New Jersey. The evening was filled with some of Woody's finest songs, along with quotes from his writings arranged by Millard Lampell. Woody was in the audience, wizened with white hair, looking much older than his forty-three years. The Folkways album *Bound for Glory* quickly appeared, with Woody's own recordings and the script read by Will Geer; a book of quotes and lyrics, *California to the New York Island*, soon followed. Since Woody had been pretty much invisible for much of the last decade, and few of his recordings were available, he now had little fame. Even the Weavers and Pete Seeger recorded few of his songs. But that would soon change, both in the United States and Great Britain, where the limited circulation magazine *Jazz Music* featured his photo on the cover in late 1957, with an accompanying short essay summarizing his life.[43]

Song sheet for *Sing Out!* May Day 1950, Pete Seeger, "Why Are We Marching?"

Cover of the first issue of *Sing Out!* (May 1950), featuring "The Hammer Song," by Lee Hays and Pete Seeger.

Flyer for concert by Earl Robinson, "Sing for Peace," California Labor School, San Francisco, June 1, 1951.

Flyer for "Art D'Lugoff presents Calypso at Carnegie," August 1956.

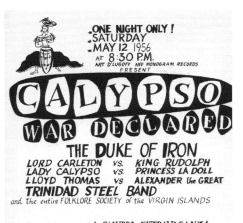

Flyer for "Calypso War Declared," Brooklyn Academy of Music, May 12, 1956.

Flyer for "Swapping Song Fair Midnight Concerts," May 11–26, 1956, Cherry Lane Theatre, New York.

Flyer for "Swapping Song Fair Midnight Concerts," March 9–24, 1956, Circle in the Square Theatre, New York.

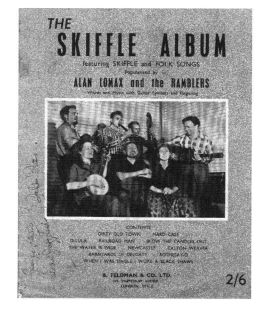

Cover of *The Skiffle Album* song-book. (London: B. Feldman, 1957.)

HOLIDAY
Swapping Song Fair

at the

Brooklyn Academy
of Music

on

FRIDAY EVE., FEB. 22nd at 8:40

FEATURING

OSCAR BRAND
N. Y.'s Most Popular Baladeer

JEAN RITCHIE
Of the Famous "Singing Ritchies of the Cumberlands"

with

ODETTA
From Chicago, "A Great New Voice"...*Variety*

and

PREMIER CONCERT APPEARANCE
of

ENID MOSIER
and her

Original Trinadad Steel Band

"Calypso"...*A la Carte from Blue Angel
& Village Vanguard*

Tickets — $2.50 - $2.00 - $1.50 (Tax Incl.) at

Brooklyn Academy - 30 Lafayette ST. - ST 3-6700
THE BOOKFAIR - 113 W. 49th ST. - JU 2-3195

Mail orders accepted — please enclose self addressed envelope

The Academy of Music is only one block from IRT, BMT, IND

Announcement for "Holiday Swapping Song Fair at the Brooklyn Academy of Music," February 22, 1957.

Cover of *Tommy Sands vs. Belafonte and Elvis*. (New York: The Girl Friend—The Boy Friend Corporation, 1957.)

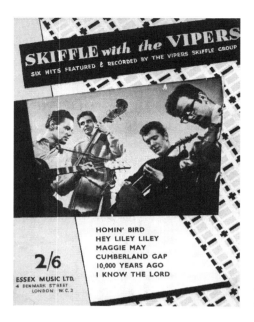

Cover of *Skiffle with the Vipers*. (London: Essex Music, 1957.)

Flyer for "Folk Festival at Midnite," Carnegie Hall, January 24, 1958.

Flyer for "Folksingers Guild Presents Folkmusic at Midnite," Sullivan St. Playhouse, New York, April 25, 1958.

Flyer for "Saturday Night Folkway Concert Series," 1958–1959, P.S. 41 Auditorium, New York.

Sheet Music for *The M.T.A.*, Atlantic Music Corp., with photo of the Kingston Trio on the cover. (Atlantic Music Corp., 1958.)

Caravan magazine front cover with drawing of folk tree, February–March 1959.

Flyer for concert sponsored by The Folklore Center with Barry Kornfeld and Rev. Gary Davis, March 7, 1959, Carnegie Chapter Hall, New York.

Cover of *Sing*, December 1959; cover photo of Jack Elliott, June Elliott, and Pete Seeger.

Flyer for "Hofstra College Folk Song Club Present a Folksong Concert," November 20, 1960, Hofstra Playhouse, Long Island.

Flyer for "Folk Music after Theatre" concert with New Lost City Ramblers and Theo Bikel, November 1960, One Sheridan Square, New York.

5

Further Developments,
1957–1958

Kingston Trio

The stifling hand of anticommunism had not lifted from popular culture—
movies, radio programs, folk music—but the latter was definitely feeling a
quickening pulse throughout the country. Then the Kingston Trio emerged
to energize the folk revival. Nick Reynolds was born in Coronado, California,
on July 27, 1933, the son of a Navy captain and a wealthy mother. He began
singing at an early age and listened to a range of musical styles, including
Mariachi music in Tijuana and the records of Augie Goupil and His Royal
Tahitians. He played a Martin 0–18 tenor guitar, along with conga and bongo
drums. Bob Shane (originally Schoen) was born in Hilo, Hawaii, on February
1, 1934, and grew up in Honolulu; his father was a local business owner. He
became steeped in Hawaiian music early and developed a wonderful voice
as well as his skill on the tenor guitar. Donald David "Dave" Guard followed
Shane on October 19, 1934, spent his teen years in Honolulu, and both attended the elite Punahou School, where they met around 1950. Guard listened
to Hawaiian music, along with English folk songs. Both Shane and Guard
played Tahitian music at local parties. For his final year in high school Guard
transferred to the Menlo School in Northern California, where Reynolds was
a student. Shane soon entered the Menlo School, while Guard wound up at
Stanford University in nearby Palo Alto. The three soon began their amazing
musical career as the Kingston Trio.[1]

At first Shane and Guard occasionally performed together, as well as separately, at local bars. One ad announced "Calpyso with Bob Shane and his guitar

Tonight at The Pagliaci [*sic*]." The three began playing at fraternity houses, where they specialized in Hawaiian and Tahitian songs, as well as comedy routines. At one point Shane returned to Honolulu and began performing in clubs and restaurants. There he met two of his musical heroes, the African American performers Stan Wilson and Josh White, who were touring the area. White talked Shane into switching from the four-string Martin to a six-string Martin D-28. Meanwhile, Nick and Dave were forming their own local groups, including a quartet named "Dave Guard and the Calypsonians" in late 1956, taking advantage of the mounting calypso craze; Guard had also learned to play the five-string banjo from Pete Seeger's instruction book. Reynolds soon left the group, which appeared to have little promise, except to the budding manager Frank Werber. The publicity and stage manager for Enrico Banducci's hungry i nightclub, Werber brought Shane, Guard, and Reynolds back together and worked hard to perfect their sound and stage presence. They chose the name The Kingston Trio because it had a Caribbean flavor as well as preppy sound. They began hanging around and learning from San Francisco's variety of performers—jazz greats Chico Hamilton and Stan Getz at the Black Hawk, comedians Mort Sahl, Lenny Bruce, Phyllis Diller, as well as folk performers Barbara Dane, Malvina Reynolds, Maya Angelou, Stan Wilson, Lou Gottlieb, Rod McKuen, Sonny Terry, and Brownie McGhee. They were particularly moved by a Weavers concert at the Opera House in San Francisco. The Trio opened at the Purple Onion in late May 1957 for a week as a replacement for the comic Phyllis Diller. Instead of a week they stayed for seven months, packing the small room each night. Lou Gottlieb, a musicologist and member of the Gateway Singers, recalled that he "started working as a stand-up comic and got a job at the Purple Onion. There were three guys there who used to hang around the hungry i all the time. . . . Well, sir, these kids really had something different. There was a magic about that act that was hard to explain." Gottlieb arranged the song "Saro Jane" for their first album, launching a close collaboration.[2]

The Trio obtained a contract with Capitol Records, and their album *The Kingston Trio* appeared in early summer 1958. They borrowed songs from various groups and sources: "Fast Freight" (Easy Riders), "Saro Jane" (Gateway Singers), "Sloop John B" (Weavers), "Hard, Ain't It Hard" (Woody Guthrie), and "Bay of Mexico" (Pete Seeger). The album slowly took off, then was given a boost by Paul Coburn, a disk jockey in Salt Lake City on KLUB, who began playing the song "Tom Dooley" on June 19. The buzz for the song led to Capitol's releasing the single in early August, and within the month it was on the charts, topping out at number 1 by year's end.

The Trio, at least in their early years, worked hard to project an apolitical image, shying away from the curse of folk music's assumed left-wing taint, while wearing their signature matching (usually striped) oxford shirts. The popularity of "Tom Dooley" partially gained from its conservative association with Thomas A. Dooley, a missionary doctor in Vietnam and Laos who fanned the flames of Catholic anticommunism after the defeat of the French in 1954. The Trio didn't shy away from this connection, although they continued their musical dependence on Pete Seeger and the Weavers. "Hanged Man in Hit Tune," *Life* announced in mid-December: "Out of the jukeboxes in almost every bar and candy store came the same three-part harmony pleas of an old folk song imploring a gay blade headed for the gallows to hang his hand in shame before the hangman fitted it through a noose." By year's end the Trio—three young men in striped shirts, their conservative look countering rock 'n' roll's greasy, long-haired, sexually charged, rebellious image—had captured much of the nation's musical imagination, which would continue for some years and proved singularly influential on the emerging folk revival. While the Kingston Trio performed numerous songs with an ethnic flair and connection, their authenticity lay in their grassroots style and appeal, with no hint of a foreign accent or language facility.[3]

Folk Festivals and Recordings

The Kingston Trio, along with Harry Belafonte and numerous others, made it clear that folk music had broad commercial appeal, contesting the stunning popularity of Elvis and so many other rock 'n' roll as well as pop performers, while it retained its traditional reach. Folkways, Stinson, Elektra, Vanguard, Decca, Riverside, and other record companies flooded the market with a variety of folk voices and styles. "A major effort in the recording of balladry, Kenneth Goldstein's five-volume series [*The English and Scottish Popular Ballads (The Child Ballads)*] for Riverside is noble in purpose," ran an article in the *Saturday Review* in early 1957. Older songs could also turn up at folk festivals then dotting the landscape. The Swarthmore College folk festival in April 1957 featured John Jacob Niles, for example, along with Mike and Peggy Seeger, Tom Paley, Tony Saletan, and Ellen Stekert. "The hordes of bathless, bearded and barefoot undesirables which were expected to over-run the campus, on the basis of stories which upperclassmen circulated to gullible freshmen and sophomores, never materialized," the campus newspaper surprisingly commented. "Instead the more than 500 guests who did register created a friendly and pleasant atmosphere here for three days." The 1955 festival, headlining Josh

White and Jean Ritchie, had attracted three thousand students, mostly from other colleges, which frightened the administration into canceling the 1956 weekend. The next year, with a much-reduced crowd, there were no problems. Odetta was the featured performer in 1958, and the festival continued into the 1960s. Joe Hickerson and others from Oberlin College had attended the 1957 event, and upon returning to Ohio they staged their own festival.[4]

In May 1958 Barry Olivier petitioned the University of California at Berkeley's Committee for Drama, Lectures, and Music to support a summer folk music festival. Having grown up in Berkeley and become an adept guitar player, Olivier was active on the local folk scene. The committee agreed, and the first festival was held during four days in late June. Ballad singer Andrew Rowan Summers, banjo player Billy Faier, Marais and Miranda, Frank Warner, and Jean Ritchie performed. Pleased with his success, Olivier followed up over the next decade with a similar lineup of traditional performers as well as workshops, and the Berkeley event became one of the most important of the college festivals. Numerous others would soon follow, giving the nation's students a taste of folk music's eclectic substance.[5]

Great Britain

"I am boiling over; I've had enough of the supercilious critics who clutter up the newspapers and magazines with attacks on skiffle," John Hasted announced in *Sing* in early 1957. "All right, granted that some skiffle groups make a dreadful noise; that many of the folksongs are badly interpreted; that some skiffle is indistinguishable from rock 'n' roll. The point that has been missed is this. Folk music has been dead in English cities for many years. Young people all over the kingdom are producing the home-made article. New songs, new tunes, above all a new style, in an age when you are supposed to Sit and Listen to What You Get." As for finding new songs, Hasted recommended obtaining Library of Congress records from the American Library, Grosvenor Square, while "Dobell's in Charing Cross Road sell Folkways, Columbia and Stinson labels which cover the most authentic material."[6]

In *Sing*'s next issue Hasted continued with his skiffle discussion. He applauded the appearance of the huge number of skiffle clubs, with more than four hundred in London alone. "Unlike the older skiffle groups, the new ones make no distinction between a rock 'n' roll number and a folk song, and I think this is only to be expected and is not a bad thing anyway," he explained. "It seems to me that good songs will last the longest, and immediate popularity is no criterion." Still, Hasted, joined by many others, retained his doubts. "All along, I had a rather ambivalent attitude to skiffle," he later explained. "What I really dreamt of was a folksong revival, but skiffle craze was the next best thing. I called my group a 'Skiffle and Folksong Group,' in the hope that a folksong revival would grow out of skiffle. It did." Alan Lomax published two rather laudatory articles in *Melody Maker* in 1957, "Skiffle: Why Is It So Popular?" and "Skiffle: Where Is It Going?" He appreciated the skifflers' interest in African American folk songs and had confidence "that their mastery of their instruments will increase, that they will get tired after a while of their monotonous two-beat imitation of Negro rhythm and that, in looking around, they will discover the song-tradition of Great Britain. . . . Then they will produce something a bit more home-grown." Skiffle would remain popular into 1958, but never without controversy, and it would soon influence a broader commercial folk music revival.[7]

Skiffle's popularity, following the Weavers success and other indications of folk music's commercial potential, encouraged Alan Lomax to begin copyrighting some of the songs that he and his father had collected, not as the composers but specifically listed as "collected, adapted, and arranged by." He was particularly incensed when Lonnie Donegan claimed composer credit for "Bring a Little Water, Sylvie," a song Lomax had recorded from Kelly Pace, a prisoner at the Arkansas State Penitentiary in 1934. Donegan also claimed copyright on "Goodnight Irene" and other Lead Belly songs, leading Lomax, morally outraged as well as always short of funds, to challenge all such claims. "Generally, I have come around to your view (which Moe Asch has come around to, on his own) that the only way to protect folk music from the Lonny [*sic*] Donegans and Mitch Millers is to do some copyrighting on your own," Pete Seeger wrote to Lomax. "I agree that your research has been fundamental to the present folksong revival. I regret that you feel it necessary, but under the circumstances of our society, in which research must suit the scholar or the big business firms (as in scientific research), there seems to be no other way for you to pay for your field work and other work which does not pay for itself directly." The nuances and ethics of the copyright issue would bedevil Lomax for many years.[8]

Various American folk performers would come and go in London, such as Sandy and Caroline Paton, popular singers from Chicago, who arrived in 1957. In a piece in the New York folk fanzine *Caravan*, Paton, while critical of skiffle, appreciated the more traditional stylings: "Here in London, a few weeks ago, Caroline and I attended a 'Ballads and Blues' concert on British Industrial Songs. Ewan MacColl, A. L. Lloyd, Seamus Ennis and Dominic Behan made up the program." He concluded, "This was a damned exciting evening of real folkmusic and there were less than 75 people in the audience." By "real" Paton meant from traditional sources rather than the hybrid skiffle. He was soon performing in local clubs and coffeehouses.[9]

The initial "Ballads and Blues" concerts, mostly at the drafty Theatre Royal, Stratford East, were followed in late 1957 by a new series with Lomax, jazzmen Jim Bray and Bruce Turner, the American performers Guy Carawan and Ralph Rinzler, the traditional musician Margaret Barry, and Seamus Ennis. Rinzler, a graduate of Swarthmore College who had moved to France for graduate work, was brought to London to fill in temporarily for Peggy Seeger on a few recordings. He moved into Bert Lloyd's house, where he remained for a year. He would recall: "Between Ewan and Bert's work, I had another vision of how people use folklore in creative ways." Peggy Seeger would also stay with Bert and Charlotte Lloyd, as well as elsewhere, until moving in with MacColl in 1959.[10]

Drawing less than a full house to the original "Ballads and Blues" concerts, MacColl soon relocated to the more-friendly Princess Louise pub on High Holborn in London, where he, Lloyd, and Ennis, along with Lomax, initiated the Ballads and Blues Club (later renamed the Singers' Club). The American musical influence was certainly pronounced, partly due to Lomax's presence. MacColl had been highly influenced by the topical songs included in *The People's Song Book*, issued by People's Songs in New York in 1948. Lomax had written the foreword, itself influenced by the Workers' Music Association, and Collet's bookshop in London quickly imported the book. Resident performers at the Ballads and Blues Club—including MacColl, Lloyd, Lomax, Rinzler, Isla Cameron, Fitzroy Coleman, Seamus Ennis, Peggy Seeger—were singing songs from a stunning variety of traditions, including Australian, American, English, Irish, Scottish, German, Dutch, Jamaican, and so many others.[11]

As for Lomax, he was getting restless after his time in England and on the continent. He had published *American Folk Guitar: A Book of Instruction* (1957) with Peggy Seeger, and then his folk-novella, based on his earlier field recordings, *Rainbow Sign* (1959). "I've had a rough time for eight years, and I have only just pulled myself out of a very nasty mess and have about 2000 dollars saved up to tide me over until I find my own way in the states," he wrote to his old friend and former radio personality (until blacklisted) John Henry Faulk in June 1958, just before his return to New York. "There are a lot of things I can do at my own level and in my own fashion. I have an idea what some of them are, and I will certainly learn more when I come, but basically I want to write, write positively and richly, and aim very high and wide."[12]

Sing Out! and Folk Music's Revival

"A phenomenon of this age of anxiety and confused revolt is the quickly-growing popularity of American Folk music in the cities of Europe," Bert Lloyd, editor of *Recorded Folk Music*, expressed in the first issue in March 1958. "It is sure that some American folk songs attract listeners by the violent rootless emotions conveyed by their texts. That the texts reflect circumstances remote from the experience and traditions of the listener seems not to count. But the real power of the U.S. folk song, the quality that gives it sanction and prestige and makes it widely accessible even at the expense of native folk music, lies not so much in the words as in the tunes. For at least a century, American traditional melody has been moving out of the domain of folk music proper towards the domain of popular music."[13]

Lloyd's expertise fueled his ability to connect and explain American folk music's international reach, but his comments could equally apply to domestic issues. In early 1958 *Variety* announced, "The folksingers are coming back into their own. With many jazz concerts finding it rough sledding around the country this past fall and winter season, the folksong packages are picking up lots of concert coin." The article mentioned Marais and Miranda, Josh White, Cynthia Gooding, Susan Reed, Oscar Brand, Bob Gibson, Richard Dyer-Bennet, Pete Seeger, and Theodore Bikel as drawing big crowds. Folk clubs, such as the Gate of Horn in Chicago, the hungry i in San Francisco, the Crystal Palace in St. Louis, the Limelight in Aspen, Colorado, and Down in the Depths in New York, began to appear, even before the Kingston Trio's leap into surprising popularity.[14]

Sing Out!, now reduced to a quarterly, continued to cover the folk scene, although it would soon have a rival or two. Editor Irwin Silber had toned down his political views, having been influenced by Soviet leader Nikita Khrushchev's 1956 revelations of Stalin's crimes. He refused to discuss his politics when testifying before HUAC in 1958, however, citing his First Amendment right of free speech. As he honestly explained in late 1957 to the folklorist Archie Green, who was highly critical of Silber's Communist Party affiliation—which ended in early 1958, as the party continued to shrink, with perhaps a few thousand members, including many government informers: "I think you will recognize that an element of sanity began to creep into SING OUT at the time it switched over to quarterly publication. It seems to me that this trend of modest, sounder political outlook has steadily developed. . . . A year ago we decided to eliminate our editorial page, thus removing from ourselves the temptation to issue the same kind of left-wing dogma for which we had achieved an unenviable reputation."[15]

Silber, with a family to support, was soon forced to seek additional income. In 1958 he began working with Folkways Records' owner Moses Asch in doing promotional work, and they became joint publishers of *Sing Out!* (each had 45 percent, with Pete Seeger holding the remaining 10 percent). They would soon launch Oak Publications, an expansive series of songbooks, instruction manuals, reprints of earlier works, and much more that would have wide circulation. The magazine's skimpy winter 1957 issue included mostly songs, along with Pete Seeger's review of Burl Ives's paperback *Sea Songs*. While rather positive, the reviewer also noted Ives's 1952 appearance before HUAC, when he "fingered, like any common stool-pigeon, some of his radical associates of the early 1940's. He did this not because he wanted to but because he felt it was the only way to preserve his lucrative contracts; and that makes his action all the more despicable." Seeger usually held his temper in check, but this was too much even for him to stomach; their relationship remained cool for many decades.[16]

Sing Out!'s next issue included John Hasted's thoughtful explanation of skiffle:

> In Britain there has never been home-grown guitar music, blues, country and western singing. There have been pops [pop songs], many of which have a genuine national flavor, descendants of the music-hall songs and of earlier popular ballads and folk-song. Now, in the last ten years, Jazz has swept into the hearts of the young people; and, more slowly, blues, Negro work songs, in fact a great deal of American folk music and country and western became popular. You can jive to it; I have seen a roomful of people jiving through a talking blues.

So, skiffle emerged: "For years, people had been battling to get youngsters to sing, and not just listen and jive to the pops. And now, there are Skiffle groups everywhere." A following article by Steve Lane explained skiffle in more detail. Bert Lloyd graced the winter 1958 cover, with the explanation that he "is a British folksinger and folklorist whose work thanks to the magic of the long-playing record, is becoming increasingly familiar to American folk music lovers."[17]

Skiffle made some slight inroads into the domestic marketplace, with Lonnie Donegan's concerts drawing crowds in 1956, when his version of "Rock Island Line" became a bestseller; as late as 1961 he had a hit with the novelty song "Does Your Chewing Gum Lose Its Flavour (On the Bedpost

Overnight)?"). Sensing an interest, in 1957 Folkways Records released the album *American Skiffle Bands*. Drawn from recent recordings of the Mobile Strugglers, The Memphis Jug Band, and others, in his notes Sam Charters explained that the "skiffle band was an instrumental group that used homemade instruments. . . . There were white skiffle bands and colored skiffle bands." Born in Pittsburgh in 1929, Charters first became enamored with jazz music, and in the early 1950s he moved to New Orleans to study the local culture, then became fascinated with studying blues performers. While his notes for the Folkways album used the term skiffle, in his groundbreaking study *The Country Blues*, published in 1959 and with a chapter on the Memphis Jug Band and the Jug Stompers, he did not mention skiffle—African American jug bands, in Memphis and elsewhere, were some of the forerunners of the British skiffle movement.[18]

While *Sing Out!* struggled to survive, Lee Hoffman, catching the musical winds, launched an upstart, essentially apolitical folk magazine in New York. Born in Chicago in 1932 and raised in the South, she attended junior college in Savannah, Georgia, graduating in 1951. She found herself drawn to science fiction and met Larry Shaw at the World Science-Fiction Convention in Cleveland; they were married in New York in 1956 but separated two years later. While holding down various jobs in New York, Hoffman became involved in publishing, and she connected science fiction to her developing interest in folk music. She published *Quandry* in the early 1950s, as well as a few issues of *The Chattahoochee, Okefenokee, & Ogeechee Occasional Gazette*, connected to the Fantasy Amateur Press Association, soon retitled *CHOOOG*. In May 1957 she produced a special "Folkmusic Issue," including songs, a review of three Oscar Brand concerts, as well as a piece on a local festival with Brand and Lord Burgess. "Folkmusic is turning into Big Business nowadays, with specialized recording companies springing up like toadstools, and everytime you turn around, you run into another Authority on the subject (including the self-appointed amateurs like me)," Hoffman explained in the next issue. "A lot of them are spending a good deal of their time 'proving that item[s] such as THE BASTARD KING OF ENGLAND, KAFOOZALUM, etc. are *not* real folk music." For Hoffman, "Songs stand or fall in the singing, and not over the moot point of authorship," including bawdy songs, which are "sung by the *common* man . . . the modern 'folk.'" She also believed: "A song may be a fine folksong, but in the hands and mouth of a singer whose style is non-folk, it loses its folk qualities and becomes just another pop or art song (depending on who's singing)." This issue of *CHOOOG* included reviews of Oscar Brand and Jean Ritchie concerts, two of her current favorites.[19]

Ever the author and publicist, Hoffman next launched the fanzine *Caravan*, focusing primarily on the New York folk scene and now including other writers. "I couldn't pick, I couldn't sing. However, I was an old hand with the mimeograph," she would recall. "Dave [Van Ronk] did a controversial column under the penname 'Blind Rafferty' and English fan John Brunner contributed a column of folk music news from the UK." Van Ronk, born in Brooklyn in 1936, dropped out of school at fifteen, and soon took to jazz as a performer. Around 1955 he discovered the magic of the folk guitar through watching Tom Paley in Washington Square, where on Sunday afternoons Van Ronk soon became a regular. While a staunch anticommunist—but no lover of the political and economic establishment—he joined the Libertarian League, an anarchist organization. Lee Hoffman met Van Ronk in the Village, and, she said, with "Dave's encouragement, I started a folkmusic fanzine." Initially free, with its increased circulation *Caravan* soon cost ten cents. Two local photographers, Aaron Rennert and Ray Sullivan, along with Joel Katz, who recorded the local concerts, launched Photo-Sound Associates, which supplied the magazine with pictures.[20]

While *Caravan* existed on a shoestring (but with some support from Jac Holzman at Elektra Records and Paddy Clancy of Tradition Records), Van Ronk, writing as Blind Rafferty, did not hesitate to attack Elektra in the first issue, "The Elektra Catalog—A Sarcophagus": "Even at my angriest, I cannot truthfully say that many of Elektra's records are actually 'bad.' They lack even that much character. . . . Whether or not this is literally true, I am amazed at Elektra's ability to turn out one innocuous little album right after another—genteel, sophisticated, and utterly false." John Brunner's expansive article "With My Ear to the Ground" covered the popularity of skiffle in England. "The more versatile and original skifflers, those not content to follow Donegan and who have taken the trouble to learn more than three chords on their guitars, expand their activities into related fields," he explained. "Calypsos are popular, especially since London has a rapidly growing West Indian population and the West Indies cricket team is currently touring Britain." In the next issue Van Ronk clarified his comments on Elektra, since he liked Tom Paley and Frank Warner. "Each record and each artist must, of course, be evaluated separately. I did not think it would be necessary to explain this, but evidently some illiterates had some semi-literates read the article to them. Anyway, my opinions on Elektra's overall approach are unchanged."[21]

Caravan served mostly to cover the local folk scene but had established a transatlantic connection, and with some national mail distribution. "*Caravan* became our forum, with page upon page of theoretical arguments about the correct stance of the modern urban folk musician or listener," according to Van Ronk. "It also served as a sort of club newsletter, with gossip, in-jokes, and commentary about whatever was happening on the Village scene." *Caravan*'s circulation greatly benefited from another Greenwich Village institution just getting off the ground: Izzy Young's Folklore Center.[22]

Born in Manhattan on March 26, 1928, Israel G. "Izzy" Young grew up in the Bronx, attended the local High School of Science and then Brooklyn College, which he ultimately left without graduating. He developed a love of square dancing early, having joined Margot Mayo's American Square Dance Group in 1945. He worked at his father's bakery as well as at Catskill resorts as a waiter during the summers, along with performers John Cohen and Tom Paley. He had no love for the Communist Party, believing himself an independent on the left. In the mid-1950s he met Kenneth Goldstein, the record producer, and plunged into buying and selling folklore books, issuing his first catalog in 1955. Then in early 1957 the folklorist Ben Botkin announced in the *New York Folklore Quarterly*, "Israel G. Young, a young bookseller with ideas (and possibly idioms) . . . has a feeling that there are going to be 'some changes made' and that new forces and movements are about to burgeon in the American folklore field." At the same, time *Sing Out!* noted that Young had opened the Folklore Center at 110 MacDougal Street in the heart of the Village, responding to those who had wondered, "Wouldn't it be wonderful if there were one place which sold everything available in the folk song field?" He had to cash in his insurance policy to rent the narrow space. "I signed the lease for my store last week and I am all ready to open up on April 6," Izzy recorded in his notebook. "Folksingers just do not buy books and they will be a problem—and if they do they expect discounts etc. I hope to interest the general public more in folklore—cater to specialists and libraries so I can sell rare books etc. and start distributing books and publishing books so I can make a living."[23]

The Folklore Center, selling books, records, instruments, and other music items, quickly became the heart of folk music in the Village and even nationally. President Dwight Eisenhower had been inaugurated for his second term in January, and while Young was no Republican—far from it—he seemed to have caught the administration's entrepreneurial optimism. Still, he hardly had the spirit of a capitalist, and during his decade and a half in business he never made any money. "When Izzy opened that little hole, there was suddenly a place where everyone went, and it became a catalyst for all sorts of things," recalled Van Ronk. "There were picking sessions, and Izzy even held a few concerts there to help out singers who needed a gig and couldn't find one elsewhere.... It became so much a club that there was a sort of running joke that Izzy never actually sold anything." Izzy also organized concerts at other locations—for example, presenting Peggy Seeger at the Actor's Playhouse in June 1957, at the request of Albert Grossman, who was then in Chicago running the Gate of Horn.[24]

The Folklore Center became the main distributor for *Caravan*. "Izzy is the one who labeled the folk music fans 'folkniks,'" Lee Hoffman commented. "There were usually a few folkniks hanging out in The Folklore Center, sometimes picking and singing. The store was very small, but Izzy occasionally held informal concerts there with the audience standing around the performers. When Izzy learned that some British merchant seamen in port had their own skiffle group, he scheduled an in-store concert with them." Hoffman had broad interests. Her third monthly issue included John Brunner's report from London, focusing on the traditional Irish singer Margaret Barrie. Van Ronk added an essay on the history of IWW songs, and Barry Kornfeld, under the name "Kafka," adopted his own view of authentic performers: "A commercial folksinger has a lack of confidence in folk music's audience appeal so he elaborates upon it and adds all sorts of saccharine sweet icings: novelty (Oscar Brand), sex (Josh White), elaborate arrangements (Marais & Miranda), and slickness (Clarence Cooper). These people are all talented and enjoyable to watch and hear but none are *folk* singers." Defining authenticity was a slippery slope, certainly a matter of taste, but the *Caravan* entourage took the side of what they perceived to be more traditional and less commercial.[25]

Van Ronk contributed no more to *Caravan*, but Kornfeld and others picked up the slack in the November issue. Hoffman gave a warm review of a Paul Clayton/Tom Paley midnight concert at the tiny Actor's Playhouse, sponsored by the Folklore Center. While scarcely known in the wider folk world, Clayton had recorded numerous albums for Riverside, Tradition, Folkways, and Stinson, which were helpfully listed in *Caravan*. Paley, born in New York in 1928, had so far appeared on two Elektra records, particularly the influential *Folksongs of the Southern Appalachian Mountains* (1953), while developing his career teaching math; he began at the University of Maryland in 1956. Clayton, born in the old whaling town of New Bedford, Massachusetts, on March 3, 1931, took to singing and playing the guitar early on. Steeped in folk and pop songs, he also encountered a wealth of old sea songs at the local Bourne Whaling Museum. He entered the University of Virginia in Charlottesville in 1949, where he uncovered collections of hillbilly songs and worked with the renowned ballad scholar Arthur Kyle Davis, who became his advisor.

He also began performing with William Marburg, who would soon become a foremost bluegrass performer under the name Bill Clifton. Clayton and Clifton performed at Bascom Lamar Lunsford's singular Virginia Folk Festival in the university's gymnasium in the spring of 1950, where Clayton was influenced by Virgil Sturgill's mastery of the mountain dulcimer. Clayton would become one of the rare young dulcimer players.

In the summer of 1951 Clayton traveled to Great Britain, where he discovered a cache of traditional songs and even performed on the BBC-TV North American Service twenty-eight program folk music series. He also traveled around the Continent, performing and collecting. Back in Charlottesville he had a folk radio show, performed with Clifton, assisted Davis on his important compilation *More Traditional Ballads of Virginia*, and collected ballads in the nearby Appalachian Mountains. His amazingly wide repertoire was represented in his plethora of early albums, starting with *Whaling Songs and Ballads* for Stinson (1954), and ending with two for Elektra, *Unholy Matrimony* (1958) and *Bobby Burns' Merry Muses of Caledonia* (1958). In April 1957, during a trip to Europe, he informed Marian Distler at Folkways Records that he would soon be returning and "hope to turn again to Folkways, the folksingers friend." He had a remarkable but surprisingly short recording career. In the late 1950s Clayton moved to Greenwich Village, where he easily joined the thriving folk scene documented by *Caravan*.[26]

Caravan's December 1957 issue led off with Dick Weissman's glowing portrait of Brownie McGhee: "To my ears, Brownie McGhee is one of the most interesting blues singers on the contemporary folk scene." The "New York Scene" column had praise for a small concert by Jeanie and Harry West, Gina Glaser, and John Cohen, sponsored by Izzy Young, but Ken Joffee's more ambitious concert lineup of Theo Bikel, Josh White, Marais and Miranda, Robin Roberts, and the Shanty Boys came in for some criticism: "Since the styles and material of the performers varied so, and since different segments of the audience had come mainly because of different performers, no one entertainer was able to capture and hold the entire audience. . . . On the whole, it was a good lot of performers in a disappointing production." The next issue praised a concert by the "Ivy Leaguers," a British skiffle group at the Folklore Center. John Cohen and Tom Paley filled in during their break, while local artists Dick Weissman, Jo Mapes, and Fred Gerlach also joined in. "It had been quite a show" Hoffman commented. The January issue included a long letter from Sandy Paton, the American then visiting in London. He had some harsh words for the local skiffle craze, although "the phenomenon does get kids up and participating, get them to making their own music."[27]

Great Britain

Sandy Paton updated *Caravan*'s readers on the activities of the American performers in London in the February 1958 issue. "Finally met Guy Carawan and his wife—just back from what sounded like an exciting and interesting trip to China—at Alan Lomax's Boxing Day party," he explained. "They told us that Peggy Seeger was expected back in England 'in a couple of days,' though we haven't run into her yet. . . . Guy sang several American traditional carols and Christmas songs with Alan helping on some of them. Shirley [Collins] played her banjo and sang the beautiful English 'Cherry Tree Carol.' . . . Shirley does a lot of American material and does it well, but we think she really stands out when she does the English ballad of her own folk tradition." Paton remarked that Carawan would soon return to the United States, as would Lomax. Indeed, Guy would be back in New York in early February. A few months later, in May, Sonny Terry and Brownie McGhee toured England with the Chris Barber band, including a concert at Festival Hall in London and in Glasgow, receiving a good reception.[28]

Meanwhile, Ramblin' Jack Elliott welcomed his old friend Derroll Adams to London in February 1957, and their duo became an immediate hit. "Jack and Derroll got a job at a society nightclub 'The Blue Angel' in Berkeley Square, and the management applied to get them proper work permits," his wife, June, recalled. "They were paid quite a good salary and the British debutantes seemed to love them. The more 'down home' they were, the more this very sophisticated crowd loved it." Known as the Rambling Boys, they soon cut an album for Topic, which got a good reception. In late spring, when the job ended, the Elliotts and Adams took off for an extended European trip. Jack would not come back to London until late 1958, when he recorded the new album *Ramblin' Jack Elliott in London* for Columbia, then he and June retuned to the United States. Within the year he would reappear in London, however. "Two musicians who played regularly in the London clubs, and who probably influenced would be players in England as much as any were Peggy Seeger and Jack Elliott," the British guitar player John Renbourn would explain. "His version of Jesse Fuller's 'San Francisco Bay Blues' and Gary Davis' 'Cocaine Blues' were imitated widely by British pickers, but his influence extended even further. After he returned home he left behind quite a number of British Rambling Jack imitators fully equipped with ten gallon hats and mid-Atlantic drawls."[29]

Folk Style, the hillbilly collectors' magazine, was published erratically until the end of the decade and would cover Kelly Harrell, Carson Robison, Woody Guthrie, Peggy Seeger, Brownie McGhee, the folklorist and record producer Kenneth Goldstein, and Topic Records. With slight circulation, it appealed to a small group of record collectors, as American folk songs were becoming increasingly available on records and in live performances.

Until his return to the United States on July 2, 1958, Alan Lomax kept up a busy schedule. "Back in London we continued to live together," Shirley Collins recalled, "working on the Columbia World Folk Song Series of LPs and the book *The Folk Songs of North America* for Cassell, in which Alan credited me as Editorial Assistant [it was published in the U.S. in 1960]. Alan and Peter Kennedy recorded in two days the thirty-seven songs that would make up my first two solo LPs, *Sweet England* for Decca in London and *False True Lovers* for Folkways in the States." The following spring Collins would join Lomax in New York. Moreover, in 1958 he appeared on a few British recordings, such as the Pye Nixa album *American Song Train* with Peggy Seeger, Guy Carawan, John Cole, and Sammy Stokes. They performed "This Train," "The Lone Green Valley," "Railroad Bill," and "Black Black," along with about a dozen other songs; it appeared simultaneously in the United States on the Kapp Records label. HMV issued *Alan Lomax Sings Great American Ballads*, accompanied by Alexis Korner (under the name Nick Wheatstraw) and Carawan, with "Jolly Roving Tar," "Jesse James," and "Darlin' Corey." While a passable guitar player with a decent voice, Lomax appeared on only a few recordings during his long career, and mostly during his stay in England.[30]

Pye Nixa had formed in 1955 and along with numerous Lonnie Donegan, Chris Barber, and Petula Clark recordings, also featured Big Bill Broonzy and Josh White. The company issued *Murderers' Home* in 1957, the first release drawn from Lomax's 1947 field recordings at the Parchman Farm in Mississippi (released in the United States the next year by Tradition Records, now titled *Negro Prison Songs*); all of the songs were copyrighted in the names of the performers. "Even in 1947 I could see that the custom of work-song singing was dying out at Parchman, where we had recorded our finest singing in the early '30s," Lomax explained on the album's cover. "The old-timers has lost their voices, and most of the young prisoners regarded the practice as 'old-fogeyism.'" Still, the British audience could hear some unique African American field recordings. In addition, in 1957 Pye Nixa released *Blues in the Mississippi Night*, based on Lomax's recordings of Big Bill Broonzy, Memphis Slim, and Sonny Boy Williamson following their appearance at a 1947 concert at Town Hall. The album remained for a few weeks on *Melody Maker*'s list of "Top Jazz Discs" in Great Britain.[31]

Peggy Seeger had attended the World Festival of Democratic Youth in Moscow in July 1957 along with Guy Carawan. From there Peggy, Guy, and three dozen others traveled to China, despite opposition from the U.S. State

Department, since such travel by Americans was then outlawed. "I returned again to England in the spring of 1958 to work with Ewan, displacing the four-string banjo player who had been accompanying him," according to Peggy. She had difficulty obtaining a work permit, however, was deported to France, and did not return to London until early 1959, where she would be based for many decades.[32]

The United States

"This week in London, Alan Lomax was preparing to return to the United States after seven years of tireless folk-song collecting across the face of Europe," *Newsweek* announced on April 14, 1958, with no hint of Alan's past political problems, only a romantic tinge. "He had traveled in a red Volkswagon, moving from one inn to another, sometimes sleeping in the fields." Leaving Shirley Collins in London for the time being, Lomax was anxious to reestablish his role as the country's foremost folklorist and folk music organizer and promoter. He had returned to an increasingly vibrant scene in New York and around the country. In his June letter to John Henry Faulk he had already thought of a return collecting trip: "The prospect of roving round through the south with you sounds glorious. I want to go south in the end of July to finish various jobs I have in hand and can think of no better companion." The plan was premature, however, and he would not take the trip until the next year, and with Collins rather than Faulk.[33]

Time greeted Lomax's return with a glowing, although not particularly accurate, report in September: "For the past eight years, fringe-bearded Alan Lomax, now 43, has been tracking down such leads, fitting together musical jigsaw pieces of many a puzzle about the family of man. He has collaborated with leading folklorists the world over, listened to miles of music already on tape, added taped material of his own and edited the best into comprehensive form. Columbia [Records] so far has issued 16 remarkable annotated albums." Alan had left the country just as the Weavers were topping the charts, but there was as yet a rather feeble folk movement. While he had not been out of touch during this years abroad, he was surely surprised by the quickening folk scene, particularly in Greenwich Village, his new home. "He left the U.S.A. as an 'enfant terrible' and he returns a legend," Pete Seeger announced in *Sing Out!* "I welcome back Alan Lomax, not just because he is an old friend, but also because, in my opinion, he is more responsible than any other single individual for the whole revival of interest in American folk music. . . . We wish him well in his many projects and hope that we will be hearing from him." It did not take long.[34]

Before Lomax returned to New York, a group of brothers would began to popularize their own infectious brand of Irish music. Paddy and Tom Clancy had migrated from Ireland to Toronto in 1947 and wound up in New York in 1951, where as actors they broke into local theater. Their younger brother, Liam, arrived in New York in early 1956 and quickly fell into the local folk scene. He soon found himself at a party at Diane Hamilton's Village apartment—she was an heir to the Guggenheim family fortune—where he met Oscar Brand, Cynthia Gooding, Logan English, Paul Clayton, Robin Roberts, and Josh White. Soon after his arrival, he and his brothers, with the help of Hamilton's funding and the advice of the record producer Kenneth Goldstein, launched Tradition Records with an album of Irish songs, *The Lark in the Morning*. The brothers next found themselves on the stage of the Woody Guthrie celebratory concert in March. They soon recorded, in Goldstein's kitchen in the Bronx, with their friend Tommy Makem, newly arrived from Ireland, an album of Irish rebel songs, *The Rising of the Moon*, which launched their musical career. During the summer of 1956 Liam joined Hamilton to visit Paul Clayton in Chapel Hill, North Carolina; Clayton had done an album of whaling songs for Tradition. The three made field recordings of numerous artists in the area, including the guitarist Etta Baker. "Fixtures at most of the early folk get-togethers were the Clancy Brothers," Theo Bikel recalled. "At first there were just two of them, Paddy and Tom Clancy. Later they were joined by their younger brother Liam and Tommy Makem, who added a more lyrical and artistic flavor to their more roughly hewn Irish country delivery."[35]

Makem would briefly return to Ireland but landed back in New York in March 1957. That summer he attended a Bob Gibson concert with Odetta. Makem recalled, "She and I went down the street to Izzy Young's Folklore Center, where the banjos and guitars were goin' at it. Paul Clayton was there singing whaling songs with his friend Jo El. It turned into a party, as it always did at Izzy's place." In early 1958 the Clancys released their second album, *Come Fill Your Glass with Us*, of Irish drinking songs. The Clancy Brothers and Tommy Makem, with their boisterous, bracing performances, backed by guitar, banjo, and tin whistle, would become a vital part of the vibrant folk scene, as would Tradition Records.[36]

New York's energized folk scene got an important boost when Art D'Lugoff opened the Village Gate nightclub on the corner of Thompson and Bleecker Streets in early 1958. A World War II veteran, D'Lugoff had graduated from New York University in 1949 and worked at various jobs while helping organize jazz and folk concerts by mid-decade. For a few years he staged a series of midnight concerts in Greenwich Village beginning in 1955 at the Cherry Lane Theatre, formed in 1924, as well as the Circle in the Square, since 1950 occupying the former home of Cafe Society on Sheridan Square. Called "Swapping Song Fair" as well as "The Midnite Special," they featured Brownie McGhee, Sonny Terry, Rev. Gary Davis, Cynthia Gooding, Leon Bibb, Robin Roberts, the Clancy Brothers, Trinidad Steel Band, the Israeli singers Hillel and Aviva, and calypso singers, demonstrating folk music's international flavor. The Village Gate would quickly become a leading folk, jazz, and comedy club, with an activist political agenda, and with Pete Seeger often performing. "We held rehearsals at the Village Gate in the afternoons," Dave Van Ronk, who was forming a group with Paul Clayton to record for Folkways, would recall. "Art D'Lugoff had just opened the club and was having trouble obtaining the necessary license to hire entertainment. . . . It being a brand new place, Art was more than happy to have some people in there." The album became *Foc'sle Songs and Chanties* by Paul Clayton and the Foc'sle Singers.[37]

Caravan focused on performers and performances in New York but did not slight the rest of the country. The March 1958 issue featured Frank Hamilton's letter detailing folk happenings in Chicago: "As you probably have heard, Chicago has had a busy season for folk music. The Gate of Horn has featured quite a few well-known folk singers like Josh White, Theo Bikel and others. The Gate has built up a terrific following but I have questions about whether or not such a specialized medium as folk music can be really appreciated for its intrinsic worth in a night club when you cater to a drinking crowd irrespective of who this crowd might be, artistic or humanitarian or perhaps musical values to a degree must be sacrificed." Albert Grossman and Les Brown, who had been students together at Roosevelt University in Chicago, founded The Gate of Horn, the premier folk venue in the Windy City, in July 1956. They opened with Robin Roberts, followed by Bob Gibson, Big Bill Broonzy, Odetta, Theo Bikel, and Sonny Terry and Brownie McGhee. In two years Allan Ribback replaced Brown as the club's co-owner. Hamilton became the house musician and Gibson a club regular, particularly during the first year. "The Gate of Horn was the very first place where folk music as such was the draw," Gibson recalled. "It had a greater effect upon a number of people than did all the clubs [in Chicago] put together in those days. . . . I started something there early on and it became some sort of a tradition."[38]

Hamilton went on to announce that a new entity, the Old Town School of Folk Music, had opened its doors in Chicago in late 1957: "Just recently a local performer who's quite excellent, Win Stracke, and I opened up a school of folk music in the 'Old Town' district of Chicago," Hamilton wrote. "The school is an attempt to start a 'social' approach to teaching versus the classical concept of a teacher being an iron-fisted slave driver over a bewildered student." Stracke had his own local children's TV show and had been involved with the actor and radio personality Studs Terkel since the 1940s, when both had been active in People's Songs. Hamilton had learned the art of teaching students in groups from Bess Hawes in Los Angeles, a technique he perfected in Chicago and set the school on its successful career (into the twenty-first century). WFMT-FM, the local classical radio station, served to promote the school's classes and concerts—the first featuring Big Bill Broonzy—with its own Saturday night Midnight Special folk show.[39]

In *Caravan*'s April 1958 issue Billy Faier (who appeared on the cover of the May issue) launched his column "Message from the West," covering the West Coast. He had been part of the San Francisco folk scene early in the decade, along with Barbara Cahn (Dane), Stan Wilson, Jo and Paul Mapes, Rolf Cahn, and Stan Wilson, and after living in New Orleans, Southern California, and New York, he returned in July 1957. "I'm writing this letter so all I'll say about myself is that I'm teaching guitar, banjo, and mandolin (stop snickering), and have a weekly radio program on KPFA, 'The Story of Folkmusic,' and I've given two concerts, at Fugazi Hall in SF and at The Berkeley Little Theater." In the following issue he announced the release of his two albums, *Art of the Five String Banjo* with Frank Hamilton on guitar (Riverside, produced by Kenneth Goldstein) and *Banjos, Banjos and More Banjos* (Judson), along with Dick Weissman and Eric Weissberg. He also mentioned that he and the folklorist Archie Green had visited Aunt Molly Jackson, the ballad singer from Harlan County, Kentucky, who had moved to New York City in the 1930s and since relocated to Sacramento: "The result of the visit, in one respect, is that we learned that Aunt Molly still has much material to offer, not just union and mining songs either, and I am going back next week to see her again." He was soon conducting Friday night concerts at the North Gate Coffee Shop in Berkeley, where his friend Barry Olivier—soon to initiate the Berkeley Folk Festival—ran a weekly folk music program. Benjamin Botkin, in his *New York Folklore Quarterly* column, praised Faier's coverage: "Speaking of the folk singers and musicians that bloom on Washington Square these spring Sundays . . . I am glad to note that a fresh wind blows over this *caravan* from the West Coast, with California getting a whole section of 'Where to's' of its own, and that the folk music cult is not only national but international, with a four-page communication from England, which now boasts three folk music journals."[40]

Having some success with her fanzine, for the August/September issue of *Caravan* Lee Hoffman switched to a more professional photo-offset, small format magazine. The issue featured a profile of Jean Ritchie and Faier's continuing "Message from the West." He gave a detailed roundup of Barry Olivier's Berkeley Folk Festival: "The weekend of folk music was the most exciting musical event of my life. It is difficult to explain about the Fraternal spirit that I felt among the singers and the audiences." Barry Kornfeld introduced the readers to an overview of Izzy Young's Folklore Center. "The variety of people to be found in the store is amazing—for it is my theory that at one time or another *everyone* drops into the Folklore Center," he explained. "The Center's fame has spread to the colleges, resulting in crowds of these intelligentsia during vacation periods." As for the store's proprietor, "A business man, Izzy is not. He's too honest to use even the subtle subterfuges that the modern business man uses. He won't sell something that he doesn't believe in without stating this to the buyer."[41]

"With *Caravan*, there was finally a place where the arguments that had previously been limited to barroom colloquies could be set down in print," Van Ronk would later explain. Sensing a folk music boom—"The college folk clubs were starting, Harry Belafonte and the Tarriers had some hit records, Elektra was doing good business, and to our way of thinking it could not be long before discerning listeners had got their fill of slick folk-fakery and must turn to us, the true keepers of the flame"—in late 1957 Van Ronk, Roy Berkeley, Roger Abrahams and others formed the Folksingers Guild, which would run its own concerts. Lee Hoffman helped with promotion. For Van Ronk, "One way and another, the Guild was a way for us to pick up a few bucks, to establish ourselves, and to learn our craft." An early concert of "Folk Songs and Songs of Protest" featured Berkeley, Abrahams, Van Ronk, Luke Faust, Gina Glazer, and Bob Yellin; another early affair included the Tarriers, Happy Traum, and Dick Weissman. No one made much money, but they had fun, and the concerts would last into 1959.[42]

Caravan's fall 1958 issue included essays on Frank Hamilton, an informative report on the "British Record Scene," focusing on the Topic label, and an obituary of Big Bill Broonzy, who had died on August 15 in Chicago. John Brunner reported on the London club scene, while lamenting that Sandy and Carolyn Paton were returning to the United States. Ron Radosh reported on the student folk club at the University of Wisconsin, which in 1956 faced resistance from the administration. Soon enough, however, Pete Seeger concerts on campus began drawing large crowds, and the administration softened its opposition to student groups charging admission for an event. A hootenanny with Guy Carawan, Marshall Brickman, and Eric Weissberg proved highly successful, followed by appearances from Seeger, Odetta, and Theo Bikel.

Similar campus clubs were springing up around the country. For example, following his successful folk festival at the University of California-Berkeley, Barry Olivier informed *Caravan*'s readers that numerous performers were appearing on campus, including Cisco Houston, Jean Ritchie, Sandy Paton, Odetta, and Bikel.[43]

In *Caravan*'s December-January 1958/59 issue, Lee Hoffman listed Kenneth Goldstein as the book review editor, with Roger Abrahams the record review editor. Moreover, she announced that Billy Faier would be replacing her as the magazine's editor. Lee Haring contributed a long profile of Cynthia Gooding, a prolific and versatile performer with an international repertoire. The issue included mostly record reviews. In fact, Hoffman was pretty burned out. "I don't remember how many offset issues of *Caravan* I turned out," she would write, "but it became more work than fun and I was being pressured to make it more serious. I didn't want to put out a scholarly publication or a professional one. Billy Faier was interested so I sold it to him and started another slim mimeographed fanzine. This one, I called *Gardyloo* (the traditional cry of warning before one dumped a bucket of slops out of an upstairs window)." Both *Caravan* and *Gardyloo* would continue for another year or so.[44]

While folk music and its musicians would proliferate in increasing locales, the popular press accelerated its own coverage, particularly in response to the proliferation of recordings. "There was a time, still remembered, when a man who wanted a folksong on record had to trudge over the meadow and through the woods before he could come close to a Josh White, a Burl Ives, Woody Guthrie, or Leadbelly," the jazz scholar Frederic Ramsey explained in the *Saturday Review* in late 1958. "We are here to say, though, that an uncommon quantity of folk-inspired material has been issued in the past four or five years." He reviewed albums by Pete Seeger, Harry Belafonte, Brother John Sellers, and Guy Carawan.[45]

"The last years of the 1950s were a great time to be in the Village," Van Ronk summed up his view on the coming end of the decade. "It was not too crazy yet, but there was an exhilarating sense of something big right around the corner. As for the folk scene, it was beginning to look as if it might have a future, and me with it." What was happening in Greenwich Village had been rapidly spreading around the country. Folk music, broadly defined, appeared to have a bright future, while spanning the Atlantic Ocean.[46]

6

The Decade Ends, 1959–1960

Popular Music and Folk Music

On April 3,1959, Alan Lomax, along with the labor union and concert organizer Lou Gordon, produced the wide-ranging "Folksong: '59" concert, subtitled "A Panorama of the Contemporary American Folk Song Revival," at Carnegie Hall. "He had been impressed on his return [from England], Mr. Lomax said, to find 'war whoops coming out of juke boxes that I used to have to go down to Mississippi to record,'" according to the *New York Times*. "Americans, he declared, have always been ashamed of the way they expressed themselves. 'The time has come for Americans not to be ashamed of what we go for, musically, from primitive ballads to rock 'n' roll songs,' he said." Jimmie Driftwood (ballad singing) [aka James Corbitt Morris], Earl Taylor and the Stoney Mountain Boys (bluegrass), the Selah Jubliee Singers and the Drexel Singers (gospel), Muddy Waters and Memphis Slim (blues), the Cadillacs (rock 'n' roll), as well as Pete and Mike Seeger headlined the wide range of musical styles. Lomax had even invited the pop star Bobby Darin to perform, but with no luck. Lomax explained his musical approach in his concert comments: "The purpose is to show that we now have a full-fledged American musical revival, with its roots deep in Americana, that reaches a wider audience every day and that must be encouraged and appreciated critically in order for it to continue to grow in the healthiest fashion. In my mind the best of this music includes the much scorned and derided rock 'n' roll and rock-a-billy. And on the concert I will show how this music has grown out of rhythm and blues, hillbilly and gospel and thus has folk roots."[1]

Upon his return from England Lomax deftly exhibited his eclectic musical tastes. "'The record business has turned America into a musical democracy.' So says Alan Lomax, folk music collector who's been in Europe for the past eight years digging up material for LP release here," Mike Cross in *Variety* explained a week before "Folksong: '59." "Lomax is tremendously impressed by rock 'n' roll which has brought the folk-blues and folk-spiritual forms into the pop market. 'Rock 'n' roll,' he says, 'is an extension of jazz and blues and it's being kicked around the same way jazz and blues were in their early days.' He also pointed out that when he left the States in 1950 there were just a handful of people actively performing pure folk songs. 'Now,' he added, 'there are more than 5,000 entertainers involved with getting the folk message across.'" Moreover, "'Rock 'n' roll,' he stated, 'is opening the door to America's genuine traditional music and freeing it from its longtime domination by the European culture.'"[2]

Lomax expanded on his views in his planned comments during "Folksong: '59":

> "They call this the beat generation. A better name would be—*the generation with the beat*. Rock and roll, rhythm and blues, gospel, hillbilly, the folk song revival, have made this generation into a singing, dancing, song-making generation. Sometimes the sounds are corny, sometimes the songs are crude—but the musical atmosphere of present day America is charged with electricity. Music is on the move. The racial bars are gone. . . . This tangy, bouncy, experimental music frightens some older people and offends others. But it has become the breath of life to the teenagers. For them it stands for the excitement of living in a dynamic and changeful world. For them it stands for the future. And who will dare to say that they are not right? And so tonight we are going to have a concert of the folk music of the city, of the folk songs of '59."[3]

While rock 'n' roll, along with much of popular music, was designed as dance music, folk songs rarely (if ever) motivated audience members to dance in the theater aisles or at home. In his remarks, however, Lomax admitted that "I've had a lot of fights with responsible grown ups since I came back to this country about the movement of a certain censored part of the human anatomy which rhymes with Elvis. Well, it is a longstanding Anglo-Saxon tradition that this highly important body area should be kept still when there's music going. I've said that it's good for the digestion to exercise this area. But maybe the best argument is that it's just a very fine and pretty thing to dance while you're singing, if you feel like dancing." Indeed, Lomax dedicated much of his fieldwork to studying dance as well as songs.[4]

Lomax's wide-ranging views of folk music generated both applause and criticism. "I think last night was a great success," Pete Seeger wrote to Lomax on April 4. "You had a hellova hard job to do, and it must have been especially hard doing it yourself. . . . If I have any constructive criticism, it would be this: you might get a more fair (objective) listening from the public if you do *not* expect them to share our enthusiasms."[5]

Aaron Rennert's report in the tradition-oriented *Gardyloo* had a critical edge. While congratulating Lomax on his creative reach, Rennert complained about the sound system and apparent lack of organization. He preferred the Stoney Mountain Boys, Memphis Slim, and Pete and Mike Seeger: "For the most part, taking each group individually, the music was enjoyable. However, the program as a whole was entirely lacking in a central point or theme." Dick Weissman's review in *Caravan* was equally mixed, concluding that "the concert was an attempt to bear out Lomax's ideas about the vitality of contemporary American folksong. Lomax's introduction to the group were beautifully written and well delivered, but alas, the groups themselves did not perform in accordance with his descriptions." Lomax quickly released an album of concert highlights on the United Artists label, *Folk Song Festival at Carnegie Hall*, featuring Jimmie Driftwood, Earl Taylor and the Stoney Mountain Boys, Memphis Slim, and Muddy Waters. [6]

Lomax attempted, with some success and much sincerity, to capture the complex nature of popular music in 1959. Since his return from England he had studied the current musical landscape and, after scouring the country for performers for the Carnegie Hall concert, demonstrated that he had a complex understanding of musical authenticity mixed with contemporary popular culture. Lomax was well aware that young people—the postwar, baby-boom generation had not yet entered college—accepted the current wide range of musical styles, with folk music only part of the mix. During 1959 Bobby Darin, Frankie Avalon, the Browns, the Platters, Elvis Presley, the Coasters, Richie Valens, and Connie Francis topped the record charts, boosted by the popularity of Dick Clark's *American Bandstand* TV show. The Grammy Award winners included Darin (record of the year), Jimmie Driftwood (song of the year, "The Battle of New Orleans"), Frank Sinatra (best male performance), and Ella Fitzgerald (best female performance); there was no folk category yet. Buddy Holly, Richie Valens, and the Big Bopper died in a plane crash in February, Little Richard had become a minster and recorded only gospel songs, Chuck Berry was charged with a criminal offense, and Elvis was in the army—although his records kept selling into 1960—all of which seriously depleted the ranks of the top rock 'n' roll performers and opened the door wider for folk music.[7]

The Kingston Trio and Popular Folk Music

"One of the regular free performances in a city park is put on every fine Sunday afternoon by ballad singers in Washington Square," the *New York Times* noted in May 1959. "Its setting is the empty fountain in the center of the park. . . . Musicians, many with guitars, some with banjos, a few with mandolins and one or two with bass viols, share the fountain with Greenwich Villagers, tourists, cats and dogs and a clicking corps of photographers." While the local Washington Square gatherings had been taking place for more than a decade, folk music had been garnering national exposure and commercial popularity. "The New York scene corresponds with a nation-wide upsurge in folk music enthusiasm," Grace Jan Waldman explained in *Mademoiselle*, the women's magazine. "This crescendo of interest has worried many strict traditionalists, who fear the effects of commercialism on folk art." For *Billboard*'s Ren Grevatt, "The folkniks are on the move as never before. The emergence of folk music and artists as big business is highlighted by more folk records in release, more periodicals on folk music in publication, more frantic activity on the doubtful front of copyrighting the largely public domain material of the folk field, and more folk music concerts, particularly on the outdoor front, than at any time in recent memory." A month later Grevatt extended his views: "The third great pillar of musical Americana is now asserting itself in the pop field. First, it was the onrush of rhythm and blues, out of the limited market of the South and onto the hit lists all over the nation. The second stage of the evolution was reached with the inroads of hillbilly music and artists on the pop charts. Finally and currently it is the arrival of folk music as a big business entity." Folk joined jazz, rhythm and blues, and country as "basic American forms which last. Calypso, on the other hand, which from time to time goes thru fits of resurgence, has not lasted as a pop force. Nor has Hawaiian music or Latin music."[8]

The Kingston Trio continued to head the list of popular folk performers. Since there was no Grammy folk music category in 1959, the Trio's "Tom Dooley" won for Best Country & Western song. However, the next year this was rectified, when the Trio garnered the first Best Ethnic or Traditional Folk Recording for their album *The Kingston Trio at Large*. "It is hard to recall an instance when as wholesome a group of entertainers as the Kingston Trio has won as swift and widespread a popularity as they have," the mainstream *Redbook* magazine explained in May 1959. "Burl Ives, our most appealing soloist in the field of folk song, took many hard years to win a substantial audience on records, while the most meteoric of recent successes have been made by singers on the rock-'n'-roll kick, by a few in the gentler vein of Pat Boone's pop balladry or, among the combos, by those employing tricky vocal effects, which tend to sound tiresome after a few listenings." A fresh contrast to the long-haired, greasy rock 'n' rollers, with their racial and sexual challenges to society's mores—similar to the calypso fad of a few years earlier—the Trio "score sensationally without catering to any of the current sure-fire vogues." Their album *From the hungry i* reached number 2 on the charts in early 1959, quickly followed by the number 1 hit for fifteen weeks, *The Kingston Trio at Large*, then *Here We Go Again* for another eight weeks. They appeared on the Roy Rogers and Dale Evans television show early in the year, alongside the country music stars Johnny Cash, Jimmy Dean, the Everly Brothers, and Roy Acuff.[9]

Slotting the Kingston Trio into a particular musical category proved difficult, although the record companies preferred attaching the niche marketing label "folk music." They appeared as headliners at both the Newport Jazz and Folk Festivals in July 1959. Folk festivals had long history in the country, with a variety of performers and formats. George Wein, a jazz musician and impresario, had launched the Newport Jazz Festival in Newport, Rhode Island, in 1954, which had proved highly successful. For 1959 he first thought of including a few folk acts for one afternoon, such as Odetta, who had appeared at his club Storyville in Boston in 1958, Pete Seeger, the Weavers (now including Erik Darling, who had replaced Seeger), and the Kingston Trio, who also had been a hit at Wein's second Storyville location on Cape Cod. "Not surprisingly, as I did more research and conferred with more people in the folk community, it grew abundantly clear that one afternoon program would not even begin to scratch the surface of this folk explosion," Wein later explained. "What Newport needed was a full-fledged Folk Festival." Wein preferred to shift the Trio from the jazz to folk festival, but their agents insisted on their appearing at both. "The Kingston Trio had no place on a program with Dave Brubeck, Red Allen, and Bobby Hackett," according to Wein. "But because I felt that the group could be a key factor to the success of the first Newport Folk Festival, I went along with their request. Their set at the Jazz Festival wasn't terrible, but it provided just the ammunition the press needed to sound the cry of 'commercialism at Newport.'" While they might have seemed out of place among such jazz giants, in fact the Trio had been part of the jazz club scene in San Francisco and were most comfortable in such company. Indeed, folk, jazz, and blues performers, as well as comedians, shared the stages of numerous clubs, such as the Village Gate in Greenwich Village.[10]

To help organize the folk festival Wein hired Albert Grossman, Odetta's manager, who owned the Gate of Horn in Chicago and was well connected to many of the performers. Grossman assembled a compelling lineup, including John Jacob Niles, Sonny Terry and Brownie McGhee, Odetta, the New Lost City Ramblers, Pete Seeger, Earl Scruggs with Hylo Brown and the Timberliners, presenting a mix of ballads, bluegrass, blues, and ethnic music. "All told, there were more different sounds and styles in one place than you could absorb," Wein concluded. "But it was all a part of the same idea, part of the folk movement. An unspoken feeling was in the air, a sense that folk music was approaching a threshold."[11]

There were two festival highlights. First, Bob Gibson presented Joan Baez, who was not listed on the program. Born in New York in 1941, Baez's family moved around until they landed in Boston in 1958. Influenced by Odetta, Pete Seeger, and Harry Belafonte, she began performing at Club 47 in Cambridge, then accepted Grossman's offer to appear at the Gate of Horn for two weeks in June 1959, along with club regular Bob Gibson, where she also met Odetta. "Bob Gibson invited me to appear as his guest at the first Newport Folk Festival," she recalled in her memoirs. "I went to Newport with Odetta and her bass player." The second night Gibson introduced Baez before a crowd of more than ten thousand: "We sang, 'Virgin Mary Had One Son.' He played the twelve-string, and with eighteen [guitar] strings and two voices we sounded pretty impressive." Joan next did one solo, then after much applause they joined together on "Jordan River." "An exorbitant amount of fuss was made over me when we descended from the stage," she noted, launching her career into full flight (although the festival's press reviews somehow slighted her appearance).[12]

The festival's other hallmark was the Kingston Trio's critical appearance, following their debut at the jazz festival. Their popularity was soaring, marked by their appearance on the cover of *LOOK* magazine on August 3, accompanied by a slick article on their clean-cut image as wealthy, married men, a safe contrast to the scruffy, interracial rock 'n' rollers. "The true folk enthusiasts at the festival accepted the presence of the Kingston Trio begrudgingly," Wein would later admit. "I had scheduled the group to close," but as Sunday night dragged on the younger fans demanded that Wein schedule them before the bluegrass star Earl Scruggs, which he agreed to do. When the trio finished their set "the audience went crazy. . . . They refused to quiet down, despite the considerable efforts of emcee Oscar Brand. . . . Dave Guard of the Kingston Trio came back out and asked the crowd to give Scruggs his due. Earl Scruggs played a brief set before the return of the Kingston Trio for a final encore." Wein had bowed to crowd pressure, but later felt "I lost a lot of friends in the folk world because of that slipup." The issue of musical authenticity would long plague this and many other folk festivals.[13]

Wein concluded that despite the Kingston Trio controversy, this "was otherwise a successful festival." The press generally agreed. Robert Gustafson in the *Christian Science Monitor* rated this "an exciting weekend. On Sunday night, however, there came a group [Kingston Trio] that not only left a bad taste, but also vividly pointed out the direction that future Newport Folk Festivals should not travel." Praise equally came from the jazz scholar Frederic Ramsey; he particularly liked Earl Scruggs, who "is, to a current generation of folk-music performers and listeners, a virtuoso equivalent in stature to that of Louis Armstrong amongst jazz aficionados of a generation or so before." Ramsey made no mention of the popular Kingston Trio. The *New York Times* music reviewer Robert Shelton praised "perhaps the most ambitious attempt ever made at delineating a cross-section of the nation's folk music." In a more detailed follow-up in *The Nation*, Shelton concluded: "The Newport Folk Festival is off to an excellent start. If it shows flexibility, digs deeply for new performers and nurtures the roots as well as the branches of folk song, it should grow in stature." He made only brief mention of the Kingston Trio. Shelton expressed a few reservations, however, in a letter to Archie Green: "I rather consciously held back on negative criticism at Newport in both my *Times* and *Nation* piece."[14]

The Greenwich Village folk pundits took a somewhat more critical stance. In his "Newport Report" in *Gardyloo*, Mark Morris gave a rather detailed rundown of the performers, also with no mention of Baez. As for the Kingston Trio: "What connection these frenetic tinselly showmen have with a folk festival eluded me, except that it is mainly folk songs they choose to vulgarize. But if their presence will assure the audience which enables the festival to present the other performers on the program, I shall grit my teeth and welcome them." For Izzy Young, writing in *Caravan*, "Every aspect of human emotion was displayed there. Folk music was proven to be a great art form, and not something to be listened to necessarily because it is cultural or traditional. Where Alan Lomax failed in FOLKSONG '59 at Carnegie Hall a few months ago, Albert Grossman succeeded at Newport without making celebrations of what the singers should sing." As for the Kingston Trio, they "put on a wild, frenetic performance of their hit tunes which was fantastic to see and ghastly to hear. . . . The audience would not quit screaming and cheering until Oscar promised to bring the trio back on after Scruggs had finished. . . . Only one person was heard booing (this writer) when the Kingston Trio returned to another great ovation." Young would later complain that *Caravan*'s editor, Billy Faier, had tampered with his review: "No two of my sentences were left in order and the rest you rewrote so that my sense, style, thought and integrity were violated grossly." As for *Sing Out!* editor Irwin Silber, "If the program seemed to be dominated by the 'city' folk-singer with the traditional performer getting only an occasional look-in this was an accurate reflection of the current folk song 'boom' and the personalities who are dominating it." Relishing their success, Wein and Grossman planned a second festival in 1960. Vanguard Records would issue three volumes of festival highlights, while Folkways would produce one album covering both 1959 and 1960.[15]

Newport featured folk performers and added the scholarly panel, "What Is American Folk Music?" on Sunday morning, featuring folklorist Willis James, Alan Lomax, Moses Asch, and literary critic Stanley Edgar Hyman. Izzy Young presented a brief summary:

> Dr. Willis James offered some Negro folk "cries" as an example of one form of American folk music. Alan Lomax concerned himself with the emotional interior of people and brought forward the idea of "process" as being the proper way of looking at folk music. Moses Asch of Folkways Records discussed the American "problem" of having to refer to Lomax to find what may or may not be considered folk music. Many of us were under the impression that he would have something to say about the recent practice of copyrighting folksongs, but if so, he left it unsaid. On the other hand his cry from the heart that he did not want folk music to be stifled was understood by everyone.

For Mark Morris in *Gardyloo*, "Alan Lomax reiterated his story of the union of Negro music with the square white European music; it is always a joy to listen to this man, a true poet among theorists." Future Newport festivals, copying the style of college festivals, would continue the practice of featuring discussion panels.[16]

"Now it has become apparent that the Newport Festival . . . will not only succeed itself, but will be followed by other folk concerts and tours of folk artists throughout the country," Frederic Ramsey predicted in the *Saturday Review*. "It has also become apparent that concert activities will be reflected in a proliferation of recordings that will help to familiarize audiences with the joys, real or imagined, of folk music." Moreover, he concluded, the "personality of the folk performer is a spicy ingredient in the complex of factors that go to make up the excitement of listening to his music, either at festival or at home."[17]

Besides George Wein, Manny Greenhill was another Boston folk promoter. A graduate of the City College of New York and a World War II veteran, Greenhill had moved to Boston in 1950 and began organizing concerts in

1956, including one for Pete Seeger at Symphony Hall on December 5, 1958. A week later at the Boston YMCA he presented the blind gospel street singer Reverend Gary Davis, a phenomenal guitar player, along with Barry Korn-feld, one of the Washington Square stalwarts. Kornfeld would accompany Davis for the next two years, combining an urban folknik with the traditional Davis, while Greenhill became Davis's manager.

Reverend Davis had become influential among white, urban blues per-formers, particularly in New York. After his birth in South Carolina in 1896 and work as a blind street corner and revival meeting singer and preacher, he first recorded for the American Record Company (ARC) in 1935 and moved to New York City in 1944. He appeared with Woody Guthrie, W. C. Handy, Count Basie, and Eubie Blake at the memorial for Lead Belly on January 28, 1950, about the time that Elizabeth Lomax, Alan's wife, was recording Da-vis's biography (which was never published). During the next decade Davis recorded for the Stinson, Riverside, and Folk-Lyric labels, appeared in many concerts, continued his street corner appearances, and taught guitar at home. Along with Brownie McGhee, Sonny Terry, and others, Davis served as a lo-cal, and vital, link to the older southern blues musicians, while developing his own masterful guitar style. He continued a busy performing schedule until his death in 1972.[18]

Alan Lomax

Following "Folksong: '59" Alan Lomax had plunged into the folk scene with his usual energy. Shirley Collins, still involved in their romantic relationship, remained in London until "one day a letter arrived from him saying that he would like me to join him in the United States," she would recall. "He was planning a collecting trip in the South and wanted me as his assistant." Collins arrived in New York in April. "Shirley from England has come for a visit and we're going to California for some lectures, then coming back to the East, to pick up a recording machine and then go south for field trip," Lomax happily wrote to John Henry Faulk. "Will camp out to save money, and I'm going after material for a novel I hope or at least a play, and certainly for records and for photographs." He was trying in a way to relive the glory days of his field trips in the 1930s and 1940s, when numerous folklorists fanned out throughout the country and sent their recordings to the Library of Congress.[19]

Lomax was then joined by only a few other folklorists in the South, such as Harry Oster in Louisiana and Robert "Mack" McCormick in Texas. A pro-fessor at Louisiana State University, Oster began compiling his field record-ings for a Louisiana Folklore Society LP in 1957, soon followed by additional albums. "He follows the folk trail in a battered 1953 Mercury, tracking down leads with the persistence of a questing lepidopterist," *Time* explained, in a glowing account in October 1959. Frederic Ramsey followed with a more detailed article in the *Saturday Review*: "These are the scholars and explorers whose work, although commercially unrewarding, is preserving and making available for us many folk musics from obscure corners of the world. The performers they record will never appear in night clubs or at folk festivals." Within a few years, however, he would be proved wrong.[20]

Lomax and Collins left New York for California on June 20, 1959, and after driving nonstop they arrived in Chicago and stayed with Studs Terkel and his wife Ida. After recording a program for Terkel's WFMT radio show, they left their car with him and took the train to Berkeley and Barry Olivier's second Berkeley Folk Festival in late June. The festival's four days were crammed with workshops, beginning with Lomax discussing "What Are Folk Songs?" and concerts with Cisco Houston, Burl Ives, Seamus Ennis, the African American blues performer Jesse Fuller, Sam Hinton, Jeannie Robertson, Pete Seeger, Sam Hinton, and Sandy Paton. This was a nice mix of British and American musicians, with Lomax performing with his guitar. "During the festival Alan upset a few young city-born singers—he called them city-billies—by suggesting that they should learn folk-song *style* at the same time they learned the words and music," according to Collins. "It was excellent advice, but they resented it. I thought *they* were arrogant—they thought *he* was. Impasse." This was another example of the continuing controversy over defining authenticity. Lomax published his views in an article, "The 'Folkniks'—and the Songs They Sing," in the summer issue of *Sing Out!*, which in turn came from his liner notes to *Guy Carawan—vol. II* (Folkways 3548): "Singing style is the means by which the singer expresses the subtle emotional nuances of the song." While the challenge was difficult, Lomax believed "that more and more of the young singers are finding their own way to standards such as those I have been attempting to set forth." John Cohen, a member of the tradition-oriented New Lost City Ramblers, attempted a response, "In Defense of City Folksigers": "It takes comments such as Lomax'[s] to crystalize the problem of emotional content as it affects city folksingers. However, any step towards acceptance of this understanding will not come from criticism as he has presented it—but from the music itself."[21]

From Berkeley Lomax and Collins flew back to Chicago, picked up their car, and drove to visit Lomax's daughter Anne, then at the progressive Circle Pines summer camp in Michigan. "On the drive up, Alan said how much he was dreading teaching at a co-operative summer camp—said he'd forgotten how to co-operate anyway," Shirley would explain. "We both cheered up though when we were taken to the little wooden cabin near the lake that was to be ours, and we quickly established a routine of lecturing in the morning, spending the afternoon on the water rowing and swimming, and giving informal workshops and concerts in the evening. The children there really enjoyed the music." The children, as well as the staff, were accustomed to folk music, with Pete Seeger and Big Bill Broonzy having performed there two years before. Next Lomax and Collins hurried back to New York, then to the Newport festival, which for Collins "was a great disappointment. . . . 'Folk' is such a debased and mis-used word, given far too wide an interpretation by some of its worst perpetrators." She didn't care for Martha Schlamme, Odetta, Bob Gibson, or the Kingston Trio, preferring instead Jean Ritchie, Jimmie Driftwood, whom she had met in Berkeley, Frank Warner, and Earl Scruggs.[22]

"I finally raised the money to pay for a southern recording trip," Lomax wrote to his brother Johnny on August 9. The funding came from Ahmet and Nesuhi Ertegun at Atlantic Records, who had recent hits with the Drifters, Ray Charles, and Bobby Darin. "The idea is to try to get a picture of Negro folksong—religious and secular, in stereo. . . . I'm leaving here August 15 and have to be back in New York about October 10 but I should be able to make a good beginning on the job in this time. All my old field contacts are stale by now and I need any help you can give me for recording sites." While it might be difficult to discover fresh material, Lomax felt that "the best area for collecting left in the South is in the country from Texakarna [sic] south to the Gulf." Referring to "my English secretary and friend, Shirley Collins," he said they would be visiting soon.[23]

Lomax and Collins finally left New York on August 21, first stopping in Virginia, then on to Kentucky and Alabama, with the focus on recording African Americans. In Virginia they recorded Texas Gladden and her brother Hobart Smith for two days; Lomax and his wife Elizabeth had also visited them almost two decades earlier, in September 1941. Retracing sections of his 1941 travels, Lomax and Collins next recorded Wade Ward in Galax, then Estil C. Ball in Virginia. "The days in Virginia were very rewarding," Collins felt, "both in terms of the people we met and the material we recorded. I loved watching Alan at work, building affection and trust. Recording in the field is a difficult task, but Alan brought to it his years of experience, wide-ranging knowledge, unfailing patience, humour, enthusiasm, judgment and integrity." In Kentucky, their next stop, they recorded Old Regular Baptists at an outdoor prayer meeting. Collins now began to feel afraid: "Amidst all the beauty was hardship and deprivation for many mountaineers. We heard of the miners' bitter conflicts with mining companies and their armed guards."[24]

In Memphis they tracked down the remaining members of the Memphis Jug Band before heading for Alabama and recording the Sacred Harp Singers, then on to the Mississippi State Penitentiary, Parchman Farm, which Lomax had first visited with his father in 1933. "We were in Parchman for three days," Collins noted. "Alan found that the music, in the intervening . . . years since he'd first recorded there, has lost something of its grandeur and despair." In northern Mississippi they found Sid Hemphill, a fiddler and "quills" (panpipes) player, and from there they traveled to Como, where they recorded blues guitarist and singer Fred McDowell, as well as Lonnie and Ed Young, a black fife and drum duo. After visiting with Jimmie Driftwood and Almeda "Granny" Riddle in Arkansas, as well as Vera Hall (who had first been recorded by John Lomax in 1940) in Alabama, they headed to St. Simons Island off the Georgia coast. "The drive down through Arkansas, Mississippi, Alabama and Georgia to reach our last destination of the field trip, St. Simons, one of the Georgia Sea Islands, made me aware again how very far from England I was," Collins would later reflect. "I saw sights that I never would at home. . . . We took a day's sightseeing at the Okefenokee Swamp, we saw further KKK signs outside many towns, we ate, to my shame, in segregated restaurants, swam in segregated pools, and in Georgia we came across a convict chain-gang working at the side of the road."[25]

Lomax had first been in St. Simons with the African American writer Zora Neale Hurston and the New York University folklorist Mary Elizabeth Barnicle in 1935, and he now recorded Bessie Jones and the Georgia Sea Island Singers, who would soon be nationally popular. After two months and eight hundred miles, Lomax and Collins ended the trip by recording J. E. Mainer's string band, who had first recorded for Bluebird in 1935, in Concord, North Carolina. "We made it safely back to New York where we had all of two hours to spare before driving up to Boston, where we were appearing in concert with Sonny Terry and Brownie McGhee. Old friends of Alan's, I had met them in London a couple of years back," Collins ended her account.[26]

Lomax remained a crucial thread connecting the energetic folklorists and political activists of the New Deal era with the thriving folk revival of the late 1950s, but his work was far from over as the decade ended. Just returned to New York, in the apartment on West 3rd, in late October he wrote to the country music star Johnny Cash. Growing up in Arkansas, Cash had in 1954 returned from a stint in the Air Force in Germany and launched his recording career at Sun Records with such hits as "I Walk the Line." He joined the Grand Ole Opry in 1956 and soon switched to Columbia Records. "It's pleasant to discover that we have been mutual admirers for sometime," Lomax began, in responding to a letter from Cash. "The best of jazz, hillbilly, and rock and roll has always belonged, in my mind, to the developing folk tradition in America, and I consider some of your ballads among the best of contemporary folk expression. It makes me feel very happy to know that you have found my 'Blues in the Mississippi Night' album so exciting." During his southern trip Lomax attempted to recapture his longstanding love for recording white and black vernacular music, but this did not mean abandoning his interest in contemporary popular music and its economic potential. In need of funds, Lomax explained: "I have an enormous backlog of American folksongs which I think would be of great use to you in your further work as an American folk bard. A field recording trip to the Deep South which I have just completed, has turned up many new exciting songs and bases for songs. It would be a great pleasure for me to work with you on developing this material for the commercial market." Unfortunately, nothing came of this intriguing possibility.[27]

Lomax's next major project was to prepare the southern recordings for commercial release, but he also penned a glowing, influential tribute of the still largely unknown bluegrass music that appeared in October in *Esquire* magazine, "Bluegrass Background: Folk Music with Overdrive." "Out of the torrent of folk music that is the backbone of the record business today, the freshest sound comes from the so-called Bluegrass band—a sort of mountain Dixieland combo in which the five-string banjo, America's only indigenous folk instrument, carries the lead like a hot clarinet," Lomax began. He traced the origins to Bill Monroe and the Bluegrass Boys in 1945, with Earl Scruggs and Lester Flatt, who drew upon English and Scottish folk songs, as well as the "hot Negro-square dance fiddle." "Today we have a new kind of orchestra suitable for accompanying the frontier tunes with which America has fallen in love," he concluded. "And now anything can happen." Bluegrass was given a simultaneous boost with Mike Seeger's Folkways Records release of *Mountain Music Bluegrass Style*, which included Earl Taylor, B. Lilly and Don Stover, and Tex Logan, as well as the young New Yorkers Eric Weissberg and Bob Yellin. In 1960 United Artists issued *Alan Lomax Presents Folk Songs from the Blue Grass—Earl Taylor and His Stoney Mountain Boys*. In his notes for the album, Lomax predicted that "bluegrass may become as important in its field as early New Orleans jazz has been in relation to Negro music. The bluegrassers have developed the first true orchestral form in five hundred years of Anglo-American music." As for the Stoney Mountain Boys, whom he met through Mike Seeger, "They attack every song and every note as if they were a wing of jet fighters on their last mission."[28]

In the midst of these activities, Lomax developed health problems. As Shirley Collins informed the English folklorist Peter Kennedy in late November, "We are in the middle of terribly hard times again. For the past week Alan has been in bed with a severe ear infection—in his good ear (he is half deaf in the other).... Alan has many prospects—but all in the future, which never seems to get any closer." They also struggled to edit their field recordings for Atlantic Records, which would result in seven albums released in 1960. An additional twelve albums appeared on the smaller Prestige International Records label, also in 1960, this time with the assistance of Carla Rotolo, a young activist and the older sister of Suze Rotolo, later famous as Bob Dylan's girlfriend.[29]

While exploring traditional folk, bluegrass, country, and various aspects of popular music, Lomax expanded his theoretical ideas, long in gestation. The famed anthropologist Margaret Mead had invited him to give a talk at the 1958 annual meeting of the American Anthropological Association in Washington, which appeared as "Folk Song Style: Musical Style and Social Context" in the December 1959 issue of *American Anthropologist*. Three years earlier he had begun the exploration of the cross-cultural comparison of musical style and social structure in the article "Folk Song Style: Notes on a Systematic Approach to the Study of Folk Song," published in the *Journal of the International Folk Music Council*. He would develop this approach, soon named cantometrics, for the next three decades.[30]

Lomax never held a regular academic position, and he struggled to enhance his scholarly reputation while continuing his role in the ongoing folk music revival. As for Shirley Collins, she later wrote, "He felt he wanted to be on his own, that he couldn't commit himself permanently to one relationship." She returned to England in January 1960, clutching a letter from Lomax appointing her his agent in working with the BBC. "I missed Alan dreadfully, but I was young and resilient and picked up the threads in England again," she would recall. "The Folk Revival was getting underway, folk clubs flourishing all over the country, and I was able to make a living as a singer." And so she did.[31]

England

"We hadn't been back in the States very long when we received a call from Pete Seeger who had had his passport taken away from him during the Mc-Carthy [*sic*] hearings," June Shelley explained about her return to England with Jack Elliott in September 1959. "We had become friendly with his kid sister Peggy when she came to London and had introduced her to Ewan Mc-Coll, whom she went on to marry." *Sing* featured a photo on their December 1959 cover, with the caption: "Pete Seeger with Jack and June Elliott during Pete's recent British tour—the event of the year for folk song fans." Before the seven-concert tour, Elliott joined with the Weavers (Erik Darling having earlier replaced Seeger), Sonny Terry, and Brownie McGhee for a matinee show at Royal Festival Hall. Shelley wrote that they "proceeded to tour all over England and Scotland by train. . . . Some nights Jack would go on stage first and other nights Pete would open the show. At the end they would do a song together. In Glasgow, Jack did a song 'I Belong to Glasgow,' Scottish accent and all, that brought the house down." "Pete Seeger must have had a great impact on England while touring the country earlier this year, for the first time," Izzy Young explained in his *Folk Music Guide*USA* in early 1960.[32]

When Seeger and the Elliotts arrived in England, the folk scene was flourishing, despite the decline of skiffle. "It is indeed encouraging and a sign of vitality that we find new contributions and developments in the wide field of folk-music going on all the time," Brian Bird concluded in *Skiffle: The Story of Folk Song with a Jazz Beat,* the first book on the style, published in 1958. He believed that skiffle would last, since "the supply of songs which can be played and sung by Skifflers is practically inexhaustible." But others did not share his optimism, and by the time the book appeared fans had moved on to a variety of musical styles, including folk.[33]

Through 1959 the British music market was flooded by recordings from the United States. Popular performers included Elvis Presley, Gene Vincent, Richie Valens, Johnny Cash, Chuck Berry, the Cheers, and Ray Charles. In February Chris Barber's Jazz Band, no longer listed under skiffle, toured in the States, while their recording "Petite Fleur" reached the charts at home. By year's end Johnny Cash, the Browns, and Gene Vincent would be touring in Great Britain, joining such locals as Billy Fury, Johnny Gentle, and the Beat Boys. Eddie Cochran would follow in January 1960. Others, such as Alexis Korner and Davy Graham, were turning to jazz and blues, paving the way for the British rock explosion of the 1960s.[34]

As for folk music, Ewan MacColl, Bert Lloyd, and numerous others continued their promotions and explorations. The English Folk Dance and Song Society (EFDSS) held down the traditional wing of the movement, located at Cecil Sharp House and led by Douglas Kennedy, the father of Peter Kennedy, until 1961. In October 1959, EFDSS hosted the Third English Folk Music Festival and Concert. The more influential political wing included the Workers' Music Association, which controlled Topic Records, the London

Youth Choir, and *Sing* magazine. Music became a vital part of the antiwar movement, spearheaded by the Campaign for Nuclear Disarmament (CND) organized in February 1958. In April they planned "a march from London to the Atomic Weapons Research Establishment at Aldermaston in Berkshire," John Hasted explained. "What songs would we sing? Songs which would give a lead, and help the marchers to march." They came up with "Ban the Bomb For Evermore," along with MacColl's "Song of Hiroshima" and John Bruner's "The H-Bomb Thunder." Bert Lloyd, as well as Ewan MacColl and Peggy Seeger, joined the marchers. Future marches would go from Aldermaston to London.[35]

   Peggy Seeger had to leave London in May 1958 because of visa problems, but she finally returned in early 1959 to began living with MacColl; their son Neill was born in March. They performed together at the Ballads and Blues Club, now located at the ACTT trade union headquarters in Soho Square, while MacColl turned out a range of new songs. They continued to record together, including the albums *Barrack Room Ballads* and *Second Shift* for Topic. The label was also reissuing various Folkways albums from the United States, such as Brownie McGhee and Sonny Terry's *Guitars, Harmonica,* Sonny Terry's *Harmonica Blues, Pete [Seeger] and Five Strings, Spirituals by the Fisk Jubilee Singers,* and particularly Woody Guthrie's *Bound for Glory.* As their popularity grew, Seeger and MacColl traveled to North America three times, beginning in late 1959 with a two-month trip through Canada. Next, during the summer of 1960, they appeared at both the Berkeley Folk Festival and the second Newport Folk Festival, then returned for a concert at Carnegie Hall on December 3, introduced by Pete Seeger. MacColl's picture appeared on *Sing Out!'s* cover in late 1959, with an accompanying article by Irwin Silber, "Ewan MacColl—Folksinger of the Industrial Age." "He is dismayed by the overwhelming American influence on the English folk song revival," Silber explained. "MacColl himself never sings an American song." Izzy Young remarked in his *Sing Out!* column in early 1961, "The largest conclave of folksingers ever to meet in NYC met at Carnegie Hall early last December to attend Ewan MacColl's and Peggy Seeger's first NYC concert."[36]

   MacColl's musical and political partner, Bert Lloyd, was also keeping busy. In 1958 he launched the periodical *Recorded Folk Music: A Review of British and Foreign Folk Music.* Peter Kennedy, Paul Oliver, Alexis Korner, Eric Hobsbawm, along with Lloyd wrote the wide-ranging articles. For example, Kennedy covered "British Folk Music on Record" in the January-February 1959 issue:

It is paradoxical but typically English that we have the finest imaginable folk songs and the most varied instrumental music, and yet next to none of it has ever appeared on a commercial gramophone record published in Britain. . . . The example of the United States gives us hope. It was our own British-born songs and tunes, brought to light in America by such collectors as Cecil Sharp and the Lomaxes, that began the folksong revival in the United States. Stage performers such as Burl Ives and Josh White introduced folk song to many city folk.

There were a few exceptions, such as the recordings by MacColl, Lloyd, Margaret Barry, Isla Cameron, Shirley Collins, Harry Cox, and Jean Robertson, but much more needed to be done. Alexis Korner wrote about "The Evolution of Muddy Waters," and Daniel J. Crowley followed in the magazine's last issue with "Toward a Definition of Calypso." The magazine's sponsor, the left-wing Collet's jazz and folk shop, pulled the plug at the end of the second year. At the same time, Lloyd was editing (with the composer Ralph Vaughan Williams) the influential *The Penguin Book of English Folk Songs*, published in 1959 by the English Folk Dance and Song Society.[37]

As the decade ended, the British folk scene bustled along, poised to experience an explosion. Ewan MacColl, Bert Lloyd, Peggy Seeger, Shirley Collins, and a host of traditional performers as well as urban upstarts would spearhead a robust revival. Topic Records would be joined in the mix by other companies, while music from the United States flooded the marketplace. *Sing* continued to provide information on the folk scene and would be joined by other specialized magazines. Musical influences flowed back and forth across the Atlantic, as they had done for countless decades.

United States

The combination of the Kingston Trio's spectacular popularity and Harry Belafonte's ongoing fame fueled folk music's continuing rise in the U.S. "Interest in folk music is burgeoning in America as its boundaries disappear in the flood of new recordings, books, magazines, newsletters, radio programs, TV Spectaculars that are devoted to folk music and that seem to appear daily now," Izzy Young wrote in his short lived publication *Folk Music Guide*USA* in late 1959, which listed folk events nationwide. "Individual groups find it hard to keep their songs to themselves as the modern folk singer doesn't hesitate to draw on a hundred traditions, if necessary, to please his new audience. Ten years ago a folksinger might have to know some 200 songs, perhaps; today he must be familiar with thousands of songs." In an early 1960 issue Young commented on a party honoring the New Lost City Ramblers (NLCR) at Alan Lomax's apartment: "I never saw so many folksingers at one time. Jean Ritchie sang some carols and later joined in some strong leading of Bluegrass singing with Bill Clifton, Tex Logan, the Greenbriar Boys and the NLCR. It was a pleasure to see Country and City Musicians playing so well together. Alan Lomax and Shirley Collins sang some early, hearty Wassail Songs in the next room that almost knew no end."[38]

Three magazines published in New York, *Sing Out!*, *Caravan*, and *Gardyloo*, kept an interested public informed on various aspects of the ongoing revival. *Sing Out!* had struggled through much of the 1950s, but with folk music's upswing it took on a new life; the forty-two-page issue of early 1959 would expand by ten pages within a year, with a focus on song lyrics and historical articles. The Spring 1959 issue included a new column by Israel "Izzy" Young, "Frets and Frails," which would be a fixture for the next decade, a bird's-eye view of the passing scene. Silber and Young, two strong personalities with often conflicting political views, made a deal that there would be absolutely no censorship, an agreement adhered to for many years. Young's Folklore Center would also issue a range of newsletters and other publications as the sheer volume of folk news escalated quickly and dramatically; Young soon became a popular fly-on-the-wall, an entertaining and informative gossip columnist. The spring issue included Ron Radosh's attack on the popular performers of the time, such as the Kingston Trio, the Weavers, and the Gateway Singers: "It is about time that fans of folk song and those who hope to spread it, sing it, or perform it in the folk tradition stop patronizing the prostitutes of the art who gain their status as folk artists because they use guitars and banjos." Issues of taste and authenticity were not new and would long remain.[39]

Sing Out!'s early 1960 issue included Bill Oliver's discussion of the Ash Grove folk club in Los Angeles. Ed Pearl, a student at UCLA in the mid-1950s, became part of the campus Folk Song Club and found himself embroiled in an attempt to bring the blacklisted Pete Seeger to campus. "I already knew what side of the political fence I was on," he would later comment, "and I truly loved that music. I was already enraptured with Burl Ives and Harry Belafonte and Pete Seeger and Woody Guthrie and John Jacob Niles." Pearl had a wide range of musical tastes, having grown up on Israeli and Yiddish songs and listened to Spade Cooley and the other local country-western performers before discovering Harry Smith's *Anthology of American Folk Music* while at UCLA. He dropped out of college to take a short-lived job at Edwards Air Force before returning to Los Angeles and launching the Folk Arts Society in February 1958 with a flamenco concert at the Jazz Concert

Hall. A month later the second program, "Folk Songs of America," featured Logan English and Marcia Berman.[40]

With such success Pearl decided to open a club, the Ash Grove, the following July, beginning with Brownie McGhee, Guy Carawan, and the flamenco guitarist Jeronimo Villarino. Soon Stan Wilson, Barbara Dane, McGhee, Bess Hawes, Sam Hinton, and others filled the small stage, along with poetry and jazz nights, and even a chamber music concert. "Surrounded by the rather garish orange outside wall, screaming its message onto Melrose Avenue, the Ash Grove stands as some sort of memorial to blind faith's paying off on rare occasion," or so claimed the liner notes to the late 1958 album *Saturday Night at the Coffee House: a Night at the Ash Grove*, featuring Bud Dashiell, Travis Edmonson, Barbara Dane, Rolf Cahn, and Lynn Gold. Dashiell and Edmonson would soon combine into a popular duo, performing many Mexican songs in Spanish.[41]

In a short piece in *Caravan*, "Folk Music, Los Angeles," Billy Faier mentioned that the Ash Grove had been temporarily closed because of license difficulties in early 1959. "It would be a shame if the ASH GROVE does not reopen because it was the only place in Los Angeles where folk singers could present their material without any commercial coating," Faier remarked. "The ASH GROVE audience came to hear ethnic type sounds." It did reopen on March 26 with Jack Elliott and the Folkniks. Faier also listed the Unicorn, Cosmo Alley, and Club Renaissance, three other local establishments featuring folk acts. McCabe's guitar shop, opened in 1958, served as another local magnet for musicians and fans. As for Ed Pearl, he kept in touch with the national folk scene and visited the first Newport Folk Festival, where he met the New Lost City Ramblers. "With the juke-box profit-takers frantically looting the public domain for folk song hits and the beatniks trying to take over folk music to give validity to their bohemianism, it is refreshing to find a folk song hub with no other avowed axe to grind than to present Folk Music in its most desirable city format," Bill Oliver wrote in *Sing Out!* in early 1960. "This place is the Ash Grove, a concert-cabaret house, which started a little more than a year and a half ago on West Melrose Avenue, Hollywood. Among the 60 or so folksong coffee houses now spotted in the Los Angeles area, the Ash Grove is easily among the most substantial and solid of the lot."[42]

While *Sing Out!* focused on song lyrics and historical articles, *Caravan's* editor Billy Faier preferred a more scholarly approach, beginning with his first issue in early 1959 and featuring discographies and book reviews. For example, the folklorist MacEdward Leach introduced readers to the American Folklore Society, while Archie Green reviewed G. Malcolm Laws's *American Balladry from British Broadsides*, published in 1957. Laws had previously published

Native American Balladry: A Descriptive Study and a Bibliographic Syllabus
(1950). Page Steger covered the folk scene in the Bay Area, and there were also
listings of concerts in New York and elsewhere, a feature in each issue. The
April-May issue featured the first part of Fred Hoeptner's fascinating exploration of "Folk and Hillbilly Music: The Background of Their Relationship,"
which concluded in the June-July issue. This was an early scholarly study of
country music.[43]

The New Lost City Ramblers

Lee Hoffman had launched *Gardyloo* in April 1959 with a concentration on
New York's folk scene. "Although I've been somewhat aware of the 'hillbilly'
field for sometime, I've only recently 'discovered' it myself," she wrote to Archie Green in early 1959. "With the release of the New Lost City Ramblers
record and several other things, including my acquisition of the Folkways
[Harry Smith] anthology, I find a whole vast genre of music before me." Beginning with Barry Kornfeld's focus on Erik Darling, the editor followed with
a glowing review of radio station WNYC's massive concert at the Cooper
Union featuring a variety of the city's folk establishment: Hally Wood, the
Shanty Boys (Mike Cohen, Roger Sprung, Lionel Kilberg), Cynthia Gooding, Pete Seeger, Jean Ritchie, Frank Warner, Oscar Brand, the Tarriers, and
the Great Calypso Orchestra with Lord Invader. Hoffman also reviewed the
New Lost City Ramblers' (Mike Seeger, John Cohen, Tom Paley) concert
with Andrew Rowan Summers on February 28 at elementary school PS 41
in Greenwich Village: "Their music, as you probably know by now, is primarily the hillbilly music of the 1920s–'30s, and they do it magnificently."
She continued, "They are three fine musicians and their emphasis is on their
instruments. . . . Their charm and humor were much in evidence." She also
had a brief mention of the Ramblers' new Folkways album *The New Lost City
Ramblers. Gardyloo* quickly became "a vehicle for promotion," Hoffman later
explained. "I ran articles and gags by and about the Ramblers."[44]

Mike Seeger (1933–2009) was born in New York City, the oldest child of
the famed ethnomusicologist Charles Seeger and the modernist composer
and folklorist Ruth Crawford Seeger, and the half-brother of Pete. He grew
up in the Washington, D.C., area surrounded by traditional music. He early
learned the banjo and soon other instruments, and in 1952 he met Dick
Spottswood and subsequently through him the local circle of avid old-time
country and blues record collectors, including Robert Travis. Such networks
of collectors had been growing, particularly on the East and West Coasts,
through such magazines as *Disc Collector* and its companion *Country Direc-*

tory, launched in 1960, subtitled "Covering Discographies and Research on Country-Folk Artists." Around this time Seeger heard Lester Flatt and Earl Scruggs and the Foggy Mountain Boys, his introduction to bluegrass music. In 1954 he moved to Baltimore, which had a thriving bluegrass scene. There he met Hazel Dickens, who performed with him in Bob Baker and the Pike County Boys. He also began his documentary recording career, beginning with his Folkways album *American Banjo Scruggs Style*, appearing in 1957; he was one of those journeying south to record traditional musicians, including Wade Ward in Virginia. On May 25, 1958, Seeger appeared on a radio program in Washington, along with Tom Paley and John Cohen, both of whom he had previously met. In early 1959 he moved back to Washington, working as a recording engineer at Capitol Transcriptions, while the New Lost City Ramblers began their stellar career.[45]

John Cohen was born in New York City in 1932 and as a youngster discovered old hillbilly records and the five-string banjo. He attended Yale University in New Haven, Connecticut, and during the summer of 1952 while working at a resort in the Catskills he met Izzy Young and Tom Paley. By the time he enrolled as an undergraduate at Yale he had set out on a southern musical pilgrimage; he met with disappointment, however, when he reached Asheville, North Carolina: "I telephoned Bascom Lunsford, the 'Minstrel of the Appalachians,' but he wouldn't see me when he learned I was from New York and I knew of Alan Lomax and Pete Seeger and my last name was Cohen." After graduating from Yale as an art major he took a photographing trip to Peru. In 1957 he moved into a loft near Greenwich Village, where he connected with the Beat literary scene, which included Jack Kerouac and Allen Ginsberg, and a number of the abstract expressionist painters, as well as the local folk establishment. While the New Lost City Ramblers were forming, Cohen ventured on a collecting trip to eastern Kentucky in 1959, where he photographed and recorded banjo player, guitarist, and singer Roscoe Holcomb. His field recordings would appear in the 1960 Folkways album *Mountain Music of Kentucky*. "These 1959 recordings present the vigorous music of Kentucky mountain people," Cohen later wrote in the liner notes to the Smithsonian Folkways expanded CD reissue. "They sang and played banjos with a terrific energy that is almost unheard of now. They learned their music in a setting totally different from our contemporary life, in an era before people got their experiences from TV or their music from Nashville, when people plowed with mules, canned beans and tomatoes from their gardens, and reclined on front porches with slatted wooden swings attached to rafters by metal chains."[46]

Paley was born in 1928 and also grew up in New York, where he first learned the guitar, then banjo and mandolin, while participating in the left-wing

Folksay and its local square dances. In 1949 he met Woody Guthrie and did some performing with him before entering graduate school in mathematics at Yale. He and Cohen reconnected in New Haven and began performing together, while Paley recorded his influential Elektra album *Folk Songs from the Southern Appalachians* (1953) before moving to College Park to teach at the University of Maryland in 1956. Izzy Young scheduled a concert for the developing trio at the Carnegie Recital Hall on September 13, 1958; the next day Moses Asch recorded them for Folkways Records, and they adopted their group name when *The New Lost City Ramblers* album soon appeared. They used a variety of instruments on this initial recording—selling fewer than four hundred rather expensive copies during its first year—slowly spreading southern old-time music to a developing audience on a parallel track with the Kingston Trio's emergence as the avatar of popular folk music. "We stood in opposition to the commercialization of folk music which was being exploited by the Kingston Trio, the Limeliters, the Highwaymen, the Chad Mitchell Trio, and other groups with collegiate appeal," John Cohen would later explain. Billy Faier gave the album a glowing review in *Caravan*, in which he mentioned the role of the hillbilly record collectors, such as D. K. Wilgus (whose pioneering *Anglo-American Folksong Scholarship Since 1898* appeared in 1959), Archie Green, and Eugene Earle, whose research and writings had a strong influence on the Ramblers' repertoire.[47]

The Ramblers had slight initial national exposure as Lee Hoffman expanded her promotional efforts in *Gardyloo*. The May 1959 issue included John Cohen's article "About Us: The NLCR," a reprint of his liner notes for their Folkways album, as well as Hoffman's review of their May 17 concert in Washington, D.C., arranged by Mike Seeger. They appeared with guitarist and singer Elizabeth "Libba" Cotten, whom Mike and Peggy Seeger had discovered while she did housework for their parents. Her 1958 Folkways album, *Folksongs and Instrumentals with Guitar*, came from home recordings by Mike Seeger. "It was a very fine evening, and indeed, it was worth the price of admission to see that incredible array of instruments," Hoffman concluded. "I heartily recommend that if you get the opportunity to hear and see Elizabeth Cotton [*sic*] in person, you jump at the chance. I would also heartily recommend your attending New Lost City Rambler concerts, but that seems redundant somehow." The Ramblers had already recorded their second Folkways album, *Old Time Songs for Children*, released during the summer. While *Gardyloo* had a New York focus, the May issue also included a review of the 23rd Annual National Folk Festival in Nashville, which had fallen on hard times since its glory days.[48]

Gardyloo continued its Ramblers coverage in the July issue, with Seeger's photo on the cover and his essay on their initial musical odyssey. Winnie Winston followed with a rave review of their June concert at local Mills College: "This concert was the greatest thing I have ever attended, and I am looking forward to the next affair with the New Lost City Guitar Smashers"—this was a reference to that part of their act where Cohen, pretending to be mad at Paley's excessive banjo tuning, smashed a (cheap) guitar on the stage. Hoffman now began losing her energy to publish *Gardyloo*, which would end in early 1960—"In time, much of the old Wash[ington] Square gang dispersed in various directions," she would write. "By early 1960 working for a living was taking up a lot of my time. After the sixth issue, I closed down *Gardyloo*. And I began to drift away from the folknik scene myself." The Ramblers became more active: they appeared in scattered concerts, at the Newport Folk Festival in July, and on the CBS Camera Three TV show in September, along with Oscar Brand and Jean Ritchie. They soon recorded their third Folkways album, *Songs from the Depression*. While the songs might have seemed to include progressive political overtones, the Ramblers, despite the trio's left-wing roots, claimed to have no protest agenda.[49]

The Ramblers visibility increased through 1960, highlighted by their fourth album, *The New Lost City Ramblers Volume II*, summer appearances at the second Newport Folk Festival and the University of California-Berkeley festival, and performances at clubs such as the Gate of Horn in Chicago and the Ash Grove in Los Angeles. Hillbilly music, heavily influenced by the Ramblers, was securing a place within the emerging folk revival. It had various champions, including Archie Green. A college graduate and a carpenter by trade in San Francisco, he was one of the zealous hillbilly record collectors scattered around the country, serving as a bridge between the folk establishment, the collectors, and academic folklorists. He was also a fierce anticommunist, with left-wing politics closer to the historic Industrial Workers of the World (IWW); he preferred the anticommunist parodies in the Joe Glazer and Bill Friedland album *Ballads for Sectarians* (1950) and the *The Bosses' Songbook: Songs to Stifle the Flames of Discontent* (1958) by Roy Berkeley and Dave Van Ronk of the Libertarian League and the Folksingers Guild. Still, Green did not hesitate introducing himself to Pete Seeger in 1956: "Books and records are my hobby. The challenge I have set for myself is to compile a descriptive checklist of American Labor and Work Songs on Records. If it is possible, I want to draw from the fields of folk, country and western, pops, blues and other musical forms to tell the stories of workers and their industries."[50]

Old-time music spread throughout northern college and universities. *Folkways: A Magazine of International Folklore*, published by the University of Michigan Folklore Society, devoted much of issue 3 to explaining its origins: "Around 1940, the Old Timey music began to die out as it was replaced by electrified Country and Western. The advent of Bluegrass revived the five-string banjo and many of the traditional songs, but with tremendous modifications of instrumental styles." In a flattering article the New Lost City Ramblers, who had appeared in a concert on campus on November 18, 1960, were praised for reviving the style: "To hear the Ramblers is not only an enjoyment but an education. You cannot help but learn something from them, not only of the music, but of the people and the emotion behind it. And this is the trademark of the truly great folk musicians." The issue also included an ad for the Folklore Society's April 1961 folk festival, with the performers Frank Hamilton and Bill McAdoo.[51]

The Archie Green–Pete Seeger correspondence lasted for some years. In early 1957 Seeger suggested that Green contribute to *Sing Out!*, which editor Irwin Silber seconded. Along with Seeger, Silber was also interested in labor songs, but Green refused. While he did write for *Caravan* and other publications, he disliked Silber's politics. In early 1959 Silber mentioned to Green, "Our biggest complaint these days is that we seem to have lost our sense of social consciousness. People think we are tending to conform too much and are beginning to border on the non-political. I'm not sure whether I should feel complimented or insulted." Later in the year, with Green still holding out, Silber wondered, "Are you the type of anti-Communist whose perennial political touchstone will be a person's attitude toward [Soviet leader Nikita] Kruschev [*sic*] and Hungary [following the 1956 uprising and subsequent Soviet invasion] rather than his attitude towards what is happening here in the United States? Do you feel that we must prove our anti-communism to your satisfaction before you will believe it legitimate for someone to write for us?" Still, their exchanges continued for some years. In October 1959 Green informed Seeger, "I have been at the University of Illinois Institute of Labor and Industrial Relations. By good fortune the faculty and staff is most interested in my research." He did send Seeger a copy of his labor songs discography, parts of which would soon appear in print. Green remained as a librarian at Illinois for about a year, returned briefly to San Francisco, then moved back to the University of Illinois with his family in the late summer of 1960, where he would play a vital role as advisor to the emerging Campus Folksong Club.[52]

Civil Rights and Guy Carawan

The folk revival had both musical and activist political connections in the South, personified by Guy Carawan's work at Highlander Folk School in Monteagle, and then Knoxville, Tennessee, even before songs became a vital part of the developing civil rights movement. Myles Horton and Don West founded the Highlander school in 1932 with an emphasis on workers' education; Zilphia Mae Johnson began as a student in 1935, soon married Horton, and became the school's music director. Under Zilphia Horton's leadership the school issued a number of labor songbooks in the 1930s. Carawan had first visited Highlander in 1953, and after an active musical life through the decade, with Pete Seeger's suggestion, in May 1959 he volunteered to replace Horton, who had died in 1956, as the school's music director. "For the next two years I was the only person that I know of in the South going around to different freedom movements and conferences singing and and teaching freedom songs," according to Carawan. Long accepting both black and white students, Highlander had switched to offering civil rights workshops in 1953, prompted by the Supreme Court's *Brown v. Board of Education of Topeka, Kansas* school desegregation case. When the court ruled that segregation was illegal in 1954, Highlander was set to move forward, but not without opposition. "During those first few months we had at least half a dozen week long residential workshops bringing Negro community leaders and liberal whites together to discuss various aspects of how to bring about democracy in the South," Carawan explained to Josh Dunson. "My role was to get singing going, and teach songs appropriate to the spirit of the freedom struggle. . . . The singing helped a bunch of strangers brought together for a week's exchange of ideas & experiences lose their inhibitions and really get into the spirit of things."[53]

"I'm going to enclose a whole batch of material on the school here," Carawan wrote to Izzy Young in August 1959, "the kind of musical program I'm engaged in developing, and a recent experience involving a raid on Highlander by local extremist elements who don't like Highlander for [its] work in integration." He mentioned spending a night in jail, charged with drunkenness and resisting arrest following a raid on the school by local and state police on July 31. During the frightening raid the students bolstered their spirits by singing "We Will Overcome," based on a 1945 picket line song by the Food and Tobacco Union workers in Charleston, South Carolina, that Zilphia Horton had taught to Pete Seeger in 1947. Soon known as "We Shall

Overcome," Carawan helped to spread it throughout the civil rights movement. "My main goal down here aside from enjoying myself and learning all
I can is to try and develop the use of singing for brotherhood," he continued
to Young. "Practically all the festivals are lily white though the music crosses
lines that people and performers can't. . . . We're planning a Cumberland Mt
Folk Festival next summer (a truly integrated one for all kinds of old and
new Negro and white music) which will be open to every one to attend."
The racial situation was tense, as Paul Endicott, Carawan's agent, informed
Moses Asch in late August: "Rev. [Martin Luther] King's church in Montgomery is under continuous police surveillance and in view of the fact that
the raid on Highlander made the front pages in Alabama, the Church people
do not think that it would be wise for Guy to appear in Montgomery at this
particular time." The Montgomery bus boycott, led by King, had ended in
November 1956 after an anxious year, following a Supreme Court decision
outlawing bus segregation, but southern segregationists were hardening their
opposition to the civil rights movement. Civil rights songs would become a
vital part of the movement, initially led by King and his Southern Christian
Leadership Conference (SCLC).[54]

While working at Highlander, Carawan continued to give concerts
throughout the North, free from threats of violence—Paul Endicott arranged for a tour on the West Coast and into Canada during April and May
1959, for example—as well as recording for Folkways Records, which had
begun in 1958 with *Songs with Guy Carawan*, followed by *Guy Carawan:
Something Old, New, Borrowed, and Blue*. Alan Lomax wrote the generous
liner notes for the latter: "The modern American folk-song revival began
back in the thirties as a cultural movement, with overtones of social re-
form. In the last ten years our gigantic amusement industry, even though
it is as yet only mildly interested in folk music, has turned this cultural
movement into a small boom. As might have been expected, a throng of
talented and ambitious city youngsters have taken over. These so-called
city-billies or folkniks make most of the LPs and perform at most of the
concerts." While Carawan certainly qualified as a folknik, whom Lomax
often criticized, nonetheless he praised the album because "Guy looks the
part he sings, that is frontier America come alive again, direct, unpreten-
tious, genuine and full of restrained feeling. . . . Right now it is a pleasure
and an education in the roots of our music to listen to him, because he is
serious and he is on the right track." Lomax was also a strong supporter of
Carawan's civil rights work.[55]

Irwin Silber featured Carawan on the cover of *Sing Out!*'s summer 1960
issue, along with a flattering article: "Somewhere in the South today there

is a tall, good-looking, clear-eyed young man with a banjo—and a mission." Following a brief biography, the magazine's editor traced Carawan's recent appearances at southern colleges and his joining a lunch counter sit-in in Nashville. In February four freshmen at North Carolina Agricultural and Technical College had initiated the sit-in movement, protesting segrega- tion at a Woolworth's in Greensboro, North Carolina, and the movement quickly spread throughout the South. "Singing has become such an impor- tant part of the integration struggle," Silber explained, "that Highlander has now scheduled a 'Singing Workshop' for this summer. . . . Guy Carawan is a phenomenon in this curious, cynical world of 1960. He does not consider himself a hero, a martyr, or a crusader. He is in the South today because he has to be."[56]

From his base at Highlander, Carawan worked closely with the gathering civil rights movement, deftly connecting folk music with racial justice. In early April 1960 Highlander hosted the "First South wide conference of 80 Sit-In participants," Carawan would comment. Two weeks later, from April 19 through April 21, the "First South-wide conference of 200 Sit-In partici- pants [was] called by SCLC at Raleigh, N.C. This was the founding gathering of SNCC [Student Non-Violent Coordinating Committee]. At both of these gatherings I introduced We Shall Overcome and Keep Your Eyes on the Prize—until then the students had not sung these songs." In August Cara- wan—joined by Gil Turner, Pete Seeger, Ethel Raim, Waldemar Hille, Ernie Marrs, Julius Lester, and Hedy West—hosted a Sing for Freedom workshop at Highlander and published a freedom songs songbook, which was distributed at a SCLC conference in Shreveport in October. He also led the singing at the SNCC gathering in Atlanta the same month, as music became an essential part of the movement.[57]

Carawan had originally found "the singing that went on at civil rights gath- erings was stiff and formal," as he explained to Josh Dunson. "It seemed that most of the leaders running the meetings were those educated types of Negroes who have gotten rid of all traces of folk speech, humor and old Baptist style in their behavior and are afraid to sing a spiritual or gospel song that might cause a foot to tap, hands to clap or bodies to sway." During the Montgomery bus boycott, for example, civil rights meetings featured "Onward Christian Soldiers" and "Old Time Religion," or perhaps "Jacob's Ladder." "In 1959 the NAACP sent out a song sheet to its branches suggesting that they use the idea of song fests for their new membership drive—the song sheets were full of parodies of songs like, 'Old Mill Stream,' 'Let Me Call You Sweetheart' and 'The More We Get Together the Happier We'll Be.' Not a single song out of Negro folk culture on it." Carawan would now devote his life to infusing the civil rights movement with spirited songs, most newly composed and based on African American folk life. "After three months at Highlander (by the end of July 1959)," he continued to Dunson, "I knew that this was something special that I could offer many of the people and situations that I was coming in contact with." Carawan became involved with the Nashville sit-in movement in the spring of 1960, spending two months documenting the escalating events in this tense city. Folkways quickly issued the album *The Nashville Sit-In Story* (Folkways FH 5590), including statements by student leaders John Lewis, Marion Berry, and Diane Nash, and songs by the Nashville Quartet (Joseph Carter, Bernard Lafayette, James Bevel, Samuel Collier), "You Better Leave Segregation Alone," "Moving On," and "Your Dog Loves My Dog." Music had become a vital part of the movement.[58]

Little Sandy Review

"I am enclosing under separate cover the first issue of a new folk magazine—THE LITTLE SANDY REVIEW—a magazine largely devoted to record reviews and record listings in the folk field," Paul Nelson informed Moe Asch on March 26, 1960. Nelson and his editorial partner Jon Pankake had met as undergraduates at the University of Minnesota in 1957 and connected through their love of folk music and films. They attended a Pete Seeger concert in 1957, but soon discovered they preferred a more rustic folk sound. Nelson requested that Asch "send us covers on all your new folk releases well in advance, and also send us two complimentary copies of each new American and English folk release." In exchange they would print a full-page Folkways ad in each issue, as they did in the first issue. Asch responded that he didn't "think it is fair to you people to give us free ads" but would send some records for review. "We are two people who love folk music very much and want to do all we can to help the good in it grow and the bad in it perish," they explained in the inaugural issue. Among the reviews in the first issue, they praised the New Lost City Ramblers, the "absolute best folk group now recording . . . and anyone who has not heard them should immediately do so."[59]

Each monthly issue of the *LSR* would include a range of record reviews and folk news, with no hesitation in picking their idea of winners and losers. For example, the second issue praised Pete Seeger's *Song and Play Time* while panning albums by the Kingston Trio and The Skifflers: "SOLD OUT, it seems to me, would be a far better-fitting title for the Skifflers' new LP then for the Kingston Trio's. One knows what to expect from Guard, Shane, and Reynolds—but no one would figure Hally Wood to be part of what is as sickeningly commercial and dishonest a folk group as I have ever heard (with the possible exception of the Limeliters or the Coachmen)." The latter they would refer to as "folkum," what Pankake later explained as distinguishing "in a market of consumer products, those artifacts that were just 'product'—out to make a buck, to entertain, some slickly and some ineptly—from those that had intellectual value, integrity, commitment, emotional depth, meaning." They received praise from Pete Seeger for "the most obdurately opinionated and interesting magazine one could wish for." Nelson and Pankake connected with Joe Nicholas, who published *Disc Collector*—they included an ad in the second issue, with the notation "Heartily endorsed by THE LITTLE SANDY REVIEW"—and now *Country Directory*. The first issue of the latter, in November 1960, with the Australian hillbilly collector John Edwards on the cover, listed the Library of Congress recordings of Woody Guthrie, Burl Ives, Lead Belly, Earl Robinson, Aunt Molly Jackson, and Bascom Lamar Lunsford, mostly *Little Sandy Review* favorites. While folk and country had become distinct commercial labels, among record collectors and the broader folk community they clearly overlapped.[60]

"Two young, ardent and extremely articulate folkniks in Minneapolis have managed to kick up more of a fuss in folksong circles over the past few months than almost anyone has done," Irwin Silber wrote in *Sing Out!* In addition to their likes, "it is their 'dislikes,'—and the sharp, unmitigated tone of their criticism—that has, perhaps, helped to win for Pankake and Nelson & Co. an enviable reputation for directness and honesty." Billy Faier in *Caravan* was equally welcoming: "Little did we know that this innocently titled, mimeographed magazine would turn out to be a crusader for marching into our midst from the wilds of the mid-west. For the editors of *LSR* have something to say and say it they do, leaving little to the imagination as to their feelings about the current folk-music-on-record scene." For the next few years the *LSR* would become increasingly controversial, particularly when it attacked those who promoted topical songs. Nelson and Pankake represented one aspect of the wide range of folk music interests and tastes at decade's end, when folk authenticity was certainly problematic. They also connected with the British scene; the sixth issue featured a listing of English records by Alan Lomax, Peggy Seeger, Jack Elliott, and Shirley Collins that were available from the bookseller Ken Lindsay in London.[61]

Old and New Faces

George Wein scheduled the second Newport Folk Festival for June 24–26, 1960, with daytime events and evening concerts. "There was an even greater degree of musical diversity this year," he would argue. "We had performers from Africa [the Nigerian Michael Olatunji], Scotland [Ewan MacColl], Spain [flamenco guitarist Sabicas], Israel [Oranim-Zabar Trio], and Ireland [Clancy Brothers and Tommy Makem]. Professionals like Will Holt, Theodore Bikel, and the Gateway Singers performed alongside more 'authentic' performers like Jesse Fuller and Frank Warner. John Lee Hooker performed his mysterious blues." Wein particularly praised Robert Pete Williams, first recorded by Harry Oster at the Louisiana State Penitentiary. "It was clear that the folk festival audience—mostly college age—found such meaning and honesty in the songs themselves." Authenticity and crowd participation seemed to be the bywords. Robert Shelton's *New York Times* review praised Flatt and Scruggs and the Foggy Mountain Boys as well as the Weavers, Pete Seeger, and the finale with Odetta, John Jacob Niles, the New Lost City Ramblers, and Frank Warner. John Greenway and Cisco Houston honored Woody Guthrie in a special segment.[62]

"According to experts, the basic cause of the bull market in folk music—which has been coming on ever since World War II—is the do-it-yourself trend: folk audiences, unlike jazz audiences, like to participate in the music they admire," *Time* expounded to its wide audience. "At Newport last week, many spectators brought along banjos and guitars with their sleeping bags and sat around campfires on the beaches strumming far into the night. (In the last three years U.S. banjo sales have increased by 500%.)" The article included a brief list of popular folk musicians: Odetta, Theodore Bikel, the New Lost City Ramblers, Pete Seeger, the Brothers Four, the Weavers, and Joan Baez. Newport's broad range of performers could satisfy about any musical taste. Susan Montgomery, in an expansive article in *Mademoiselle*, agreed that the "intensity of students' current passion for folk music—and the nature of the love affair—is demonstrated vividly at a festival like the one at Newport. Each night the music continued long after the regular performances were over, when it became the property not of professionals but of small groups of students who carried their sleeping bags and instruments down to the beach." And she added: "Folk music, like a beard and sandals, has come to represent a slight loosening of the inhibitions, a tentative step in the direction of the open road, the knapsack, the hostel." Jack Kerouac, no lover of folk music, had published *On the Road* only three years earlier, but his spirit had become increasingly pervasive.[63]

"Ewan MacColl was heard for the first time in America at the Newport Folk Festival," Izzy Young remarked in his *Sing Out!* column. "He has an absolute air of tradition about him and he delightfully ignores his own implacable rules for singing and composing songs within a tradition. The twenty or so minutes of ethnic music presented at the Festival more than held its own against the fifteen hours of commercial music heard. I think that good folk music is good entertainment and doesn't have to be watered down into 'sugar and treacle' for the people to like it."[64]

Newport was not the only folk festival in 1960, but it captured the headlines. Barry Olivier staged the third Berkeley festival in July with a broad lineup: Ewan MacColl and Peggy Seeger, Sam Hinton, the cowboy singer Slim Critchlow, Sandy Paton, the New Lost City Ramblers, John Lomax Jr., and the bluesman Lightnin' Hopkins. Two Yale students had invited Odetta, Tom Paley, Robin Roberts, and Logan English to the first Indian Neck Folk Festival in 1957, located on Long Island Sound. Three years later two new students, Jack Burgis and Bill Arnold, organized the second festival, limited to 450 invited guests in early May. Robert Shelton's glowing review in *Caravan* mentioned the performers Sandy Bull, Carolyn Hester, Billy Faier, Eric von Schmidt, Jackie Washington, and the Highwaymen (five sophomores from Wesleyan University). "The absence of any 'big-name' performers at Indian Neck was not a detriment," Shelton concluded. "The unknowns and little-knowns are making beautiful music and persuasive good sense in their performances." They certainly represented the new crop of performers.[65]

"Folk music—the authentic and the commercial blends—is rapidly reaching the fad stage," Jay Milner announced in the *New York Herald* in February 1960. "You might say there's a grassroots movement in the nation's popular music tastes. The teenagers provide the momentum for most of the fads these days and, as they did with rock and roll, teenagers are singing and playing folk music as well as listening to it." Harry Belafonte and the calypso fad had kicked off the current interest, while "Alan Lomax, son of a famous folk lore collector, is representative of a branch of what is now a booming industry that promotes the authentic forms of the music." Carroll Calkins, joined by Alan Lomax, followed with an article in *House Beautiful*, explaining, "Folk songs and singing are more popular than ever before. But unless we learn to distinguish the real from commercial versions, we will never know the world of emotion and experiences from which folk music comes. This is the stuff of folk music. The farther it gets from such roots, the less impact it has." While they recognized the popularity of Belafonte, the Kingston Trio, the Tarriers, and Frankie Laine, Calkins and Lomax preferred the authenticity of traditional southern mountain singers, bluegrass performers such as Earl Scruggs, the Stoney Mountain Boys, as well as Jean Ritchie.[66]

While folk music was relatively scarce on TV, on June 16 CBS did feature a one-hour tribute, "Folk Sound USA," sponsored by Revlon, with Joan Baez,

Cisco Houston, John Jacob Niles, John Lee Hooker, Earl Scruggs and Lester Flatt, Frank Warner, and Peter Yarrow. *Variety* gave it a mixed review: "Sumup on this one is good performances, ingenious integration and staging, but not quite ingenious enough to overcome the problem of an all-music stanza of brief selections all in the same general vein. Good try, though." Harriet Van Horne, a popular newspaper critic, countered with a snooty column in the *New York World-Telegram & Sun*, "Square Toe Blues": "It's the kind of folk music I associate with far-out Bohemian types. I mean the types who wear leather thong sandals and who entertain you after dinner (a casserole of garlic bulbs and goat hearts in bad wine) with their scratchy old recordings of blues songs by Leadbelly [*sic*] and Blind Willie Johnson. . . . No, this kind of music is not for Miss Square Toes." At least she didn't try any red baiting, only beatnik slurs.[67]

Robert Shelton, popular music critic at the *New York Times*, covered "Folk Music Makes Mark on City's Night Life" in a November column: "Folk music is leaving the imprint of its big country boots on the night life of New York in unparalleled fashion from the grimiest Greenwich Village espresso joint to the crooked-finger elegance of the Waldorf Astoria." He mentioned Gerde's Folk City, the Gaslight Cafe, the Bizarre, the Flamenco room of the Chateau Madrid, the Commons, Cafe Society Downtown, and Art D'Lugoff's Village Gate. "The last years of the 1950s were a great time in the Village," Dave Van Ronk would fondly recall. "It was not too crazy yet, but there was an exhilarating sense of something big right around the corner. As for the folk scene, it was beginning to look as if it might have a future, and me with it." He first established himself at the Commons, then the Gaslight coffeehouse, where he was a regular performer for some years, described by Robert Shelton as a "24-year-old droopy-mustached city boy . . . [with] a great fluency with Negro folk song."[68]

Gerde's Folk City had begun as one of Izzy Young's experiments in January 1960. Along with his partner Tom Prendergast, they initiated folk nights at Mike Porco's bar on West Fourth Street, which they named the Fifth Peg. Porco, along with his brother John and his cousin Joe Bastone, had originally purchased William Gerdes's restaurant on West Third in 1952, which they moved to West Fourth a few years later. The Fifth Peg opened with Ed Mc-Curdy and Brother John Sellers, soon followed by the Clancy Brothers, Billy Faier, the Tarriers, Brownie McGhee and Sonny Terry, and Dick Weissman. But for some reason the crowds soon dropped off, with Theo Bikel drawing only a handful. In late April Porco took over, changed the name to Gerdes Folk City, with Logan English as the emcee, and opened with Carolyn Hester. It quickly became the heart of the local folk scene.[69]

The Future: Dylan, Collins, Makeba

With the presidential election of John F. Kennedy in November, following eight years of Republican (generally conservative) domination, the political ground was shifting as the folk revival began to soar. Pete Seeger still faced a prison sentence, however, after a federal grand jury indictment in 1957 for contempt of Congress following his appearance before the House Un-American Activities Committee in 1955; he would finally be convicted by a federal court in March 1961 and receive a sentence of a year and a day in federal prison (but would be acquitted the next year by the Court of Appeals). The trial postponements required continual fundraising. Moses Asch at Folkways pledged one thousand dollars in late 1959, for example. Still, a youthful energy seemed to be taking hold of the country, leaving the apparently stodgy 1950s behind. Folk music was certainly becoming more popular, led by such stalwarts as Seeger, Odetta, Belafonte, Jean Ritchie, Rev. Gary Davis, the Kingston Trio, the Tarriers, John Jacob Niles, Richard Dyer-Bennet, Cisco Houston, Joan Baez, Earl Scruggs, Bob Gibson, and so many others. Simultaneously, a new crop of performers had begun to emerge, energized by a combination of the John Kennedy and Jack Kerouac mystiques.

Robert Zimmerman was born in Duluth, Minnesota, in 1941, and the family soon moved to Hibbing, a small, rugged town on the iron range. Early on he took to rock 'n' roll, rhythm and blues, and rockabilly, playing the electric guitar in a local high school band while honing his piano playing. In 1959 he began adopting the name Bob Dylan, and during that summer, before enrolling at the University of Minnesota in Minneapolis, he visited Denver. At the local folk club, the Exodus, opened that year, he met the teenage Judy Collins and the creative bluesman Jesse Fuller. "I suppose what I was looking for was what I read about in *On the Road*—looking for the great city, looking for the speed, the sound of it, looking for what Allen Ginsburg had called the 'hydrogen jukebox world,'" Dylan expressed in his memoir, *Chronicles: Volume One.* "Folk music was a reality of a more brilliant dimension. It exceeded all human understanding, and if it called out to you, you could disappear and be sucked into it."[70]

Arriving in Minneapolis, Dylan initially moved into a fraternity house and traded his electric guitar for a Martin acoustic. He began collecting folk records, starting with Odetta, and met local musician John Koerner (later known as Spider John Koerner), who became his initial musical mentor. A musical sponge, Dylan began picking up songs from the recordings of the New Lost City Ramblers, Dave Van Ronk, Peggy Seeger, John Jacob Niles, as well as Blind Lemon Jefferson, Blind Blake, and Charlie Patton. He discovered Woody Guthrie and was in thrall: "Folk songs automatically went up against the grain of all these things and Woody's songs even went against that. In comparison everything else seemed one-dimensional. The folk and blues tunes had already given me my proper concept of culture, and now with Guthrie's songs my heart and mind had been sent into another cosmological place of that culture entirely." Next he met Paul Nelson and particularly Jon Pankake, who shared with him their growing record collection of traditional musicians. "Pankake was authoritative and a hard guy to get past," according to Dylan. "He was part of the folk police if not the chief commissioner, wasn't impressed with any of the new talent." Pankake introduced Dylan to Jack Elliott's recordings, among many others. Dylan also met the local musicians Dave Ray and Tony Glover (who would later be part of the Koerner-Ray-Glover blues group). Dylan played in the local folk clubs but in December 1960 took off for Greenwich Village.[71]

"On a sunny afternoon in the spring of 1954, when I was fifteen, the Great Folk Scare, like a beautiful wild bird, flew into my living room and made a perfect landing," Judy Collins has explained. Growing up in Denver, Colorado, in a middle-class family, she had been studying classical piano and voice. But hearing "The Gypsy Rover" on the soundtrack of the Alan Ladd film *The Black Knight* led to getting a guitar and listening to Jo Stafford's album *American Folk Songs*. Within a few years the "country was falling in love with folk songs, as was I. I looked for material wherever I could, haunting the record stores with my previous babysitting money in hand, buying records of old sea chanties and English folk songs." She began performing locally after high school graduation, including stints at the Gilded Garter in Central City, Colorado, and the Exodus in Denver: "Hal Neustaedter had opened the club in 1958 [1959], and by the time I worked there for the first time in the fall of 1959, it was *the* club in the Rockies for folk music." She was now married and living in Boulder. At the Exodus she met and worked with Bob Gibson, the Tarriers (Eric Weissberg, Bob Carey, Clarence Cooper), and Josh White. In January 1960 she performed at the Limelight in Aspen, Colorado, with the Smothers Brothers (Dick and Tom), then that summer at the Gate of Horn in Chicago. There she met Studs Terkel and worked with Theo Bikel, Sonny Terry, Cynthia Gooding, Odetta, and Miriam Makeba. That fall Collins moved with her family to Storrs, Connecticut, and began her active professional career appearing throughout the country, one of the few female folk singers, including Carolyn Hester, Jo Mapes, Gooding, and now Joan Baez. Elektra would issue her first album, *A Maid of Constant Sorrow*, in 1961, and her career would continue well into the next century.[72]

While Dylan and Collins began their folk odyssey from the outposts of the Middle West, Mariam Makeba (1932–2008) was born a world away in Johannesburg, South Africa. She developed as a singer with the Cuban Brothers, next the Manhattan Brothers, who made a number of records. She appeared in the local film *Come Back, Africa*, which brought her to the attention of Harry Belafonte. He met her in London and served as her mentor when she traveled to the United States in November 1959 to appear on the *Steve Allen Show* in Los Angeles, then at the Village Vanguard in New York. "The Village Vanguard is a little jazz club on Eighth Street," she would write. "I do not know what I am doing here, because I am not a jazz singer, but Mr. Max Gordon, who did so much to bring me to the United States, seems very happy to have me." She immediately drew rave reviews and began performing in Belafonte's concerts, including at Carnegie Hall in May 1960 with Odetta and the Chad Mitchell Trio; the concert recording *Belafonte Returns to Carnegie Hall* received a Grammy nomination. International music had long been part of the folk revival, including calypso, and now Makeba added to this incredible mix. She appeared on her first album in 1960, *Mariam Makeba* (RCA Victor), and her voice and personal stature would continue for many decades.[73]

Decade Ends

On May 14, 1960, Izzy Young wrote in his notebook:

> I had supper with Alan Lomax on Thursday. . . . Alan tells me that city folk-singing in America is still unformed—especially since it is so young—some 30 years. He thinks the Kingston Trio is great and he still believes in rock 'n' roll as an important force. After listening to all the city music, he still feels there is nothing he can turn to and point out to a foreigner and say, "Listen to this," and look for its beauty. He said, now that the Fifth Peg is closed, that I should have a combination bookstore-coffeehouse (since coffeehouses are so impor-tant today) and have only the finest singers appear and never compromise my standards, the bookstore to be the central force as that is the best thing I've done. And then exciting things would happen. He would love to do a TV show, but he's hampered by money. I think he could do a greater job than anyone in America. He still doesn't trust me completely, and he was accurate, because I haven't made up my mind to be an "entrepreneur" or a "pater."

Both Young and Lomax had played important roles in the ongoing folk re-vival and would continue to so.[74]

In the record collectors' magazine *Record Research* in mid-1959, Izzy pre-sented his thoughts about folk music's current issues and possible future:

> There will be so much money to be made in Folk Music in the next two to three years that politics and personal differences will be forgotten in the desperate

attempts to copyright every folksong that was ever written. Hundreds of arrangements will be copyrighted by scholars, collectors, etc. The left-wing will cease attacking Tin Pan Alley as they get more and more used to the fact that more money can be made by copyright than protest. I have nothing against Tin Pan Alley as they are in the business to make money. I feel bad about all the new music that will parade as Folk Music just the way a lot of new music was called Calypso a few years ago. However, Calypso goes on just the way Folk Music will go on—despite the temporary, frenzied interest of the Alley.[75]

While Young plunged into the day-to-day aspects of the Revival, as a store owner, journalist, concert producer, pundit, and seer, Alan Lomax was developing a somewhat more distant perspective, although he continued in his longstanding, interactive, and highly influential roles. *The Folk Songs of North America* was published in 1960 to widespread praise, and that January the American Council of Learned Societies (ACLS) granted Lomax six thousand dollars for "nine months of study and research in the field of folk song . . . aimed at refinement of hypotheses . . . about the importance of vocal style and behavioral traits in the analysis and classification of folk songs." With the assistance of Margaret Mead, Lomax developed a relationship with the Department of Anthropology at Columbia University through the year of his grant.[76]

In *Sing Out!* Lomax celebrated the life of Zora Neale Hurston, the African American folklorist and novelist, who had died on January 28, 1960. Lomax, Hurston, and the folklorist Mary Elizabeth Barnicle had made a collecting trip to Georgia and Florida in 1935. In recent years Hurston had been living in relative obscurity and poverty in Florida, which Lomax lamented:

> This was the week that three Kingston Trio records were among the top twenty albums in the country. . . . This was also the week that the most skillful and talented field collector and writer that America has thus far produced died in a third rate hotel in Florida without a penny in her purse or a friend in the world. There is no one to replace Zora Hurston, but her contributions to American life and literature will long outlive the noisy and easily won successes of the market-place.

Lomax was continually looking backward as well as forward. At year's end he informed his sister-in-law Margaret: "I am going to spread Christmas between Margaret Mead's family and Anne [his daughter] in Princeton, then go onto the American Folklore meeting in Philadelphia. Meantime I am digging at my books and writing papers, just to what end I am not quite sure, except my own further education."[77]

In the *Corpus Christie [Texas] Caller-Times*, Jay Milner, with pride in his state's native son, wrote: "Hike a southern backroad today and you're likely to meet a college professor carrying a tape recording machine or a backwoodsman toting a banjo. Or both. The professor will be looking for a backwoodsman with a banjo and the backwoodsman for some one with a recording machine. But if the road is worth a folksong collector's time, an Alaskansized Texan named Alan Lomax has already traveled it." Milner presented a brief overview of his life, with the reflection: "In England the impact of his BBC programs has been so great one commentator wrote not long ago, 'the names Leadbelly [*sic*] and Woody Guthrie have become household names in England. Walk down the streets of London now and you can hear the skiffle boys pounding banjos and guitars to "John Henry" or the "Midnight Special.""78

Along with *Billboard* editor Paul Ackerman, Lomax considered writing a book on "The Folky Fifties," with much intellectual and musical scope. "For the first time, in this decade, folk songs and pseudo folk songs turned up in the hit parade," they began their proposal. "IRENE began the trend in 1950; THE BATTLE OF NEW ORLEANS, in 1959, emphasized again that this was no fad, but represented a change in public taste." They included rock 'n' roll, "a new musical bridge between white and Negro artists. It has prepared America to accept the blues and the swinging spirituals of today, the gospel songs." As for "hillbilly. . . . It has now produced America's most exciting contemporary orchestral style—blue grass. It has also reacted to the thrust of rock and roll and rhythm and blues to give rise to a new style—rockabillly, where singers can still make ballads like their mountain ancestors or swing out like jive men." Their book would "define the various styles and trends which have preoccupied the teenagers and mystified or terrified their parents. . . . It will be a portrait of an era and a wonderful book to sing from [including 150 songs]. And it will tell the stories of such characters as Muddy Waters, Fats Domino, Elvis Pressley [*sic*], The Kingston Trio, The Weavers, Mahalia Jackson, Jimmy [*sic*] Driftwood, Peter Seeger—all new to American bigtime, but now elbowing our slick, European-based pop-song industry into the shadows." Unfortunately, such an expansive, creative approach, from two of the foremost authorities on popular music never saw the light of day, but it expressed Lomax's lifelong pursuit of all forms of music, vernacular and otherwise.79

Growing up in the 1950s, the daughter of Communist Party members, Alix Dobkin, later a folk singer and feminist activist, early absorbed much of the developing folk revival. "Woody Guthrie, the Weavers and Almanac Singers,

John Jacob Niles, Leadbelly [*sic*], Josh White, Jean Ritchie, Brownie McGhee and Sonny Terry, Reverend Gary Davis, Cynthia Gooding, Oscar Brand, and so many others had for years been sowing the seeds that blossomed into a folk music boom," she would recall in her autobiography, "and no one deserves more credit that the tireless Pete Seeger. . . . Singing Seeger's songs bonded and revitalized people of good will working for the common good, and in the late 1950s, the first generation he raised began to come of age. The songs promoted broad themes of peace and social justice, were simple enough to learn, and were known by many." The musical stage was now set for the folk eruption just around the corner, where Lomax, Seeger, and their colleagues would play a vital role. The British folk revival of the 1950s, heavily indebted to the influx of songs and performers from the United States, would also mature into the ensuing 1960s folk and rock explosion, with obvious political transatlantic overtones.[80]

Notes

Introduction

1. Scott Alarik, *Revival: A Folk Music Novel* (Portsmouth, N.H.: Randall, 2011), 135.

2. Maurice Isserman and Michael Kazin, *America Divided: The Civil War of the 1960s* (New York: Oxford University Press, 2000).

3. *Folk Songs of the United States* (Sacramento: California State Department of Education, 1951), iii; David Bonner, *Revolutionizing Children's Records: The Young People's Records and Children's Record Guild Series, 1946–1977* (Lanham, Md.: Scarecrow, 2007).

4. Robert Cantwell, *When We Were Good: The Folk Revival* (Cambridge, Mass.: Harvard University Press, 1996), 281; Dick Weissman, *Which Side Are You On? An Inside History of the Folk Music Revival in America* (New York: Continuum, 2005), 72. To date, the most thorough discussion of the decade can be found in Ronald D. Cohen, *Rainbow Quest: The Folk Music Revival and American Society, 1940–1970* (Amherst: University of Massachusetts Press, 2002), chapters 3–5.

Chapter 1. Background in the U.S. and Great Britain

1. Stith Thompson, ed., *Four Symposia on Folklore: Held at the Midcentury International Folklore Conference, Indiana University, July 21–August 4, 1950* (Bloomington: Indiana University Press, 1953), 160, 161, 171; John Szwed, *Alan Lomax: The Man Who Recorded the World* (New York: Viking, 2010).

2. D. K. Wilgus, *Anglo-American Folksong Scholarship since 1898* (New Brunswick, N.J.: Rutgers University Press, 1959).

3. Nolan Porterfield, *Last Cavalier: The Life and Times of John A. Lomax* (Urbana: University of Illinois Press, 1996).

4. Benjamin Filene, *Romancing the Folk: Public Memory and American Roots Music* (Chapel Hill: University of North Carolina Press, 2000), chap. 1.

5. Tim Brooks, *Lost Sounds: Black and the Birth of the Recording Industry, 1890–1919* (Urbana: University of Illinois Press, 2004); Karl Hagstrom Miller, *Segregating Sound: Inventing Folk and Pop Music in the Age of Jim Crow* (Durham, N.C.: Duke University Press, 2010); Susan Curtis, "Black Creativity and Black Stereotype: Rethinking Twentieth-Century Popular Music in America," in *Beyond Blackface: African Americans and the Creation of American Popular Culture, 1890–1930,* ed. W. Fitzhugh Brundage (Chapel Hill: University of North Carolina Press 2011), 124–46; Grace Elizabeth Hale, "Hear Me Talking to You: The Blues and the Romance of Rebellion," in Brundage, *Beyond Blackface,* 239–58; Marybeth Hamilton, *In Search of the Blues: Black Voices, White Visions* (London: Cape, 2007); Elijah Wald, *Escaping the Delta: Robert Johnson and the Invention of the Blues* (New York: Amistad, 2004), 98–102; Robert Gordon and Bruce Nemerov, eds., *Lost Delta Found: Rediscovering the Fisk University–Library of Congress Coahoma County Study, 1941–1952* (Nashville: Vanderbilt University Press, 2005); Ted Gioia, *Delta Blues* (New York: Norton, 2008); David Evans, ed., *Ramblin' on My Mind: New Perspectives on the Blues* (Urbana: University of Illinois Press, 2008). On work songs from both white and African American roots, see Ronald D. Cohen, *Work and Sing: A History of Occupational and Labor Union Songs in the United States* (Crockett, Calif.: Carquinez, 2010).

6. Debora Kodish, *Good Friends and Bad Enemies: Robert Winslow Gordon and the Study of American Folksong* (Urbana: University of Illinois Press, 1986).

7. Robert Gordon, *Folk-Songs Of America* (Washington, D.C.: National Service Bureau, 1938), 1–3.

8. Scott B. Spencer, ed., *The Ballad Collectors of North America: How Gathering Folksongs Transformed Academic Thought and American Identity* (Lanham, Md.: Scarecrow, 2012).

9. Karen L. Cox, *Dreaming of Dixie: How the South Was Created in American Popular Culture* (Chapel Hill: University of North Carolina Press, 2011); Anthony Harkins, *Hillbilly: A Cultural History of an American Icon* (New York: Oxford University Press, 2004).

10. Ronald D. Cohen, *A History of Folk Music Festivals in the United States* (Lanham, Md.: Scarecrow, 2008), 1–29.

11. Bill Malone and Jocelyn R. Neal, *Country Music, U.S.A.*, 3rd rev. ed. (Austin: University of Texas Press, 2010); Michael Ann Williams, *Staging Tradition: John Lair and Sarah Gertrude Knott* (Urbana: University of Illinois Press, 2006); Chad Berry, ed., *The Hayloft Gang: The Story of the National Barn Dance* (Urbana: University of Illinois Press, 2008); Peter La Chapelle, *Proud to Be an Okie: Cultural Politics, Country Music, and Migration to Southern California* (Berkeley: University of California Press, 2007); Jeffrey J. Lange, *Smile When You Call Me a Hillbilly: Country Music's Struggle for Respectability, 1939–1954* (Athens: University of Georgia Press, 2004); Ronald D.

Cohen, "Music Goes to War: California, 1940–1945," in *The Way We Really Were: The Golden State in the Second World War*, ed. Roger W. Lotchin (Urbana: University of Illinois Press, 2000), 47–67; Tracey E. W. Laird, *Louisiana Hayride: Radio and Roots Music along the Red River* (New York: Oxford University Press, 2005).

12. Pete Seeger, "Progressives and Fascists Both Sing Folk Songs," c. 1942, in *Pete Seeger in His Own Words*, ed. Rob Rosenthal and Sam Rosenthal (Boulder: Paradigm, 2012), 78; Richard A. Reuss with JoAnne C. Reuss, *American Folk Music and Left-Wing Politics, 1927–1957* (Lanham, Md.: Scarecrow, 2000).

13. "Miserable but Exciting Songs," *Time*, November 26, 1945, 52; "Americana on Record," *Newsweek*, September 22, 1947.

14. B. A. Botkin, ed., *A Treasury of American Folklore* (New York: Crown, 1944), 819–20; Lawrence Rodgers and Jerrold Hirsch, eds., *America's Folklorist: B. A. Botkin and American Culture* (Norman: University of Oklahoma Press, 2010).

15. E. David Gregory, *Victorian Songhunters: The Recovery and Editing of English Vernacular Ballads and Folk Lyrics 1820–1883* (Lanham, Md.: Scarecrow, 2006); Gregory, *The Late Victorian Folksong Revival: The Persistence of English Melody, 1878–1903* (Lanham, Md.: Scarecrow, 2010). For a study that discusses the songs and ballads that nineteenth-century collectors had ignored and overlooked, see Roy Palmer, *The Sound of History: Songs and Social Comment* (London: Faber and Faber, 2008).

16. Sheila Tully Boyle and Andrew Bunie, *Paul Robeson: The Years of Promise and Achievement* (Amherst: University of Massachusetts Press, 2001).

17. Nick Clarke, *Alistair Cooke: A Biography* (New York: Arcade, 1999).

18. Alan Lomax to John Lomax, June 3, 1938, and Alan Lomax to D. G. Rowse, December 8, 1938, in *Alan Lomax, Assistant in Charge: The Library of Congress Letters, 1935–1945*, ed. Ronald D. Cohen (Jackson: University Press of Mississippi, 2011), 79, 111.

19. Christina Baade, "Airing Authenticity: The BBC Jam Sessions from New York, 1938/39," *Journal of the Society For American Music* 6, no. 3 (August 2012): 271–314.

20. *The Ballad Operas: The Martins and the Coys*, Rounder 11661-1819-2; Elijah Wald, *Josh White: Society Blues* (Amherst: University of Massachusetts Press, 2000), 107–8; Christina L. Baade, *Victory through Harmony: The BBC and Popular Music in World War II* (New York: Oxford University Press, 2102), 122–23.

21. A. L. Lloyd, *Folk Song in England* (London: Lawrence & Wishart, 1975), 5–6; Dave Arthur, *Bert: The Life and Times of A. L. Lloyd* (London: Pluto, 2012).

22. A. L. Lloyd, *Corn on the Cob: Popular and Traditional Poetry of the U.S.A.* (London: Fore, 1945), 7, 8; Daniel J. Walkowitz, *City Folk: English Country Dance and the Politics of the Folk in Modern America* (New York: New York University Press, 2010), 178–80; Duncan Hall, *"A Pleasant Change from Politics": Music and the British Labour Movement between the Wars* (Cheltenham, U.K.: New Clarion, 2001). While Lloyd would become enamored with folk songs from the United States, the American Ernie Lieberman, passing through London on his way to the World Youth Festival

in Prague in 1947, found that the WMA chorus "have no American songs, however (except for 'Battle Hymn of the Republic') and tend to consider us thoroughly reactionary." "Workers Music Association," *People Songs* 2, no. 9 (October 1947): 2.

23. The complete Topic Records discography can be found in Michael Brocken, *The British Folk Revival, 1944–2002* (Aldershot, U.K.: Ashgate, 2003), 146–216.

24. Carl Sandburg, *New American Songbag* (New York: Broadcast Music, 1950), iii, vi; Bing Crosby message inside front cover.

25. Carl Haverlin to Eugene Raynal, October 13, 1949; Carl Haverlin to Carl Sandburg, March 31, 1950, Carl Haverlin Papers, 144, University of Delaware Library, Newark, Delaware. Penelope Niven, *Carl Sandburg: A Biography* (New York: Scribner's, 1991), states: "Sandburg's schedule pulled him back and forth across the continent in 1950, and fall found him settled at the Royalton Hotel in New York for final work on *Complete Poems*. He had done some perfunctory work on a *New American Songbag*, published in 1950 by Broadcast Music Incorporated with a foreword by Bing Crosby," 598.

26. Note from Carl Haverlin to Bob Sour, August 3, 1950, copy in possession of R. Cohen.

27. Clipping from *Billboard*, June 10, 1950; Carl Haverlin to Bing Crosby, November 20, 1950, Haverlin Papers, 144.

28. Ben Gray Lumpkin, ed., *Folksongs on Records, Issue Three* (Boulder, Colo.: Folksongs on Records, 1950), 1, 2–3.

Chapter 2. The Weavers and the Resurgence of Folk Music

1. Oliver Stone and Peter Kuznick, *The Untold History of the United States* (New York: Gallery, 2012), chap. 5; Richard Lingeman, *The Noir Forties: The American People from Victory to Cold War* (New York: Nation, 2012). On labor union songs at the time, still somewhat popular, see Ronald D. Cohen, *Work and Sing: A History of Occupational and Labor Union Songs in the United States* (Crockett, Calif.: Carquinez, 2010).

2. Among the many important books on the Red Scare, see David Caute, *The Great Fear: The Anti-Communist Purge under Truman and Eisenhower* (New York: Touchstone, 1979); Ellen Schrecker, *Many Are the Crimes: McCarthyism in America* (Boston: Little, Brown, 1998); Robert Justin Goldstein, *American Blacklist: The Attorney General's List of Subversive Organizations* (Lawrence: University Press of Kansas, 2008); Landon R. Y. Storrs, *The Second Red Scare and the Unmaking of the New Deal Left* (Princeton, N.J.: Princeton University Press, 2013); David Everitt, *A Shadow of Red: Communism and the Blacklist in Radio and Television* (Chicago: Ivan Dee, 2007); Scott Martelle, *The Fear Within: Spies, Commies, and American Democracy on Trial* (New Brunswick, N.J.: Rutgers University Press, 2011); Steven J. Ross, *Hollywood Left and Right: How Movie Stars Shaped American Politics* (New York: Oxford University Press, 2011); Larry Ceplair and Steven Englund, *The Inquisition in Hollywood: Politics in the Film Community, 1930–60* (Urbana: University of Illinois Press, 2003); Robert M. Lichtman, *The Supreme Court and McCarthy-Era Repression: One Hundred Deci-*

sions (Urbana: University of Illinois Press, 2012); Robert M. Lichtman and Ronald D. Cohen, *Deadly Farce: Harvey Matusow and the Informer System in the McCarthy Era* (Urbana: University of Illinois Press, 2008).

3. Howard Fast, *Peekskill USA* ([New York]: Civil Rights Congress, 1951), 83; Jordan Goodman, *Paul Robeson: A Watched Man* (London: Verso, 2013), 115–37.

4. John Strausbaugh, *The Village: A History of Greenwich Village* (New York: HarperCollins, 2013), 377–97.

5. Bernard Rubin, "Broadway Beat," *Daily Worker*, June 1, 1949, 13; Pete Seeger to Ron Cohen and Dave Samuelson, May 4, 2000, copy in author's possession.

6. Pete Seeger, *Where Have All the Flowers Gone: A Singalong Memoir* (New York: Sing Out!, 2009), 43; "What's On?" *Daily Worker*, January 27, 1950, 8; "Folksong at 8 at Panel Room," *Daily Worker*, May 5, 1950, 10; Strausbaugh, *The Village*, chap. 25.

7. Gordon Allison, Dining and Dancing," *Herald Tribune*, January 4, 1950; Robert W. Dana, "Village Vanguard Has Real Hoe-Down," *World-Telegram*, January 11, 1950. The preferred spelling is Lead Belly, which we will use, but we will retain Leadbelly in quoted material.

8. Leonard Lyons, "The Lyons Den," *New York Post*, June 11, 1950; Albin J. Zak III, *I Don't Sound Like Nobody: Remaking Music In 1950s America* (Ann Arbor: University of Michigan Press, 2010), 60–65.

9. Bernie Asbell, "Folk Songs Do It Again: Weavers Hit First Try," *Spin*, July–August 1950; all of their recordings can be found in Dave Samuelson, producer, *Goodnight Irene: The Weavers, 1949–1953*, 4 CD box with illustrated book, Bear Family Records BCD 15930, 2000.

10. "Goodnight, Irene," *Time*, August 14, 1950, 38; Gilbert Millstein, "Very Good Night," *New York Times Magazine*, October 15, 1950, 41. See also, James Dugan, "Birth of a Song Hit," *Maclean's*, September 15, 1950, 18–19, 49–51.

11. "Out of the Corner," *Time*, September 25, 1950, 69.

12. Harold Leventhal with Robert Santelli, "Remembering Woody," in *Hard Travelin': The Life and Legacy of Woody Guthrie*, ed. Robert Santelli and Emily Davidson (Middletown, Conn.: Wesleyan University Press, 1999), 15; Woody Guthrie to Moe Asch, October 23, 1950, and Moe Asch to Woody, October 29, 1950, Moses and Frances Asch Collection, Ralph Rinzler Folklife Archives and Collections, Center for Folklife and Cultural Heritage, Smithsonian Institution, Washington, D.C.

13. Paul V. Coates, "Well, Medium and Rare," *Mirror*, February 3, 1951; "Ciro's," *Variety*, February 5, 1951; "Weavers Warble in Emerald Room," *Houston Press*, February 28, 1951.

14. Pete Seeger, liner notes, *Negro Prison Camp Work Songs*, Folkways Records FE 4475, 1956.

15. "Weavers' Yarn," *Newsweek*, August 6, 1951, 80; Virginia Wicks, "They Told Weavers 'You're Good—But Not Commercial,'" *Compass*, August 12, 1951.

16. *Red Channels: The Report of Communist Influence in Radio and Television* (New York: Counterattack, 1950), 2, 6; Everitt, *Shadow of Red*, chap. 3.

17. *Counterattack*, Letter 159 (June 9, 1950); *Counterattack*, Letter 174 (September 22, 1950).

18. "The Inside on 'Counterattack,'" *Billboard*, September 9, 1950, 4; Jerry Wexler and David Ritz, *Rhythm & the Blues: A Life in American Music* (New York: St. Martin's, 1993), 66.

19. Liner notes, The Weavers, *Folk Songs of America and Other Lands*, Decca DL5285, 1951.

20. Frederick Woltman, "Melody Weaves On, along Party Line," *New York World Telegram*, August 25, 1951; "Weavers Show Up at O. State Fair but Are Nixed; Heidt Puts $ With AFM," *Variety*, August 29, 1951; Bill Coss, "The Weavers," *Metronome*, October 1951, 14.

21. Wicks, "They Told Weavers."

22. Milt Freudenheim, "Weavers Give Show Despite Legion Disfavor," *Akron Beacon Journal*, February 5, 1952, 2; "Singers at Cafe Here Called Reds by Tipster in Ohio: They Deny It," *New York Journal-American,* February 6, 1952, 6.

23. "Testimony of Harvey M. Matusow of Dayton, Ohio, February 25, 1952," *Report of the Un-American Activities Commission, State of Ohio, 1951–1952* (Columbus, Ohio: 1953), 106, 109.

24. Liner notes to *The Weavers: Wasn't That a Time* (Vanguard, VCD 4-147/50), 21; Aviva Shen interview with Pete Seeger, *Smithsonian*, April 2012, available at http://www.smithsonianmag.com/arts-culture/Pete-Seeger-Where-Have-All-the-Protest-Songs-Gone.html (accessed October 22, 2013).

25. Alan Lomax to Robin Roberts, Easter Sunday [1950], John and Alan Lomax Manuscript Collection, American Folklife Center, Library of Congress (hereafter cited as Lomax, Library of Congress).

26. Lomax to ?, from Paris but no date; Lomax to ?, first page missing, no date, manuscripts in the collection of Barry Ollman, Denver, Colorado. For Alan Lomax's time in the United Kingdom and Europe, see John Szwed, *Alan Lomax: The Man Who Recorded the World* (New York: Viking, 2010), 251–305.

27. Tony Judt, "On Being Austere and Being Jewish," *New York Review of Books* 67, no. 8 (May 13, 2010): 20; Rob Young, *Electric Eden: Unearthing Britain's Visionary Music* (New York: Faber and Faber, 2010); Dave Arthur, *Bert: The Life and Times of A. L. Lloyd* (London: Pluto, 2012).

28. N. E. Wadsley to Miss Dabell, December 17, 1951; Dabell to Wadsley, December 31, 1951; J. Philip O'Brien to John H. Marriott, March 7, 1952; Letter to K. A. L. Parker at the Home Office, November 2, 1953: Lomax file, National Archives, Special Branch, Kew, UK. See also Gerald Porter, "The World's Ill-Divided: The Communist Party and Progressive Song," in, *A Weapon in the Struggle: The Cultural History of the Communist Party in Britain*, ed. Andy Croft (London: Pluto, 1998), 171–91; Giora Goodman, "The British Government and the Challenge of McCarthyism in the Early Cold War," *Journal of Cold War Studies* 12, no. 1 (Winter 2010): 62–97.

29. *Patterns in American Folksong*, No. 1, "Love," and *Patterns In American Folksong*, No. 2, "Violence," copies in Lomax, Library of Congress. See also E. David Gregory,

"Lomax in London: Alan Lomax, the BBC and the Folk-Song Revival in England, 1950–1958," *Folk Music Journal* 8, no. 2 (2002): 136–69; Ronald D. Cohen, "Alan Lomax: An American Ballad Hunter in Great Britain," in *Transatlantic Roots Music: Folk, Blues and National Identities,* ed. Jill Terry and Neil Wynn (Jackson: University Press of Mississippi, 2012), 119–37.

30. Undated clipping from *London Times,* courtesy of Robin Roberts.

31. Ronald D. Cohen, ed., *Alan Lomax: Selected Writings, 1934–1997* (New York: Routledge, 2003), 182–83.

32. Paul Oliver, "Taking the Measure of the Blues," in *Cross the Water Blues: African American Music in Europe,* ed Neil A. Wynn (Jackson: University Press of Mississippi, 2007), 34; Roberta Freund Schwartz, "Preaching the Gospel of the Blues: Blues Evangelists in Britain," in Wynn, *Cross the Water,* 145–66; Elijah Wald, *Josh White: Society Blues* (Amherst: University of Massachusetts Press, 2000), 210–14, 218–21; Bob Riesman, *I Feel So Good: The Life and Times of Big Bill Broonzy* (Chicago: University of Chicago Press, 2011), 163–66, 171–74, 182–84, 213–16, 227–31; Paul Oliver, "'Early Morning Blues': The Early Years of the Transatlantic Connection," in Terry and Wynn, *Transatlantic Roots Music,* 20–35; Christian O'Connell, "Dreaming Up the Blues: Transatlantic Blues Scholarship in the 1950s," in Terry and Wynn, *Transatlantic Roots Music,* 37–56.

33. Ewan MacColl, *Journeyman: An Autobiography* (London: Sidgwick & Jackson, 1990), 269–71; Ben Harker, *Class Act: The Cultural and Political Life of Ewan MacColl* (London: Pluto, 2007), 95–96.

34. MacColl, *Journeyman,* 275; Harker, *Class Act,* 111, 126–27; Fred Woods, *Folk Revival: The Rediscovery of a National Music* (Poole, 1979), 56; Michael Verrier, "Folk Club or Epic Theatre: Brecht's Influence on the Performance Practice of Ewan MacColl," in *Folk Song: Tradition, Revival, and Re-Creation,* ed. Ian Russell and David Atkinson (Aberdeen, 2004), 112; Ben Harker, "'Workers' Music': Communism and the British Folk Revival," in *Red Strains: Music and Communism Outside the Communist Bloc,* ed. Robert Adlington (Oxford: Oxford University Press, 2013), 89–104.

35. Alan Lomax to Ruby P. Tartt, March 7, 1952, Lomax, Library of Congress; Nina Jaffe, *A Voice for the People: The Life and Work of Harold Courlander* (New York: Holt, 1997), 92–98

36. "Golden Age of Hootenanny," *Saturday Review of Literature,* November 24, 1951, 75.

37. "The First Issue," *Sing Out!* 1, no. 1 (May 1950): 16 (ellipses in original); Irwin Silber, "The Weavers—New 'Find' of the Hit Parade," *Sing Out!* 1, no. 9 (February 1951): 6, 12.

38. Milt Okun as told to Richard Sparks, *Along the Cherry Lane: Tales from the Life of Music Industry Legend Milt Okun* (Beverly Hills, Calif.: Classical Music Today, 2011), 2; "Adironack Folk Song and Dance Festival Planned for Summer," *American Folk Music* 1, no. 1 (April 1953): 4.

39. Sam Hinton, "Old Man Atom," Columbia 38 929, 1950.

40. Article in *Movie Stars Parade*, August 1950; Harold Bernz, "Atom Discs for Peace," *Sing Out!* 1, no. 5 (September 1950): 11; article in *San Diego Union Tribune*, August 1950; "No Private Censors," *Life*, September 11, 1950.

41. Pete Seeger, liner notes, *Waist Deep in the Big Muddy and Other Love Songs*, Columbia Records CL 2705, 1967.

42. Lawrence Gellert, "Atom Bomb Blues," *Sing Out!* 1, no. 10 (March 1951): 9; "Wanted: Peace Songs," *Sing Out!* 1, no. 12 (May 1951): 2; Lewis Allen, "Long Way from Home," *Sing Out!* 1, no. 12 (May 1951): 6–7; Lewis Allen, "Oh Beautiful Day," *Sing Out!* 2, no. 1 (July 1951): 13; "A Letter from Woody Guthrie," *Sing Out!* 3, no. 3 (September 1951): 2; Robbie Lieberman, *The Strangest Dream: Communism, Anticommunism, and the U.S. Peace Movement, 1945–1963* (Syracuse, N.Y.: Syracuse University Press, 2000).

43. Bob Claiborne, "Folk Music of the United States," *Sing Out!* 2, no. 4 (October 1951): 12; "People Artists' Leaders Subpoenaed," *Sing Out!* 2, no. 8 (February 1952): 2.

44. Betty Sanders and Irwin Silber, "Talking Un-American Blues," *Sing Out!* 2, no. 10 (April 1952): 10; Albert Wood, "The Dying Soldier," *Sing Out!* 2, no. 11 (May 1952): 3; "SING OUT for Hallinan and Bass," *Sing Out!* 3, no. 1 (September 1952); Malvina Reynolds, "Swivel Chair Reserves," *Sing Out!* 3, no. 4 (December 1952): 3.

45. Joseph Starobin, "'The Songs of the Hootenanny Are Still Ringing in My Ears,'" *Daily Worker*, undated clipping (1953).

Chapter 3. Blacklisting and Folk Developments

1. The actual release date for the anthology was November 1952.

2. Dave Van Ronk with Elijah Wald, *The Mayor of MacDougal Street: A Memoir* (Cambridge, Mass.: Da Capo, 2005), 46–47.

3. Luis Kemnitzer, "West Coast Record Collector," in *A Booklet of Essays, Appreciations, and Annotations Pertaining to the Anthology of American Folk Music*, ed. Harry Smith (Washington, D.C.: Smithsonian Folkways Recordings, 1997), 29–30.

4. "Editorial," *Disc Collector* 1, no. 1 (January/February/March 1951): 2; "The Perfesser [D. K. Wilgus]" and "Discography," *Disc Collector* 1, no. 3 (July/August/September 1951): 13; Marshall Wyatt, "A Visit with Joseph E. Bussard, Jr.," *Old-Time Herald* 6, no. 7 (Spring 1999): 12–17; Marshall Wyatt, "'The Music Has Always Held Sway': An Interview with Bob Pinson," *Old-Time Herald* 6, no. 4 (Summer 1998): 15–22; Marybeth Hamilton, *In Search of the Blues: Black Voices, White Visions* (London: Cape, 2007), chap. 6.

5. See Jon Pankake, "The Brotherhood of the Anthology," in Smith, *A Booklet of Essays*, 26–28.

6. "'The Coo-Coo Bird' and Others," *New York Times*, undated clipping (1952).

7. Sarah Gertrude Knott, "The Folk Festival Movement in America," *Southern Folklore Quarterly* 17, no. 2 (March 1953): 146–47; Stith Thompson, "Folklore and Folk Festivals," *Midwest Folklore* 4, no 1 (1954): 11; Ronald D. Cohen, *A History of*

Folk Music Festivals in the United States: Feasts of Musical Celebration (Lanham, Md.: Scarecrow, 2008), chap. 2.

8. Flyer for Carolina Folk Festival, June 15, 16, 17, 1950.

9. Ray Lawless, *Folksingers and Folksongs in America* (New York: Duell, Sloan and Peirce, 1960), 445; Gladys Best Henley, "Down among the Suwannee," *Etude* 72 (April 1954): 12.

10. "Disks Spread Folk Fame to Every Corner of Country," *Billboard Music Year Book: Section 6, American Folk Music* (New York: Billboard, 1946), 489; Richard A. Peterson, *Creating Country Music: Fabricating Authenticity* (Chicago: University of Chicago Press, 1997), 199.

11. Richard Carlin, *Worlds of Sound: The Story of Smithsonian Folkways* (New York: Collins, 2008).

12. Jac Holzman and Gavan Daws, *Follow the Music: The Life and High Times of Elektra Records in the Great Years of American Pop Culture* (Santa Monica: FirstMedia, 1998), 18, 25.

13. Oscar Brand, "The Authentic Version," *Saturday Review of Literature*, August 29, 1953, 54; Ron Pen, *I Wonder as I Wander: The Life of John Jacob Niles* (Lexington: University Press of Kentucky, 2010). See also, Donald Ritchie, "A Survey of Folk Music on Long Play," *American Record Guide*, October 1953, 35–38; Oscar Brand, "Old Folk Songs at Home," *Saturday Review of Literature*, December 12, 1953, 43.

14. Paul O. Jenkins, *Richard Dyer-Bennet: The Last Minstrel* (Jackson: University Press of Mississippi, 2010).

15. Ives, quoted in Ronald D. Cohen, *Rainbow Quest: The Folk Music Revival and American Society, 1940–1970* (Amherst: University of Massachusetts Press, 2002), 74; White quoted in Cohen, *Rainbow Quest*, 81; Holzman and Daws, *Follow the Music*, 26; Elijah Wald, *Josh White: Society Blues* (Amherst: University of Massachusetts Press, 2000), 177–209.

16. *American Folk Music* 1, no. 1 (April 1953): 1.

17. "Dear Reader," *Sing Out!* 4, no. 7 (Fall 1954): 2; "Don't Read This Now!" *Sing Out!* 5, no. 1 (Winter 1955): 2.

18. *More Than 'Pye In the Sky': Lonnie Donegan*, Bear Family Records BCD 15700, 1994, liner notes 16; Pete Frame, *The Restless Generation: How Rock Music Changed the Face of 1950s Britain* (London: Rogan, 2007), 31–76; Chas McDevitt, *Skiffle: The Definitive Inside Story* (London: Robson, 1997), 60–63. On the Lindsay-Guthrie correspondence, see Ronald D. Cohen, *Woody Guthrie: Writing America's Songs* (New York: Routledge, 2012), 43.

19. *More Than 'Pye In the Sky': Lonnie Donegan*, Bear Family Records, 10.

20. Paul H. Oliver, "Hometown Skiffle," *Music Mirror* 3, no. 11 (February 1956): 10; Frame, *Restless Generation*, 77–83.

21. *Theo: The Autobiography of Theodore Bikel* (New York: HarperCollins, 1994), 89; Special Branch Report, January 8, 1954, Lomax file, National Archives, Special Branch, Kew, UK.

22. Alan Lomax to Shirley and family, January 2, 1954, Lomax Papers, 3D222, folder 6, Center for American History, University of Texas at Austin, Texas; Bob Groom, *The Blues Revival* (London: Studio Vista, 1971), 12–13 (and see a photo of Lomax with Broonzy in 1951 on p. 13).

23. Ewan MacColl, *Journeyman: An Autobiography* (London: Sidgwick & Jackson, 1990), 277.

24. A. L. Lloyd, comp., *Coaldust Ballads* (London: Workers' Music Association, 1952), np.

25. Letter from Irwin Silber, *Sing* 1, no. 2 (July–August 1954): 15; Editorial, *Sing* 1, no. 2 (July–August 1954): 14.

26. Editorial, *Sing* 1, no. 3 (September–October 1954): 36; Dave Arthur, *Bert: The Life and Times of A. L. Lloyd* (London: Pluto, 2012).

27. John Hasted, *Alternative Memoirs* (Itchenor, West Sussex: Greengates, 1992), 121, 124, 128.

28. "Ballads and Blues at the Festival Hall," *Sing* 1, no. 3 (September–October1954): 40–41; Ewan MacColl, ed., *The Shuttle and Cage: Industrial Folk-Ballads* (New York: Hargail Music, 1954), 1.

29. John Hasted, "A Singer's Notebook," *Sing* 1, no. 4 (November–December 1954): 71.

30. Robert M. Lichtman and Ronald D. Cohen, *Deadly Farce: Harvey Matusow and the Informer System in the McCarthy Era* (Urbana: University of Illinois Press, 2004); Ellen Schrecker, *Many Are the Crimes: McCarthyism in America* (Boston: Little, Brown, 1998).

31. Irwin Silber, "The Time of the Lists," *Sing Out!* 4, no. 2 (January 1954): 2; Guido van Rijn, *The Truman and Eisenhower Blues: African-American Blues and Gospel Songs, 1945–1960* (New York: Continuum, 2004).

32. R. P., "Folk Music on Disks," *New York Times*, February 7, 1954. On the recording of *Leadbelly's Last Sessions,* see Frederick Ramsey Jr., "Leadbelly's Last Sessions," *High Fidelity*, November–December 1953, 49–51, 133–35.

Chapter 4. Popular Folk Music Comes of Age

1. "Ewan McColl," *Hillbilly-Folk Record Journal* 1, no. 3 (July/August/September 1954): 11.

2. "Editors Page," *Hillbilly-Folk Record Journal* 2, no. 2 (April/May/June 1955): 1; Burl Ives, "What Is a Folk Song and Why It Is Important," *Hillbilly-Folk Record Journal* 2, no. 2 (April/May/June 1955): 2. See also, Burl Ives, "What Is a Folk Song," *Variety*, January 5, 1955.

3. Tony Wales, "Folk Record Roundabout," *Hillbilly-Folk Record Journal* 3, no. 2 (April/May/June 1956): 21

4. Paul H. Oliver, "Down the Line," *Music Mirror* 1, no. 1 (May 1954): 41; Paul H. Oliver, "The Folk Blues of Sonny Terry," *Music Mirror* 2, no. 10 (October 1955): 7; Paul

H. Oliver, "Odetta," *Music Mirror* 5, no. 7 (April 1958): 6–7; Paul H. Oliver, "Brownie McGhee and Sonny Terry," *Music Mirror* 5, no. 11 (June 1958): 6–7, 17; and see also Paul H. Oliver, "Rock Island Line," *Music Mirror* 4, no. 1 (January 1957): 6–8.

5. Noel Clad, "Greenwich Village—1955," *Cosmopolitan*, April 1955, 87.

6. Erik Darling, *"I'd Give My Life!": From Washington Square to Carnegie Hall; A Journey by Folk Music* (Palo Alto, Calif.: Science and Behavior, 2008), 20.

7. Alex Korner, "Ragtime, Ringshouts and Hollers: A Study of Pre-Jazz Forms," in *Jazzbook 1955*, ed. Albert J. McCarthy (London: Cassell, 1955), 81; Pete Frame, *Restless Generation* (London: Rogan House, 2007), 8177–83; Bob Riesman, *I Feel So Good: The Life and Times of Big Bill Broonzy* (Chicago: University of Chicago Press, 2011), 212–16; Elijah Wald, *Josh White: Society Blues* (Amherst: University of Massachusetts Press, 2000), 243–46; Harry Shapiro, *Alexis Korner: The Biography* (London: Bloomsbury, 1996); Bob Groom, "Whose 'Rock Island Line'?: Originality in the Composition of Blues and British Skiffle," in *Cross the Water Blues: African American Music in Europe*, ed. Neil A. Wynn (Jackson: University Press of Mississippi, 2007), 167–82. For an excellent and extensive selection of skiffle recordings, see *The History of Skiffle*, Bear Family Records BCD 16099.

8. "Greetings from Paul Robeson," *Sing* 2, no. 2 (June/July 1955): 28; "Music Hath Charms," *Sing* 2, no. 5 (December 1955): 76; Alan Lomax, *Harriett and Her Harmonium* (New York.: Barnes, [1955]); Arnold H. Lubasch, *Robeson: An American Ballad* (Lanham, Md.: Scarecrow, 2012).

9. Alan to Johnny, November 13, 1955, Lomax Family Papers, Center for American History, University of Texas at Austin, Texas, 3D222, folder 6 (hereafter Lomax Family Papers, CAH). The known Communist was probably MacColl.

10. Shirley Collins, *America over the Water* (London: SAF, 2005), 19–20.

11. June Shelley, *Even When It Was Bad . . . It Was Good* (np: Xlibris, 2000), 50–51.

12. *Joan's Book: Joan Littlewood's Peculiar History As She Tells It* (London: Minerva, 1995), 466–67; Shelley, *Even When It Was Bad*, 57; Hank Reineke, *Ramblin' Jack Elliott: The Never-Ending Highway* (Lanham, Md.: Scarecrow, 2010), 69–74.

13. John Hasted, "A Singer's Notebook," *Sing* 3, no. 4 (December 1956–January 1957): 70; John Hasted, *Alternative Memoirs* (Itchenor, West Sussex: Greengates, 1992), 129, 130; Frame, *Restless Generation*, 102–11.

14. Alan to Shirley, April 25, 1956, 3D222, folder 6, Lomax Family Papers, CAH; Ewan MacColl, *Journeyman: An Autobiography* (London: Sidgwick & Jackson, 1990), 277.

15. *The Peggy Seeger Songbook: Warts and All: Forty Years of Songmaking* (New York: Oak, 1998), 11, 48; *The Skiffle Album, featuring Skiffle and Folk Songs Popularised by Alan Lomax and the Ramblers* (London: Feldman, 1957), inside front cover. *Dark of the Moon* was an American dramatic stage play with a few folk songs.

16. Shelley, *Even When It Was Bad*, 64.

17. John Hasted, "A Singer's Notebook," *Sing* 4, no. 2 (June–July 1957): 22.

18. Alan to Family, (Christmas) 1956, 3D222, folder 6, Lomax Family Papers,

CAH; Roberta Freund Schwartz, *How Britain Got the Blues: The Transmission and Reception of the American Blues Style to the United Kingdom* (Hants: Ashgate, 2007), 63–71.

19. Philip H. Ennis, *The Seventh Stream: The Emergence of Rocknroll in American Popular Music* (Hanover: Wesleyan University Press, 1992), 216–29; Larry Birnbaum, *Before Elvis: The Prehistory of Rock 'n' Roll* (Lanham, Md.: Scarecrow, 2013).

20. Alec Wilkinson, *The Protest Singer: An Intimate Portrait of Pete Seeger* (New York: Knopf, 2009), 128, 136.

21. "Un-Americans," *Sing Out!* 5, no. 4 (Autumn 1955): 2.

22. David Hajdu, *The Ten-Cent Plague: The Great Comic-Book Scare and How It Changed America* (New York: Farrar, Straus & Giroux, 2008); Linda Martin and Kerry Segrave, *Anti-Rock: The Opposition to Rock 'n' Roll* (New York: Da Capo, 1993); J. Hoberman, *An Army of Phantoms: American Movies and the Making of the Cold War* (New York: New Press, 2011); Michael Barson and Steven Heller, *Red Scared! The Commie Menace in Propaganda and Popular Culture* (San Francisco: Chronicle, 2001); James Gilbert, *A Cycle of Outrage: America's Reaction to the Juvenile Delinquent in the 1950s* (New York: Oxford University Press, 1988); Ronald D. Cohen, "*The Delinquents*: Censorship and Youth Culture in Recent U.S. History," *History of Education Quarterly*, 37, no. 3 (Fall 1997): 251–70.

23. Lisa Phillips et al., *Beat Culture and the New America: 1950–1965* (New York: Whitney Museum of American Art, 1995); Stephen E. Kercher, *Rebel with a Cause: Liberal Satire in Postwar America* (Chicago: University of Chicago Press, 2006).

24. Joyce Johnson, *Minor Characters: A Young Woman's Coming of Age in the Beat Generation* (New York: Washington Square, 1990), 28; Dan Wakefield, *New York in the Fifties* (Boston: Houghton Mifflin, 1992), 116; Sean Wilentz, *Bob Dylan in America* (New York: Doubleday, 2010), chap. 2; John Strausbaugh, *The Village: A History of Greenwich Village* (New York: HarperCollins, 2013), chap. 25.

25. Bob Riesman, *I Feel So Good: The Life and Times of Big Bill Broonzy* (Chicago: University of Chicago Press, 2011), 136–37, 180–82.

26. [Irwin Silber,] "Five Years Old," *Sing Out!* 6, no. 1 (Winter 1956): 2. For the history of "Black and White," see Earl Robinson with Eric Gordon, *Ballad of an American: The Autobiography of Earl Robinson* (Lanham, Md.: Scarecrow, 1998), 241–43.

27. Irwin Silber, "Carnegie Hall Rocks as the Weavers Return," *Sing Out!* 6, no. 1 (Winter 1956): 31; Pete Seeger, "Johnny Appleseed, Jr.," *Sing Out!* 6, no. 1 (Winter 1956): 44; "Tin Pan Alley, Folk Songs and The Weavers," *Sing Out!* 6, no. 2 (Spting 1956): 2.

28. Donald R. Hill, *Calypso Calaloo: Early Carnival Music in Trinidad* (Gainesville: University Press of Florida, 1993); Donald Hill, "'I Am Happy Just to Be in This Sweet Land of Liberty': The New York Calypso Craze of the 1930s and 1940s," in *Island Sounds in the Global City: Caribbean Popular Music and Identity in New York*, ed. Ray Allen and Lois Wilckin (New York: New York Folklore Society and Institute for Studies in American Music, 1998), 74–92; *West Indian Rhythm: Trinidad Calypsos, 1938–1940*, Bear Family Records 2006.

29. Harry Belafonte with Michael Shnayerson, *My Song: A Memoir* (New York: Knopf, 2011), 56, 64; Judith E. Smith, *Becoming Belafonte: Black Artist, Public Radical* (Austin: University of Texas Press, 2014); *Harry Belafonte: Island in the Sun*, Bear Family Records, BCD 16262, 2002.

30. Max Gordon, *Live at the Village Vanguard* (New York: St. Martin's, 1980), 87, 88; Belafonte, *My Song*, 99.

31. Belafonte, *My Song*, 114; Howard Taubman, "A Folksinger's Style," *New York Times*, February 7, 1954.

32. Belafonte, *My Song*, 151; "Belafonte's Best Year," *Ebony*, March 1956, 58, 60; Smith, *Becoming Belafonte*; for Belafonte's popular music context, Elijah Wald, *How The Beatles Destroyed Rock 'n' Roll: An Alternative History of American Popular Music* (New York: Oxford University Press, 2009), 190–98.

33. Belafonte, *My Song*, 155.

34. Belafonte, *My Song*, 156; Irving Burgie, *Day-O!!! The Autobiography of Irving Burgie* (New York: Caribe, 2006), 183–84. In 1957 Attaway published *Calypso Song Book* (New York: McGraw-Hill, 1957), beginning with the essay "What Is Calypso?"

35. Darling, *"I'd Give My Life!,"* 97.

36. Belafonte, *My Song*, 158–59; Ted Hilgenstuhler, "The Belafonte Secret," *'Teen*, July 1957, 10; Ray Funk and Donald R. Hill, "'Will Calypso Doom Rock 'n' Roll?': The U.S. Calypso Craze of 1957," in *Trinidad Carnival: The Cultural Politics of a Transnational Festival*, ed. Garth L. Green and Philip Scher (Bloomington: Indiana University Press, 2007), 178–97. While Belafonte was not greatly exaggerating, there is no mention of him or any such rivalry in Peter Guralnick's *Last Train to Memphis: The Rise of Elvis Presley* (Boston: Little, Brown, 1994).

37. Michael S. Eldridge, "Bop Girl Goes Calypso: Containing Rice and Youth Culture in Cold War America," *Anthurium: A Caribbean Studies Journal* 3, no. 2 (2005): 1–28, available at scholarlyrepository.miami.edu/anthurium/vol3/iss2/2.

38. Harry Belafonte letter to the *New York Mirror*, May 5, 1957; Belafonte, *My Song*, 174.

39. Tom Glazer, Introduction, Jim Morse, *Folk Songs of the Caribbean* (New York: Bantam, 1958), ix–x.

40. See *Folkways Records* catalog number 4-1957 for an extensive list, including such recent releases as "Tunes and Songs of Finland," "Hebrew Folk Songs," "Arabic and Druse Music," and "Music From South Asia." Tradition Records in the early years issued albums by Paul Clayton, Odetta, John Langstaff, John Jacob Niles, as well as the Clancy Brothers.

41. For Seeger's prodigious output during the 1950s, see David King Dunaway, *A Pete Seeger Discography: Seventy Years of Recordings* (Lanham, Md.: Scarecrow, 2011). At the same time, the exotica musical fad developed, begun by Yma Sumac's *The Voice of the Xtabay* (1950) and Les Baxter's *Ritual of the Savage* (1952), followed by *Tamboo!* (1956), *Caribbean Moonlight* (1956), and *Ports of Pleasure* (1957). The term "exotica" often referred to stylized music from the South Pacific, made popular when Martin

Denny covered Baxter's "Quiet Village," with exotic bird calls and a vibraphone instead of strings, in 1957, which reached number 2 on the *Billboard* chart in 1959, the same year Denny's *Exotica* album reached number 1. There were numerous other recordings for a few years, which had no connection to folk music. Philip Hayward, ed., *Widening the Horizon: Exoticism in Post-War Popular Music* (Sidney: Libbey, 1999); Francesco Adinolfi, *Mondo Exotica: Sounds, Visions, Obsessions of the Cocktail Generation* (Durham, N.C.: Duke University Press, 2008).

42. Jac Holzman and Gavan Daws, *Follow the Music: The Life and High Times of Elektra Records in the Great Years of American Pop Culture* (Santa Monica, Calif.: FirstMedia, 1998), 34.

43. Pete Seeger, "Johnny Appleseed, Jr.," *Sing Out!* 7, no. 3 (Fall 1957): 32; Ronald D. Cohen, *Woody Guthrie: Writing America's Songs* (New York: Routledge, 2012), 45–49.

Chapter 5. Further Developments

1. For the history of the Trio see William J. Bush, *Greenback Dollar: The Incredible Rise of the Kingston Trio* (Lanham, Md.: Scarecrow, 2013).

2. "Lou Gottlieb," in *"Wasn't That a Time!": Firsthand Accounts of the Folk Music Revival*, ed. Ronald D. Cohen (Metuchen, N.J.: Scarecrow, 1995), 149.

3. "Hanged Man in Hit Tune," *Life*, December 15, 1958, 81.

4. W. Hugh Jansen, "Balladry and Ballad Singers," *Saturday Review*, March 30, 1957, 50; Paul Berk, "Folk Characterized by Shoes, Shaves," *Phoenix*, April 16, 1957, 1.

5. Ronald D. Cohen, *A History of Folk Music Festivals in the United States: Feasts of Musical Celebration* (Lanham, Md.: Scarecrow, 2008), chap. 2.

6. John Hasted, "A Singer's Notebook," *Sing* 3, no. 6 (February–March 1957): 81.

7. John Hasted, "A Singer's Notebook," *Sing* 4, no. 1 (April–May 1957): 13; John Hasted, *Alternative Memoirs* (Itchenor, West Sussex: Greengates, 1992), 138; Alan Lomax, "Skiffle: Why Is It So Popular? and Where Is It Going," in *Alan Lomax: Selected Writings, 1934–1997*, ed. Ronald D. Cohen (New York: Routledge, 2003), 137.

8. Pete Seeger to Alan Lomax, ca. 1957, in *Pete Seeger in His Own Words*, ed. Rob Rosenthal and Sam Rosenthal (Boulder, Colo.: Paradigm, 2012), 276; John Szwed, *Alan Lomax: The Man Who Recorded the World* (New York: Viking, 2010), 292–96.

9. Sandy Paton, "A Letter from London," *Caravan* 6 (1958), 7; on Lomax and Broonzy, see Roberta Freund Schwartz, "Preaching the Gospel of the Blues: Blues Evangelists in Britain," in *Cross the Water Blues: African American Music in Europe*, ed. Neil A. Wynn (Jackson: University Press of Mississippi, 2007), 155.

10. Rinzler quotes in Dave Arthur, *Bert: The Life and Times of A.L. Lloyd* (London: Pluto, 2012), 288.

11. Britta Sweers, "Ghosts of Voices: English Folk(-rock) Musicians and the Transmission of Traditional Music," in *Folk Song: Tradition, Revival, and Re-Creation*, ed. Ian Russell and David Atkinson (Aberdeen: The Elphinstone Institute, 2004), 132.

12. Alan Lomax to John Henry Faulk, June 23 [1958], John Henry Faulk Papers, Center for American History, University of Texas at Austin, Texas, 3E169.

13. A. L. Lloyd, "American Folk Song: The Present Situation," *Recorded Folk Music* 1 (March–April 1958), 13.

14. "Flock of Names in New Cycle," *Variety*, February 26, 1958, 43.

15. Irwin Silber to Archie Green, November 26, 1957, Richard Reuss Papers, Indiana University Archives, Indiana University, Bloomington, Indiana. While Silber had toned down his political rhetoric, he would remain involved with left-wing politics until his death in 2010.

16. Pete Seeger, "Sea Song Paperback," *Sing Out!* 6, no. 4 (Winter 1957): 21.

17. John Hasted, "Don't Scoff at Skiffle!," *Sing Out!* 7, no. 1 (Spring 1957): 28–29; "On the Cover," *Sing Out!* 7, no. 4 (Winter 1958): 2.

18. Samuel Barclay Charters, "The Skiffle Band: An Introduction," *American Skiffle Bands*, Folkways Records FA 2610, 1957. Blues historians never refer to skiffle in their studies. For Charters's musical activities in the 1950s, see Samuel Charters, *A Language of Song: Journeys in the Musical World of the African Diaspora* (Durham, N.C.: Duke University Press, 2009), where he has a chapter on "Skiffles, Tubs, and Washboards: Good Time Music before the Blues," 62–80.

19. Lee Shaw, "No Matter How You Sing It," *CHOOOG*, 2–5 (Summer 1957): 2, 3, 4 (emphasis and ellipsis in original). Lee Hoffman went by Lee Shaw for a few years, then changed back to Hoffman, which we will use throughout.

20. "Lee Hoffman's Biography: My Folknik Days," available at http://www.civil. wustl.edu/~gary/Lee/bio-folknik.html. The Photo-Sound photographs and recordings can be located in the Southern Folklife Collection, Louis Round Wilson Library, University of North Carolina at Chapel Hill.

21. Blind Rafferty, "The Elektra Catalog—A Sarcophagus," *Caravan* 1 (August 1957): 4; John Brunner, "With My Ear to the Ground," *Caravan* 1 (August 1957): 8; "Blind Rafferty," *Caravan* 2 (September 1957): 9.

22. Dave Van Ronk with Elijah Wald, *The Mayor of MacDougal Street: A Memoir* (Cambridge: Da Capo, 2005), 65–66.

23. B. A. Botkin and William G. Tyrrell, "Upstate, Downstate," *New York Folklore Quarterly*, Spring 1957, 66; "Folklore Center," *Sing Out!* 7, no. 1 (Spring 1957): 33; Scott Barretta, ed., *The Conscience of the Folk Revival: The Writings of Israel "Izzy" Young* (Lanham, Md.: Scarecrow, 2013), 5.

24. Van Ronk with Wald, *The Mayor of MacDougal Street*, 62–63.

25. "Lee Hoffman's Biography: My Folknik Days"; "Kafka," *Caravan* 3, October 1957, 8.

26. Paul Clayton to Marian, April 1, 1957, Moses and Frances Asch Collection, Ralph Rinzler Folklife Archives and Collections, Center for Folklife and Cultural Heritage, Smithsonian Institution, Washington, D.C. For Clayton's amazing life see Bob Coltman, *Paul Clayton and the Folksong Revival* (Lanham, Md.: Scarecrow, 2008).

27. Dick Weissman, "Brownie McGhee," *Caravan* 5 (December 1957): 3; "New York Scene," *Caravan* 5 (December 1957): 24; "Skiffle Stateside," *Caravan* 6 (January 1958): 5; Sandy Paton, "A Letter From London," *Caravan* 6 (January 1958): 7.

28. Sandy Paton, "London Letter," *Caravan* 7 (February 1958): 7; *Great Bluesmen in Britain: Big Bill Broonzy, Sonny Terry-Brownie McGhee, Josh White,* liner notes by Chris Smith, AVID AMSC 736, 2002.

29. June Shelley, *Even When It Was Bad . . . It Was Good* (np: Xlibris, 2000), 70; John Renbourn, "Born of Skiffle and Blues," *FRETS* 10, no. 6 (June 1988).

30. Shirley Collins, *America over the Water* (London: SAF, 2005), 26. Lomax appeared on a Melodisc EP performing four songs: "Ain't No Mo' Cane on This Brazis [*sic*]," "Long Summer Day," "I'm a Rambler And A Gambler," and "The Red River Shore"—backed by Guy Carawan and John Cole; and the Nixa Jazz Today EP *Alan Lomax Sings,* accompanied by Dave Lees Bandits. Tradition Records issued an LP in 1958, *Texas Folksongs,* from the Melodisc session with Lomax, Carawan, and Cole.

31. Liner notes, *Murderers' Home,* Pye Nixa NJL 11, 1957; *Blues in the Mississippi Night* was released by United Artists in the United States in 1959; Bob Riesman, *I Feel So Good: The Life and Times of Big Bill Broonzy* (Chicago: University of Chicago Press, 2011), 126–31.

32. *The Peggy Seeger Songbook: Warts and All; Forty Years of Songmaking* (New York: Oak, 1998), 11.

33. "Folk Song as It Is," *Newsweek,* April 14, 1958, 80; Alan Lomax to John Henry Faulk, June 23 [1958], John Henry Faulk Papers.

34. "Just Folk," *Time,* September 22, 1958, 68; Pete Seeger, "Welcome Back, Alan," *Sing Out!* 8, no. 3 (Winter 1959): 7.

35. *Theo: The Autobiography of Theodore Bikel* (New York: HarperCollins, 1994), 155.

36. Liam Clancy, *The Mountain of the Women: Memoirs of an Irish Troubadour* (New York: Doubleday, 2002), 199.

37. Van Ronk with Wald, *The Mayor of MacDougal Street,* 87–88.

38. Frank Hamilton, "Old Town School of Folkmusic," *Caravan* 8 (March 1958): 23; Bob Gibson and Carole Bender, *Bob Gibson: I Come for to Sing* (Naperville, Ill.: Folk Era, 1999), 36; "Frank Hamilton," in Cohen, *"Wasn't That a Time!,"* 155–60.

39. Hamilton, "Old Town School of Folkmusic," 23.

40. Billy Faier, "Message from the West," *Caravan* 9 (April 1958): 19; Faier, "Message from the West," *Caravan* 10 (May 1958): 19; B. A. Botkin and William G. Tyrrell, "Upstate, Downstate," *New York Folklore Quarterly* 14 (Summer 1958): 153.

41. Billy Faier, "Message from the West," *Caravan* 12 (August–September 1958): 17; Barry Kornfeld, "The Folklore Center," *Caravan* 12 (August–September 1958): 29–30.

42. Van Ronk with Wald, *The Mayor of MacDougal Street,* 67, 70–71, 72.

43. Broonzy, always popular, had stayed in touch with his friends in England, and as his health deteriorated they held a benefit concert for him at the London Coliseum on March 9, 1958, with a second on March 15 at the Dominion Theatre with Lonnie Donegan and the Chris Barber and Ken Colyer bands; Riesman, *I Feel So Good,* 242–44.

44. "Lee Hoffman's Biography: My Folknik Days."

45. Frederic Ramsey, "Popular Folk," *Saturday Review* 41 (October 25, 1958): 60.

46. Van Ronk with Wald, *The Mayor of MacDougal Street,* 83.

Chapter 6. The Decade Ends

1. John S. Wilson, "Program Given by Alan Lomax," *New York Times*, April 4, 1959, 13; John Szwed, *Alan Lomax: The Man Who Recorded the World* (New York: Viking, 2010), 308–11; Alan Lomax to Mr. Caida, ca. March 1959, Alan Lomax Collection (AFC 2004/004), American Folklife Center, Library of Congress (hereafter ALC).

2. Mike Gross, "U.S. Now a 'Musical Democracy' As Result of Disk Spread: Lomax," *Variety*, March 25, 1959, 58.

3. [Alan Lomax], "Folk Song '59," ALC.

4. [Alan Lomax], "Folk Song '59," ALC.

5. Pete Seeger to Alan Lomax, [April 4, 1959], ALC.

6. Aaron Rennert, "Folksong '59: A Review," *Gardyloo* 2 (mid-May 1959): 9; Dick Weissman, "Folksong '59," *Caravan* 17 (June–July 1959): 31.

7. Ben Sidran, *There Was a Fire: Jews, Music and the American Dream* (n.p.: Nardis, 2012), chap. 7.

8. Michael James, "Balladeers Lure Crowd to Washington Sq.," *New York Times*, May 25, 1959, 1; Grace Jan Waldman, "Life among the Guitars," *Mademoiselle*, May 1959, 14; Ren Grevatt, "Folkniks on March; Hill Sound Upsurge," *Billboard*, June 8, 1959, 1; Ren Grevatt and Paul Ackerman, "Folk Music Becomes Big Business in Pop Field," *Billboard*, July 13, 1959, 4, 8.

9. Carlton Brown, "Three Daring Young Men," *Redbook*, May 1959, 12. For country music at the time, Bill C. Malone and Jocelyn R. Neal, *Country Music, U.S.A.*, 3rd rev. ed. (Austin: University of Texas Press, 2010).

10. George Wein with Nate Chinen, *Myself among Others: A Life in Music* (Cambridge: Da Capo, 2003), 314, 192; Ronald D. Cohen, *A History of Folk Music Festivals In The United States* (Lanham, Md.: Scarecrow, 2008).

11. Wein, *Myself among Others*, 314.

12. Joan Baez, *And a Voice to Sing With: A Memoir* (New York: Summit, 1987), 59, 60.

13. Wein, *Myself among Others*, 315–16,

14. Wein, *Myself among Others*, 316; Robert Gustafson, "First Newport Folk Festival," *Christian Science Monitor*, July 14, 1959; Frederic Ramsey Jr., "Newport Ho! The Folk Festival," *Saturday Review*, July 25, 1959, 37; Robert Shelton, "Folk Joins at Newport," *New York Times*, July 19, 1959; Robert Shelton, "Folk Music Festival," *The Nation*, August 1, 1959, 59; Robert Shelton to Archie Green, Archie Green Papers, Southern Folklife Collection, Wilson Library, University of North Carolina—Chapel Hill (hereafter SFC).

15. Mark Morris, "Newport Report," *Gardyloo* 5 (September 1959): 12; Israel G. Young, "Newport Folk Festival," *Caravan* 18 (August–September 1959): 25, 27, reprinted in *The Conscience of the Folk Revival: The Writings of Israel "Izzy" Young*, ed. Scott Barretta (Lanham, Md.: Scarecrow, 2013), 12; Israel G. Young, "Dear Billy," *Caravan* 19 (January 1960): 7; Irwin Silber and Dave Gahr, "Top Performers Highlight 1st Newport Folk Fest," *Sing Out!* 9, no. 2 (Fall 1959): 21–22.

16. Young, "Newport Folk Festival," *Caravan* 18 (August–September 1959): 26; Morris, "Newport Report," *Gardyloo* 5 (September 1959): 11.

17. Frederic Ramsey, Jr., "An Arena for Folk Music," *Saturday Review*, October 31, 1959, 51, 52.

18. Robert Tilling, *"Oh, What A Beautiful City": A Tribute to Rev. Gary Davis, 1896–1972* (Jersey, U.K.: Paul Mill, 1992).

19. Shirley Collins, *America over the Water* (London: SAF, 2005), 26; Alan to Johnny and Lynn, ca. May 1959, John Henry Faulk Papers, Center for American History, University of Texas–Austin, 3E169; http://www.wirz.de/music/osterfrm.htm; Harry Oster, *Living Country Blues* (Detroit: Folklore Assoc., 1969); John H. Cowley, "Don't Leave Me Here: Non-Commercial Blues; The Field Trips, 1924–60," in *Nothing But the Blues: The Music and the Musicians*, ed. Lawrence Cohn (New York: Abbeville, 1993), 265–311.

20. "Folk Hunter," *Time*, October 12, 1959, 91; Frederic Ramsey Jr., "The Lyre of Leadbelly and Django," *Saturday Review*, December 5, 1959, 57.

21. Collins, *America over the Water*, 50; Alan Lomax, "The 'Folkniks'—and The Songs They Sing," *Sing Out!* 9, no. 1 (Summer 1959): 31; John Cohen, "In Defense of City Folksingers," *Sing Out!* 9, no. 1 (Summer 1959): 34. Lomax's photo appeared on that issue's cover.

22. Collins, *America over the Water*, 56–57.

23. Alan to Margaret and Johnny, August 9, 1959, Lomax Family Papers, Center for American History, University of Texas at Austin, Texas, 3D222, folder 6 (hereafter Lomax Family Papers, CAH).

24. Collins, *America over the Water*, 81, 87; Stephen Wade, *The Beautiful Music All Around Us: Field Recordings and the American Experience* (Urbana: University of Illinois Press, 2012), 21–22, 237–65; Szwed, *Alan Lomax*, 316–19; Tom Piazza, *The Southern Journey of Alan Lomax: Words, Photographs, and Music* (New York: Library of Congress / Norton, 2012). Lomax had included Texas Gladden, Hobart Smith, and Vera Hall in the program "Ballads, Hoe-Downs, Spirituals (White and Negro), and Blues" at Columbia University in New York on May 15, 1948. While in the city at that time, Alan recorded Gladden and Smith for Moe Asch, who released albums by each on his Disc label, with notes by Lomax.

25. Collins, *America over the Water*, 127, 165, 173–74.

26. Collins, *America over the Water*, 174.

27. Alan Lomax to Johnny Cash, October 22, 1959, ALC.

28. Alan Lomax, "Bluegrass Background: Folk Music with Overdrive," *Esquire*, October 1959, 108, reprinted in *Alan Lomax: Selected Writings, 1934–1997*, ed. Ronald D. Cohen (New York: Routledge, 2003), 200–202; Alan Lomax, liner notes, *Alan Lomax Presents Folk Songs from the Blue Grass—Earl Taylor and His Stoney Mountain Boys*, United Artists Records, UAL 3049, 1960; Neil V. Rosenberg, *Bluegrass: A History* (Urbana: University of Illinois Press, 1985), 150–54.

29. Collins, *America over the Water*, 178–79. For a complete discography of the southern albums, see Piazza, *Southern Journey*, 128–30.

30. Gage Averill, "Cantometrics and Cultural Equity: The Academic Years," Cohen, *Alan Lomax*, 233–47.

31. Collins, *America over the Water*, 180–81.

32. June Shelley, *Even When it Was Bad . . . It Was Good* (np: Xlibris, 2000), 82–83; *Sing* 5, no. 2 (December 1959): cover; *Folk Music Guide*USA* 2, no. 1 (January 1960); Barretta, *Conscience of the Folk Revival*, 23; *Pete Seeger in Concert*, Folklore Records F-Laut/1. Seeger had appeared before the House Un-American Activities Committee, not Senator Joe McCarthy's Permanent Subcommittee on Investigations of the Senate Committee on Government Operations.

33. Brian Bird, *Skiffle: The Story of Folk Song with a Jazz Beat* (London: Hale, 1958), 117. Bird was an Anglican minister with a love for both jazz and skiffle.

34. Pete Frame, *Restless Generation: How Rock Music Changed the Face of 1950s Britain* (London: Rogan House, 2007), 356–58.

35. John Hasted, *Alternative Memoirs* (Itchenor, West Sussex: Greengates, 1992), 155.

36. Irwin Silber, "Ewan MacColl—Folksinger of the Industrial Age," *Sing Out!* 9, no. 3 (Winter 1959/60): 9; Barretta, *Conscience of the Folk Revival*, 54 . For a list of Topic Records, see Michael Brocken, *The British Folk Revival, 1944–2002* (Aldershot: Ashgate, 2003), 146–216. MacColl and Seeger compiled *The Singing Island: A Collection of English and Scots Folksongs* (London: Mills Music, 1960).

37. Peter Kennedy, "British Folk Music on Record," *Recorded Folk Music: A Review of British and Foreign Folk Music* 2 (January–February 1959): 1.

38. Barretta, *The Conscience of the Folk Revival*, 16, 27.

39. Ron Radosh, "Commercialism and the Folk Song Revival," *Sing Out!* 8, no. 4 (Spring 1959): 29. See Barretta, *Conscience of the Folk Revival*, which includes all "Frets and Frails" columns as well as a wide range of Young's other publications.

40. Ronald D. Cohen interview with Ed Pearl, Los Angeles, June 25, 1990, transcription corrected by Pearl, January 30, 1993, in Ronald Cohen Collection, Southern Folklife Collection, Wilson Library, University of North Carolina–Chapel Hill.

41. Liner notes, *Saturday Night at the Coffee House: A Night at the Ash Grove*, World Pacific Records WP-1254, 1958.

42. Billy Faier, "Folk Music, Los Angeles," *Caravan* 16 (April–May 1959): 5; Bill Oliver, "LA's Ash Grove Shelters Folk Music Beehive," *Sing Out!* 9, no. 3 (Winter 1959/60): 36.

43. Hoeptner's article appeared six years before his friend Archie Green's influential "Hillbilly Music: Source and Symbol," *Journal of American Folklore*, July 1965, reprinted in Archie Green, *Torching the Fink Books and Other Essays on Vernacular Culture* (Chapel Hill: University of North Carolina Press, 2001), 8–46.

44. Lee Shaw to Archie Green, February 5, 1959, Archie Green Papers, Southern Folklife Collection, Wilson Library, University of North Carolina—Chapel Hill; Lee Shaw, "New York Notes," *Gardyloo* 1 (April 1959): 17–18; "Lee Hoffman's Biography: My Folknik Days," http://www.civil.wustl.edu/~gary/Lee/bio-folknik.html.

45. Bill C. Malone, *Music from the True Vine: Mike Seeger's Life and Musical Journey* (Chapel Hill: University of North Carolina Press, 2011). See also Hazel Dickens and

Bill C. Malone, *Working Girl Blues: The Life and Music of Hazel Dickens* (Urbana: University of Illinois Press, 2008).

46. *There Is No Eye: John Cohen Photographs* (New York: PowerHouse, 2001), 24; John Cohen, "Field Trip—Kentucky," *Sing Out!* 10, no. 2 (Summer 1960): 13–15; John Cohen liner notes, *Mountain Music of Kentucky*, Smithsonian Folkways Recordings SWF40077, 1996. For Guy Carawan, Frank Hamilton, and Jack Elliott's similar problems with conservative politics and anti-Semitism among southern folk musicians in 1953, see Ronald D. Cohen, *Rainbow Quest: The Folk Music Revival and American Society, 1940–1970* (Amherst: University of Massachusetts Press, 2002), 3–7.

47. "John Cohen I," Ronald D. Cohen, ed., *"Wasn't That a Time!" Firsthand Accounts of the Folk Music Revival* (Metuchen, N.J.: Scarecrow, 1995), 35; B. F., "*Caravan*'s Recommended Record of the Bi-month," *Caravan* 15 (February–March 1959), 29, 32; Ray Allen, *Gone to the Country: The New Lost City Ramblers and the Folk Music Revival* (Urbana: University of Illinois Press, 2010).

48. Lee Shaw, "A New Lost City Ramblers Is a Real Picnic," *Gardyloo* 2 (mid-May 1959): 18. On the history of the National Folk Festival, see Ronald D. Cohen, *A History of Folk Music Festivals in the United States: Feasts of Musical Celebration* (Lanham, Md.: Scarecrow, 2008), 32–34,

49. Winnie Winston, "New Lost City Ramblers," *Gardyloo* 4 (late July 1959): 18; "Lee Hoffman's Biography: My Folknik Days," http://www.civil.wustl.edu/~gary/Lee/bio-folknik.html. There was perhaps a seventh issue dated Spring 1960, with contributions from Pete Seeger, Billy Faier, and Paul Nelson.

50. Archie Green to Pete Seeger, June 20, 1956, Archie Green Papers, SFC; Sean Burns, *Archie Green: The Making of a Working-Class Hero* (Urbana: University of Illinois Press, 2011).

51. "Old-Timey Music," *Folkways*, issue 3, [1961], 9; "New Lost City Ramblers," *Folkways*, issue 3, [1961], 15.

52. Irwin Silber to Archie Green, January 15,1959, Irwin Silber to Archie Green, September 21, 1959, Archie Green to Pete Seeger, October 7, 1959, Archie Green Papers, SFC. See also Archie Green, *Only a Miner: Studies in Recorded Coal-Mining Songs* (Urbana: University of Illinois Press, 1972); Richard A. Reuss, ed., *Songs of American Labor, Industrialization and the Urban Work Experience: A Discography* (Ann Arbor: Labor Studies Center, University of Michigan, 1983), afterword by Archie Green.

53. Manuscript notes by Guy Carawan, undated, copy held by Ronald Cohen; Guy Carawan to Josh Dunson, undated, copy held by Ronald Cohen; John M. Glen, *Highlander: No Ordinary School, 1932–1962* (Lexington: University Press of Kentucky, 1988); Ronald D. Cohen, *Work and Sing: A History of Occupational and Labor Union Songs in the United States* (Crockett, Calif.: Carquinez, 2010), 92.

54. Guy Carawan to Izzy Young, August 24, 1969, Richard A. Reuss Papers, University Archives, Indiana University, Bloomington, Indiana; "Folk Singer Arrested in Highlander Frame-Up," *Sing Out!* 9, no. 3 (Winter 1959/60): 44–45; Paul Endicott to Moe Asch, August 29, 1959, Moses and Frances Asch Collection, Ralph Rinzler

Folklife Archives and Collections, Center for Folklife and Cultural Heritage, Smithsonian Institution, Washington, D.C.; Pete Seeger, *Where Have All the Flowers Gone: A Singalong Memoir* (New York: Sing Out!, 2009), 32–33; Guy and Candie Carawan, *Sing for Freedom: The Story of the Civil Rights Movement through Its Songs* (Bethlehem, Pa.: Sing Out!, 1990).

55. Alan Lomax liner notes, *Guy Carawan: Something Old, New, Borrowed, and Blue*, Folkways FG 3548, 1959.

56. Irwin Silber, "He Sings for Integration," *Sing Out!* 10, no. 2 (Summer 1960) 4–6; Bernice Johnson Reagon, "Songs of the Civil Rights Movement, 1955–1965: A Study in Cultural History," PhD diss., Howard University, 1975.

57. Manuscript notes by Guy Carawan, undated, copy held by Ronald Cohen.

58. Guy Carawan to Josh Dunson, undated, copy held by Ronald Cohen; Peter D. Goldsmith, *Making People's Music: Moe Asch* (Washington: Smithsonian Institution Press, 1998), 358–67; Reagon, "Songs of the Civil Rights Movement," 93–98.

59. Paul Nelson to Moses Asch, March 26, 1960, Moses Asch to Paul Nelson, April 26, 1960, Moses and Frances Asch Collection, Ralph Rinzler Folklife Archives and Collections, Center for Folklife and Cultural Heritage, Smithsonian Institution, Washington, D.C.; Paul Nelson and Jon Pankake, "Editor's Column," *Little Sandy Review* 1 (March 1960): 2, 18; Kevin Avery, *Everything Is an Afterthought: The Life and Writings of Paul Nelson* (Seattle: Fantagraphics, 2011), 12–20.

60. Review of "THE KINGSTON TRIO: SOLD OUT[;] THE SKIFFLERS: FOLK SONGS[;] THE COACHMEN: SUBWAYS OF BOSTON, *Little Sandy Review* 2:25; "Jon Pankake," in Cohen, "*Wasn't That a Time!*" 111; Pete Seeger letter, *Little Sandy Review* 4:40.

61. Irwin Silber, "The Little Sandy Review," *Sing Out!* 10, no. 3 (October–November 1960): 26; Billy Faier, "LITTLE SANDY REVIEW," *Caravan* 20 (June–July 1960): 34–35. A few years earlier Lindsay had corresponded with Woody Guthrie and even invited him to travel to London, but Woody's health problems made this impossible.

62. Wein, *Myself among Others*, 316–17.

63. "Folk Frenzy," *Time*, July 11, 1960, 81; Susan Montgomery, "The Folk Furor," *Mademoiselle*, December 1960, 98, 99.

64. Israel G. Young, "Frets and Frails," *Sing Out!* 10, no. 3 (October–November 1960): 48, reprinted in Barretta, *Conscience of the Folk Revival*, 50. Vanguard, Elektra, and Folkways released a sampling of the festival's performances on five albums; Cohen, *History of Folk Music Festivals*, 50–51.

65. Robert Shelton, "Indian Neck Folk Festival," *Caravan* 20 (June–July 1960): 30.

66. Jay Milner, "The Folk Music Craze," *New York Herald Tribune*, February 11, 1960 (the article was reprinted in the *Washington Post* on April 24, 1960); Carroll Calkins with Alan Lomax, "Getting to Know Folk Music," *House Beautiful*, April 1960, reprinted in *Alan Lomax: Selected Writings, 1934–1997*, ed. Ronald D. Cohen (New York: Routledge, 2003), 203.

67. "Folk Sound USA," *Variety*, June 22, 1960, 29; Harriet Van Horne, "Square Toes Blues," *New York World-Telegram & Sun*, June 17, 1960.

68. Robert Shelton, "Folk Music Makes Mark on City's Night Life," *New York Times,* November 17, 1960; Dave Van Ronk with Elijah Wald, *The Mayor of MacDougal Street: A Memoir* (Cambridge: Da Capo, 2005), 83.

69. Robbie Woliver, *Bringing It All Back Home: 25 Years of American Music at Folk City* (New York: Pantheon, 1986).

70. Bob Dylan, *Chronicles: Volume One* (New York: Simon & Schuster, 2004), 235–36; Robert Shelton, *No Direction Home: The Life and Music of Bob Dylan,* rev. ed. (Milwaukee: Backbeat, 2011).

71. Dylan, *Chronicles,* 247–48.

72. Judy Collins, *Sweet Judy Blue Eyes: My Life in Music* (New York: Crown Archetype, 2011), 14, 35, 55; Paul Malkoski, *The Denver Folk Music Tradition* (Charleston: History Press, 2012).

73. Miriam Makeba, *Makeba: My Story* (New York: New American Library, 1987), 85.

74. Barretta, *Conscience of the Folk Revival,* 31.

75. Israel G. Young, "Predictions of the Folklore Center for the Future," *Record Research* 23 (June/July 1959): 2, reprinted in Barretta, *Conscience of the Folk Revival,* 7.

76. Szwed, *Alan Lomax,* 326.

77. Alan Lomax, "Zora Neale Hurston—A Life of Negro Folklore," *Sing Out!* 10, no. 3 (October–November 1960): 13; Alan Lomax to Margaret [Lomax], December 19, 1960, Lomax Family Papers, CAH, 3D222, folder 6; Valerie Boyd, *Wrapped in Rainbows: The Life of Zora Neale Hurston* (New York: Scribner, 2003).

78. Jay Milner, "Texan Lomax Travels Backroad of Folk Songs," *Corpus Christie Caller-Times,* October 1, 1960.

79. Alan Lomax and Paul Ackerman, "The Folky Fifties," manuscript book proposal, n.d., AFC 2004/004, ALC.

80. Alix Dobkin, *My Red Blood* (New York: Alyson, 2009), 111.

Index

academic interest in folk songs, 7–13, 151; and founding of the Archive of American Folk Song, 10
Adams, Derroll, 106
Adams, Samuel C., 10
Adirondack Folk Song and Dance Festival, 47
African American music, 9, 10, 11, 125; relationship to skiffle, 73
African American performers, 72
Alan Lomax and the Ramblers (skiffle group), 77
Alan Lomax Presents Folk Songs from the Blue Grass, 127
Allen, William Francis, 9
Almanac Singers, 15
Ambrose, Johnny, 65
American Ballads and Folk Songs (book), 14
American Folk Guitar: A Book of Instruction, 78, 98
American Folk Music (magazine), 60, 62
American Folk Music Series (Decca), 16, 31
American Folk Song Festival (Ashland, KY), 13, 53
American Negro Theater, 84
American Skiffle Bands (album), 101
American Songbag, The, 14, 21, 22, 23
American Song Train (album), 107
Angelou, Maya, 88
Anglo-American Folksong Scholarship Since 1898, 136
Anthology of American Folk Music, 51–52

Appalachian music, 105
Archive of American Folk Song, 10; record albums, 16
Arkin, Alan, 87
Art of the Negro, The (BBC series), 42–43
Asbell, Bernie, 31
Asch, Moses, 33, 45, 53; becomes a *Sing Out!* publisher, 100; interest in world music, 90
Ash Grove (club), 132, 133
Associated Booking Corp., 33
authenticity question, 124, 132, 144, 145; at folk festivals, 121. *See also* musical purity idea

Baez, Joan, 120
Ballads and Blues (BBC radio series), 44–45, 71
"Ballads and Blues" (club), 76, 98
Ballads and Blues concerts, 63, 66–67, 97–98
"Banana Boat Song," 87
Barber, Chris, 62–63, 73
Barry, Phillips, 7, 11, 12
bawdy albums, 57, 91
Beat movement, 81, 82
Belafonte, Harry, 69, 84–87, 149; on Elvis, 86; recordings, 85–86
Belafonte Returns to Carnegie Hall, 149
Belden, Henry M., 7
Berkeley Folk Festival, 96, 112, 145; workshops, 124
Bikel, Theodore, 63

blacklisting, 34–36, 38, 48–49; in the fifties, 79
Blue Angel (club), New York, 32, 37, 85
Blue Angel, The (club), Berkeley Square, 106
bluegrass, 127–28, 151
Blue Note (jazz club), 82
blues, 43, 45, 57; Ballads and Blues (club), 76, 98; early interest in, 9, 14
Blues in the Mississippi Night (album), 107
Botkin, Benjamin A., 16–17, 111
Bound for Glory (album), 92
Brackman, Al, 30
Brand, Oscar, 15, 28, 48, 57, 91; semi-blacklisting, 58
British Broadcasting Corporation (BBC): and American music, 18, 19, 40–42; and British folk music, 17, 19; Third Programme, 43
British folk clubs, 67
British folk music: and the BBC, 17, 19; beginnings, 17–21; festivals, 129; left-leaning, 21, 65–66
British folk music community, 75, 131; interaction with American folk community, 73
British Folk Song and Dance Ensemble, 67
British radio, 18, 21
Brockway, Howard, 8
Broonzy, Big Bill, 43, 44, 45, 82, 111
Brown, Les, 110
Burdage, Gordon, 60
Burgess, Lord, 86
Burgie, Irving, 86–87, 89

"Calypso at Carnegie" concerts, 89
calypso films, 88
calypso music, 84–90, 94; commercial, 87–89; rivalry with rock 'n' roll, 88–89; teenage interest in, 88; on television, 87
Cameron, Isla, 44
Campbell, Olive, Dame, 7
Campbell, Paul (pseudonym), 30, 86
Canadian Broadcasting Corporation (CBC), 48
Capitol Records, 94
Caravan (magazine), 102, 104–6, 110–13; scholarly nature, 133–34; sources, 132
Carawan, Guy, 59, 60, 107, 139–42; concerts, 139–40; recordings, 140
Carey, Bob, 87
Carson, Fiddlin' John, 11, 14

Cash, Johnny, 126–27
Charter Records, 28
Chattahoochee, Okefenokee, & Ogechee Occasional Gazette, 101
Chicago: bohemian culture, 81, 82; folk community, 59, 110–11
Child, Francis James, 7, 8, 17
Child Ballads, 7
Child Ballads, The, 90, 95
Chisholm Trail radio program, 19
"Cindy, Oh Cindy," 87
City Ramblers, 77–78
civil rights movement, 139–42
Clancy Brothers, 90, 109
Clayton, Paul, 104–5
Clifton, Bill, 105
Club Renaissance, 133
Cohen, John: on commercialized folk music, 136; recordings, 135
Collet's Bookshop, 62, 131
Collins, Judy, 148
Collins, Shirley, 74–75, 76; on Alan Lomax, 128; on field recording, 25; impressions of southern U.S., 126; on Newport Folk Festival, 125; recordings, 107; recording trip with Lomax, 123–28
Columbia Records, 55
Columbia World Library of Folk and Primitive Music (album series), 39, 90
Come Fill Your Glass with Us (album), 109
Communist Party, 26–27; Great Britain, 20, 61–62, 64, 66
Cooke, Alistair: and Alan Lomax, 18; radio programs, 18–19, 42
copyright questions, 97
Cotten, Elizabeth "Libba," 136
Counterattack magazine, 26, 34, 35, 36
countercultural movement in the fifties, 80–82
Country Blues, The, 101
country dancing, 20
Country Directory (magazine), 135, 143
country music, 13–14; relationship to folk music, 55
Courlander, Harold, 45
cowboy songs, 7
Cox, John Harrington, 11, 13
Crosby, Bing, 22, 23
Cross, Bill, 37
Crystal Palace, 99

Darling, Erik, 73, 87, 91
Davies, Cyril, 76
Davis, Arthur Kyle, 13, 104
Davis, Reverend Gary, 123
Decca, 6, 21, 39, 56; Folk Music Series, 16, 31; skiffle recordings, 77; Weaver's records, 36
Disc Collector (magazine), 52, 134
Disc label, 45
D'Lugoff, Art, 89, 109–10
Dobkin, Alix, 151–52
Donegan, Lonnie, 75–76; biographical information, 62; recordings, 63; "Rock Island Line," 100
Donegan Jazz Band, 62
Down in the Depths, 99
Duke of Iron, 87
D'Urfey, Thomas, 17
Dyer-Bennet, Richard, 15, 31, 55, 58
Dylan, Bob, 146–48

Elecktra Records, 57, 69, 90, 91
Elliott, Ramblin' Jack, 59, 60, 72–73, 106; move to England, 73, 75; personal life, 129
English and Scottish Popular Ballads, The, 7, 95
English Folk Dance and Song Society, 20, 40, 61, 129
Ethnic Folkways Library, 45
ethnic music festivals, 13
Exodus, 148

Faier, Billy, 60, 111, 133, 143
Fantasy label, 56
Farrakhan, Louis, 88
Fast, Howard, 27
Faulk, John Henry, 108
fiddle contests, 13, 53
Fifth Peg, 146
Fisk Jubilee Singers, 9
folk clubs, 56, 82, 99, 112
folk festivals, 13, 47, 53–55, 145; British, 129; on college campuses, 95–96, 112, 124, 145; international music, 54; and musical authenticity, 121; at Newport, 119–22, 143, 144
Folklore Center, 103–4, 112; informal concerts, 104
folk music: authenticity question, 124; collegiate interest in, 112, 113, 138, 142; commercialization, 25, 55; defined, 24, 52, 60;

and popular culture, 99, 115; relationship to country music, 55; relationship to skiffle, 97; on television, 145–46; urban, 17, 103, 124
Folk Music Guide*USA, 131
folk recordings, commercial, 55
folk singers, female, 148
Folksingers Guild, 112
Folksong: '59 concert, 115–17
folk song compilations, 14–15
Folk Song Festival at Carnegie Hall (album), 117
folk songs: commercial success, 83–84; defined, 11, 24
Folk Songs from the Southern Appalachians (album), 136
Folk-Song Society of the Northeast, The, 12
Folk Songs of North America, The (book), 76–77
Folk Songs of the Caribbean, 90
Folksongs on Records, 23
Folk Style (magazine), 72, 106–8
Folkways: A Magazine of International Folklore, 138
Folkways Records, 53, 56; *Bound for Glory* album, 92; international music, 90
Ford, Tennessee Ernie, 84
Forty-Four Skiffle & Folksong Club, The, 67, 76
freedom songs, 139, 141
From the hungry i (album), 119

Gabler, Milt, 30, 33, 36
Gardyloo (magazine), 113, 132, 134
Garrison, Lucy McKim, 9
Gate of Horn (folk club), 82, 99, 110, 148
Geer, Will and Herta, 59, 92
Gellert, Lawrence, 9
Gerasi, Tom, 91
Gerde's Folk City, 146
Gilded Garter, 148
Gilliland, Henry, 11
Ginsberg, Alan, 82
Glaser, Joe, 33
Glazer, Tom, 58, 90
Glory label, 87
Goldstein, Kenneth, 78, 95
Good Earth, The (club), 67
"Goodnight Irene," 31–32
Gordon, Max, 85, 149

Gordon, Robert, 10–11
Granada Television, 77
Grand Ole Opry, 14
Green, Archie, 52, 137, 138
Grossman, Albert, 110, 120
Guard, Dave, 93
Guthrie, Woody, 55; BBC programs, 19–20; career ends, 69; Carnegie Hall concert, 1946, 57; fragile health, 60, 72; moves to Topanga Canyon, 59; recordings, 56; relationship with The Weavers, 32; tribute concert, 91–92

Hamilton, Frank, 59, 60, 110–11
"Hammer Song, The" 28, 35
Harriet and Her Harmonium (children's book), 74
Hasted, John, 65, 66, 96; forms The Ramblers, 65; on skiffle, 76, 100
Haverlin, Carl, 22, 23
Hellerman, Fred, 33, 34
Here We Go Again, 119
Highlander Folk School, 139–42
Hillbilly-Folk Record Collectors' Club, 71
Hillbilly-Folk Record Journal, 71–72
hillbilly music, 11, 13, 24, 137; defined, 52; early recordings, 16
Hinton, Sam, 47–48
Hoffman, Lee, 101–2, 111, 136; on Folklore Center, 104; on Libba Cotten, 136; on modern folk music, 202; on New Lost City Ramblers, 134, 136–37; sells *Caravan,* 113
hootenannies, 47, 50
Hootenanny label, 28, 50
Horton, Myles, 139
Horton, Zilphia, 139
House, Son, 10
House Un-American Activities Committee (HUAC), 26, 38, 49, 79–80
Hudson, Arthur Palmer, 11, 13
hungry i, 82, 99
Hurston, Zora Neale, 150

I Come for to Sing (musical group), 82
"If I Had a Hammer," 28
Indian Neck Folk Festival, 145
industrial songs, 67
international music, 90–91, 149
Ives, Burl, 15, 19, 43, 58, 71

jazz, 19, 62, 81
Jazz Music (magazine), 92
Jenkins, Gordon, 30–31, 32
Johnson, Guy B., 9
Johnson, Robert, 10
Jones, Lewis Wade, 10
Josh White Guitar Method, The (book), 74
Jubilee label, 85
jubilee songs, 9
jug bands, 62, 101

Kameron, Pete, 30, 31, 33, 35
Kapp, Dave, 30–31
Karpeles, Maude, 8
"Keep Your Eyes on the Prize," 141
Kerouac, Jack, 144
Kidson, Frank, 17
King, Martin Luther, Jr., 86
Kingston Trio, 93–95, 118–21; Grammy, 118; at Newport Folk Festival, 120–21; at Newport Jazz Festival, 119; recordings, 94, 118–19
Kingston Trio at Large, The (album), 118, 119
Kittredge, George Lyman, 8
Knott, Sarah Gertrude, 13, 53–54
Korner, Alexis, 76
Kornffeld, Barry, 104
Korson, George, 12, 13

labor songs, 15, 20, 137, 138
Lane, Larry, 82
"Last Night I Had the Strangest Dream," 48–49
Ledbetter, Huddie (Lead Belly), 9, 15, 29, 30, 31, 55; Carnegie Hall concert, 1946, 57; recordings, 56
Leventhal, Harold, 30, 32
Lieberman, Ernie, 50
Limelight, 99, 148
"Little Red Songbook," 14
Little Sandy Review (magazine), 142–43
Lloyd, A. L., 20, 64–65
Lloyd, Bert, 41, 44, 64, 99, 100; semi-blacklisting, 66
Lomax, Alan, 7, 9, 10; *American Ballads and Folk Songs,* 14; *American Folk Guitar: A Book of Instruction,* 78, 98; on authenticity question, 145; Ballads and Blues, 63; at Berkeley Folk Festival, 124; biographical information, 5, 7, 9, 16; on

bluegrass music, 127–28; children's book, 74; on city folksingers, 124; collecting trips, 45, 108; concerts for People's Songs, 6, 28; Decca Folk Music Series, 31; Folksong: '59 concert, 115–17; *The Folk Songs of North America*, 76–77, 150; fosters British interest, 18, 19, 21; guitar instruction book, 78, 98; on Guy Carawan, 140; health, 128; interest in world music, 6–7, 43, 44, 45, 90; and Johnny Cash, 127; moves to England, 6, 39–45, 64, 74; radio programs, 5–6, 15, 40–43; *Rainbow Sign*, 98; recordings, 34, 128; recording trips, 125, 128; research grant, 150; returns to US, 98, 108, 115–16; on rock 'n' roll, 115–16; scholarly articles, 128; on skiffle, 97; studies dance, 116; on urban performers, 140; work with Shirley Collins, 107; on Zora Neale Hurston, 150
Lomax, John, 5, 7, 9; at Archive of American Folk Song, 10; recordings, 34; songbooks, 14
Lumpkin, Ben Gray, 23–24
Lunsford, Bascom Lamar, 13, 53, 54
Lyricord, 21
lyrics books, 61

McCabe's guitar shop, 133
McCarthyism, 27, 36, 38, 67–68, 85. *See also* blacklisting
MacColl, Ewan, 44–45, 61, 64, 71; Ballads and Blues concert, 1954, 66–67; at Newport Folk Festival, 144; relationship with Peggy Seeger, 77
McCurdy, Ed, 48, 91
McGhee, Brownie, 105
McGill, Josephine, 8
magazines about folk music, 10, 14; *American Folk Music*, 60, 62; *Country Directory*, 135, 143; *Folk Style*, 72, 106–8; *Gardyloo*, 113, 132, 134; *Little Sandy Review*, 142–43; *Sing!*, 65. See also *Caravan* and *Sing Out!*
Maid of Constant Sorrow, A (album), 148
Makeba, Mariam, 148–49
Makem, Tommy, 109
Man Who Went to War, The (radio program), 19
"Mark Twain" (song), 85, 86
Martins and the Coys, The (radio program), 19

Matusow, Harvey, 38, 68
"Midnight Special" radio program, 111
Milner, Jay, 145, 151
mining songs, 63
Mohr, Larry, 56
Monogram label, 86
Monroe, Bill, 127
More Traditional Ballads of Virginia, 105
Morse, Jim, 90
Mountain Dance and Folk Festival, Asheville, North Carolina, 13, 53
Mountain Music Bluegrass Style, 127
Mountain Music of Kentucky (album), 135
Muddy Waters, 61
Murderers' Home, 107
musical purity idea: regarding African American music, 10, 11; regarding southern music, 8, 9, 13
Music Mirror, 72
Musicraft, 21

National Barn Dance, 14
National Jazz Federation, 75
National Play Bureau, 11
National Service Bureau, 10–11
Negro Prison Songs, 107
Nelson, Paul, 142–43, 148
New American Songbag, 21–23
Newell, William Wells, 7
New Lost City Ramblers, 134–38; appearances, 137; campus concerts, 138; at folk festivals, 137; recordings, 136, 137; reviews, 136, 137
New Lost City Ramblers, The (album), 134, 136
Newport Folk Festival, 119–20, 143; audience participation, 144; reviews, 121–22
Newport Jazz Festival, 119
Niles, John Jacob, 55, 57–58
Nixa label, 76
North Gate Coffee Shop, Berkeley, 111

Oak Publications, 100
occupational songs, 12
Odetta, 56
Odum, Howard, 9
Okeh label, 9, 11
"Old Man Atom," 35, 47–48
Old Time Songs for Children (album), 136
Old Town School of Folk Music, 110–11

Oliver, Paul, 43, 72
Olivier, Barry, 96, 111
Oster, Harry, 123–24

Paley, Tom, 56, 57, 104, 135–36
Pankake, Jon, 142–43, 148
Partlow, Vern, 47–48
Paton, Sandy, 97–98, 105
peace songs, 48, 49
Pearl, Ed, 132–33
Peekskill riot, 27
Penguin Book of English Folk Songs, The, 131
People's Artists, 26, 27, 35, 46, 47
People's Song Book, The, 98
People's Songs, 6, 15–16, 28, 46, 84; organized, 25–26
Perrow, E. C., 8
Pettit, Katherine, 8
phonograph records, 11
popular folk music, 118–23; evaluation, 118
popular music, 15–16; and folk music, 115
popular singers, 15–16
Porco, Mike, 146
Pound, Louise, 12, 14
prison camps, 9, 34
prisoners' work songs, 107
protest songs, 14
"Put My Name Down" (song), 65
Pye Nixa label, 107

race records, 11, 24
racial equality, 50
radio programs, 13–14, 15; American, 111; British, 18–19, 21, 40–45, 71, 78
railway songs, 63
Rainbow Sign, 98
Ramblers, The, 66
Ramblers, The (television program), 77
Rambling Boys, 106
Ramsey, Frederic, 113
RCA, 85, 86
record collectors, 51–52, 71, 134
record companies, 11–13
Recorded Folk Music, 99
Record Research (magazine), 149
Red Channels: The Report of Communist Influence in Radio and Television, 6, 34–35
Renbourn, John, 106
Rennert, Aaron, 117
Reynolds, Nick, 93

Richmond, Howie, 30
Rinzler, Ralph, 98
Rising of the Moon, The (album), 109
Ritchie, Jean, 43. 44–45
Riverside label, 80, 90
Roberts, Robin, 40, 41, 42
Robeson, Paul, 17, 19, 21, 74; career in England, 27; as role model, 84
Robinson, A. C. "Eck," 11
rockabilly, 151
"Rock Island Line," 73, 74, 100
rock 'n' roll: beginnings, 78; as a countercultural phenomenon, 81; early image, 79; repression of, 81; rivalry with calypso music, 88–89
Rodgers, Jimmie, 71
Roost label, 85
Rotolo, Carla, 128
Roundhouse (skiffle club), 76

Sandburg, Carl, 14, 21–24; books, 21, 22, 23; Carnegie Hall concert, 1946, 57; recordings, 21; on The Weavers, 31
Sanders, Betty, 49
San Francisco, 94; Beat movement, 82; folk music community, 60, 111
Saturday Night at the Coffee House: a Night at the Ash Grove (album), 133
Saturday Skiffle Club (radio program), 78
Scarborough, Dorothy, 9
sea songs, 10
Seeger, Mike, 127–28, 134–35, 136
Seeger, Peggy: career start, 77; guitar instruction book, 78; personal life, 98, 129; travels, 107–8
Seeger, Pete, 15, 19, 55; on Alan Lomax's legacy, 108; appearance before the HUAC, 79; becomes a *Sing Out!* publisher, 100; on Burl Ives, 100; Carnegie Hall concert, 1946, 57; college concerts, 39; on copyright questions, 97; English tour, 129; on Folksong: '59 concert, 117; forms The Weavers, 27–28; impact, 152; indictment, conviction, acquittal, 147; on lack of grassroots singing groups, 83; politics, 36; recordings, 56; on the Village Vanguard, 29; writing for *Sing Out!*, 61, 83
Shane, Bob, 93
Sharp, Cecil, 8–9, 17
Shelton, Robert, 146

Shuttle and Cage: Industrial Folk-Ballads, 67
Silber, Irwin, 68, 79–80; exchanges with Archie Green, 138; founds Hootenany label, 50, 65; on Guy Carawan, 140–41; launches *Sing Out!,* 60–61, 65; on the *Little Sandy Review,* 143; testimony before HUAC, 49, 99–100
Sing! (magazine), 65
Singers' Club, 98
Sing Out! (magazine), 46, 49, 83–84; and calypso music, 91; focus, 133; internationalist position, 68, 80, 90–91; launch, 60–61, 65; political tone, 99–100; sources, 132
skiffle, 75, 100–101; in Britain, 96–97, 102; relationship to African American music, 73
Skiffle Album, The, 77
Skiffle and Folksong Group, 97
skiffle bands, 62–63
skiffle clubs, 76, 96
skiffle groups, 77–78
Skiffle: The Story of Folk Song with a Jazz Beat, 129
Smith, Harry, 51–53
Smith, Mamie, 9, 11
"So Long (It's Been Good to Know You)," 32–33
Song Hunter (television series), 63
Songmakers Workshop, 59
Songs from the Southern Appalachians, 57
Song Swappers, 73, 91
southern regional publications, 13
spirituals, 9
square dancing, 20–21, 31
Stinson label, 56
Stone, May, 8
Stoney Mountain Boys, 127–28
"Story of John Henry, The" (recording), 59
Storyville Records, 78
Stracke, Will, 82, 110–11
string band contests, 53
Student Non-Violent Coordinating Committee (SNCC), 141

"Talking Atomic Blues." *See* "Old Man Atom"
Tarriers, 73
Tartt, Ruby Pickens, 45
Terkel, Studs, 82, 124
Third Programme, 43
Thorp, N. Howard "Jack," 7

Tin Angel (club), 56
"Tom Dooley" (song), 94–95; Kingston Trio Grammy, 118
topical comics, 82
topical songs, 20, 59, 98, 143
Topic Records, 72, 75, 78, 129; Ewan MacColl recordings, 44; relationship with Communist Party, 61; workers' music focus, 21, 40
Town Hall concerts, 1946–1947, 6
Tradition label, 58, 90, 109
Travers, Mary, 91
Treasury of American Folklore, A, 16
"Tzena, Tzena, Tzena," 31

Unicorn Cosmo Alley, 133
Unique Quartet, 9
University of California–Berkeley, 113
University of Michigan Folklore Society, 138
University of Minnesota, 142–43
University of Wisconsin folk club, 112–13

Vanguard Records, 57
Van Ronk, Dave, 51, 104, 137; on Caravan, 112; on Elektra Records, 102; on Folklore Center, 103–4; on the Greenwich Village folk scene, 113, 146
Victor Records, 11
Victor studios, 9
Village Gate, 109
Village Vanguard, 29, 85, 149

Walker, George, 9
Ware, Charles Pickard, 9
Washington Square, Greenwich Village, 72–73, 81–82; Sunday afternoon gatherings, 60, 118
Weavers, The: become mainstream, 31–32; blacklisting, 36–38; career ends, 67; at Carnegie Hall, 83; commercial success, 33–34, 36; concerts, 28–30, 39; early reviews, 29–30, 31, 32; emerge from blacklisting, 83; formation, 27–28; international outlook, 68; political attacks against, 35–38; political involvement, 29; recordings, 28–29, 33, 38; repetoire, 36, 37
Weavers at Carnegie Hall, The (album), 57, 83
Wein, George, 119, 143
Weissman, Dick, 117

Werber, Frank, 94
"We Shall Overcome," 139–40, 141
West, Don, 139
Westminster Records, 76
WFMT-FM, Chicago, 111
whaling songs, 104
When Dalliance Was in Flower and Maidens Lost Their Heads, 91
White, Josh, 35, 43, 56, 57, 74; in Almanac Singers, 15; appearance before HUAC, 58; *The Josh White Guitar Method* (book), 74; *The Man Who Went to War,* 19; "The Story of John Henry," 59; at the Village Vanguard, 29
White Horse Tavern, 82
Whitman, Slim, 73
Wilgus, D. K., 52
Williams, Bert, 9
Williams, Hank, 71
"Wimoweh," 36, 39

Winter, Eric, 65
Woltman, Frederick, 36
women folklorists, 7–8, 12
Woody Guthrie's Blues (album), 75
Work, Frederick, 9
Work, John W., 10
Workers' Music Association, 20, 40, 61, 64, 129; American members, 64
workers' songs, 21, 61, 64, 67
work songs, 14, 34, 137
World Library of Folk and Primitive Music, 45
Wyman, Loraine, 8

Young, Israel G. "Izzy," 112; on Alan Lomax, 149; on burgeoning folk repertoire, 131–32; on copyright question, 150; on folk music craze, 149–50; Folk Music Guide*USA, 131; "Frets and Frails" column, 132; opens Folklore Center, 103

RONALD D. COHEN is professor emeritus of history at Indiana University Northwest and the author of *Rainbow Quest: The Folk Music Revival and American Society, 1940–1970.*

RACHEL CLARE DONALDSON is the author of *I Hear America Singing: National Identity and Folk Music.*

Only a Miner: Studies in Recorded Coal-Mining Songs   *Archie Green*
Great Day Coming: Folk Music and the American Left   *R. Serge Denisoff*
John Philip Sousa: A Descriptive Catalog of His Works   *Paul E. Bierley*
The Hell-Bound Train: A Cowboy Songbook   *Glenn Ohrlin*
Oh, Didn't He Ramble: The Life Story of Lee Collins, as Told to Mary Collins
   Edited by Frank J. Gillis and John W. Miner
American Labor Songs of the Nineteenth Century   *Philip S. Foner*
Stars of Country Music: Uncle Dave Macon to Johnny Rodriguez
   Edited by Bill C. Malone and Judith McCulloh
Git Along, Little Dogies: Songs and Songmakers of the American West
   John I. White
A Texas-Mexican *Cancionero*: Folksongs of the Lower Border   *Américo Paredes*
San Antonio Rose: The Life and Music of Bob Wills   *Charles R. Townsend*
Early Downhome Blues: A Musical and Cultural Analysis   *Jeff Todd Titon*
An Ives Celebration: Papers and Panels of the Charles Ives Centennial
   Festival-Conference   *Edited by H. Wiley Hitchcock and Vivian Perlis*
Sinful Tunes and Spirituals: Black Folk Music to the Civil War   *Dena J. Epstein*
Joe Scott, the Woodsman-Songmaker   *Edward D. Ives*
Jimmie Rodgers: The Life and Times of America's Blue Yodeler   *Nolan Porterfield*
Early American Music Engraving and Printing: A History of Music Publishing
   in America from 1787 to 1825, with Commentary
   on Earlier and Later Practices   *Richard J. Wolfe*
Sing a Sad Song: The Life of Hank Williams   *Roger M. Williams*
Long Steel Rail: The Railroad in American Folksong   *Norm Cohen*
Resources of American Music History: A Directory of Source Materials
   from Colonial Times to World War II   *D. W. Krummel, Jean Geil,
   Doris J. Dyen, and Deane L. Root*
Tenement Songs: The Popular Music of the Jewish Immigrants   *Mark Slobin*
Ozark Folksongs   *Vance Randolph; edited and abridged by Norm Cohen*
Oscar Sonneck and American Music   *Edited by William Lichtenwanger*
Bluegrass Breakdown: The Making of the Old Southern Sound   *Robert Cantwell*
Bluegrass: A History   *Neil V. Rosenberg*
Music at the White House: A History of the American Spirit   *Elise K. Kirk*
Red River Blues: The Blues Tradition in the Southeast   *Bruce Bastin*
Good Friends and Bad Enemies: Robert Winslow Gordon and the Study
   of American Folksong   *Debora Kodish*
Fiddlin' Georgia Crazy: Fiddlin' John Carson, His Real World, and the World
   of His Songs   *Gene Wiggins*
America's Music: From the Pilgrims to the Present (rev. 3d ed.)   *Gilbert Chase*
Secular Music in Colonial Annapolis: The Tuesday Club, 1745–56   *John Barry Talley*
Bibliographical Handbook of American Music   *D. W. Krummel*

Goin' to Kansas City *Nathan W. Pearson, Jr.*
"Susanna," "Jeanie," and "The Old Folks at Home": The Songs of Stephen C. Foster
  from His Time to Ours (2d ed.) *William W. Austin*
Songprints: The Musical Experience of Five Shoshone Women *Judith Vander*
"Happy in the Service of the Lord": Afro-American Gospel Quartets
  in Memphis *Kip Lornell*
Paul Hindemith in the United States *Luther Noss*
"My Song Is My Weapon": People's Songs, American Communism, and the Politics
  of Culture, 1930–50 *Robbie Lieberman*
Chosen Voices: The Story of the American Cantorate *Mark Slobin*
Theodore Thomas: America's Conductor and Builder of Orchestras, 1835–1905
  Ezra Schabas
"The Whorehouse Bells Were Ringing" and Other Songs Cowboys Sing
  Collected and Edited by Guy Logsdon
Crazeology: The Autobiography of a Chicago Jazzman *Bud Freeman,*
  as Told to Robert Wolf
Discoursing Sweet Music: Brass Bands and Community Life in Turn-of-the-Century
  Pennsylvania *Kenneth Kreitner*
Mormonism and Music: A History *Michael Hicks*
Voices of the Jazz Age: Profiles of Eight Vintage Jazzmen *Chip Deffaa*
Pickin' on Peachtree: A History of Country Music in Atlanta, Georgia
  Wayne W. Daniel
Bitter Music: Collected Journals, Essays, Introductions, and Librettos
  Harry Partch; edited by Thomas McGeary
Ethnic Music on Records: A Discography of Ethnic Recordings Produced
  in the United States, 1893 to 1942 *Richard K. Spottswood*
Downhome Blues Lyrics: An Anthology from the Post–World War II Era
  Jeff Todd Titon
Ellington: The Early Years *Mark Tucker*
Chicago Soul *Robert Pruter*
That Half-Barbaric Twang: The Banjo in American Popular Culture *Karen Linn*
Hot Man: The Life of Art Hodes *Art Hodes and Chadwick Hansen*
The Erotic Muse: American Bawdy Songs (2d ed.) *Ed Cray*
Barrio Rhythm: Mexican American Music in Los Angeles *Steven Loza*
The Creation of Jazz: Music, Race, and Culture in Urban America *Burton W. Peretti*
Charles Martin Loeffler: A Life Apart in Music *Ellen Knight*
Club Date Musicians: Playing the New York Party Circuit *Bruce A. MacLeod*
Opera on the Road: Traveling Opera Troupes in the United States, 1825–60
  Katherine K. Preston
The Stonemans: An Appalachian Family and the Music That Shaped Their Lives
  Ivan M. Tribe
Transforming Tradition: Folk Music Revivals Examined *Edited by Neil V. Rosenberg*
The Crooked Stovepipe: Athapaskan Fiddle Music and Square Dancing
  in Northeast Alaska and Northwest Canada *Craig Mishler*

Traveling the High Way Home: Ralph Stanley and the World of Traditional
Bluegrass Music   *John Wright*
Carl Ruggles: Composer, Painter, and Storyteller   *Marilyn Ziffrin*
Never without a Song: The Years and Songs of Jennie Devlin, 1865–1952
Katharine D. Newman
The Hank Snow Story   *Hank Snow, with Jack Ownbey and Bob Burris*
Milton Brown and the Founding of Western Swing   *Cary Ginell,*
with special assistance from Roy Lee Brown
Santiago de Murcia's "Códice Saldívar No. 4": A Treasury of Secular Guitar Music
from Baroque Mexico   *Craig H. Russell*
The Sound of the Dove: Singing in Appalachian Primitive Baptist Churches
Beverly Bush Patterson
Heartland Excursions: Ethnomusicological Reflections on Schools of Music
Bruno Nettl
Doowop: The Chicago Scene   *Robert Pruter*
Blue Rhythms: Six Lives in Rhythm and Blues   *Chip Deffaa*
Shoshone Ghost Dance Religion: Poetry Songs and Great Basin Context
Judith Vander
Go Cat Go! Rockabilly Music and Its Makers   *Craig Morrison*
'Twas Only an Irishman's Dream: The Image of Ireland and the Irish
in American Popular Song Lyrics, 1800–1920   *William H. A. Williams*
Democracy at the Opera: Music, Theater, and Culture in New York City,
1815–60   *Karen Ahlquist*
Fred Waring and the Pennsylvanians   *Virginia Waring*
Woody, Cisco, and Me: Seamen Three in the Merchant Marine   *Jim Longhi*
Behind the Burnt Cork Mask: Early Blackface Minstrelsy and Antebellum American
Popular Culture   *William J. Mahar*
Going to Cincinnati: A History of the Blues in the Queen City   *Steven C. Tracy*
Pistol Packin' Mama: Aunt Molly Jackson and the Politics of Folksong   *Shelly Romalis*
Sixties Rock: Garage, Psychedelic, and Other Satisfactions   *Michael Hicks*
The Late Great Johnny Ace and the Transition from R&B to Rock 'n' Roll
James M. Salem
Tito Puente and the Making of Latin Music   *Steven Loza*
Juilliard: A History   *Andrea Olmstead*
Understanding Charles Seeger, Pioneer in American Musicology
Edited by Bell Yung and Helen Rees
Mountains of Music: West Virginia Traditional Music from *Goldenseal*
Edited by John Lilly
Alice Tully: An Intimate Portrait   *Albert Fuller*
A Blues Life   *Henry Townsend, as told to Bill Greensmith*
Long Steel Rail: The Railroad in American Folksong (2d ed.)   *Norm Cohen*
The Golden Age of Gospel   *Text by Horace Clarence Boyer; photography by*
Lloyd Yearwood
Aaron Copland: The Life and Work of an Uncommon Man   *Howard Pollack*

Louis Moreau Gottschalk *S. Frederick Starr*
Race, Rock, and Elvis *Michael T. Bertrand*
Theremin: Ether Music and Espionage *Albert Glinsky*
Poetry and Violence: The Ballad Tradition of Mexico's Costa Chica *John H. McDowell*
The Bill Monroe Reader *Edited by Tom Ewing*
Music in Lubavitcher Life *Ellen Koskoff*
Zarzuela: Spanish Operetta, American Stage *Janet L. Sturman*
Bluegrass Odyssey: A Documentary in Pictures and Words, 1966–86
    Carl Fleischhauer and Neil V. Rosenberg
That Old-Time Rock & Roll: A Chronicle of an Era, 1954–63 *Richard Aquila*
Labor's Troubadour *Joe Glazer*
American Opera *Elise K. Kirk*
Don't Get above Your Raisin': Country Music and the Southern Working Class
    Bill C. Malone
John Alden Carpenter: A Chicago Composer *Howard Pollack*
Heartbeat of the People: Music and Dance of the Northern Pow-wow *Tara Browner*
My Lord, What a Morning: An Autobiography *Marian Anderson*
Marian Anderson: A Singer's Journey *Allan Keiler*
Charles Ives Remembered: An Oral History *Vivian Perlis*
Henry Cowell, Bohemian *Michael Hicks*
Rap Music and Street Consciousness *Cheryl L. Keyes*
Louis Prima *Garry Boulard*
Marian McPartland's Jazz World: All in Good Time *Marian McPartland*
Robert Johnson: Lost and Found *Barry Lee Pearson and Bill McCulloch*
Bound for America: Three British Composers *Nicholas Temperley*
Lost Sounds: Blacks and the Birth of the Recording Industry, 1890–1919 *Tim Brooks*
Burn, Baby! BURN! The Autobiography of Magnificent Montague
    Magnificent Montague with Bob Baker
Way Up North in Dixie: A Black Family's Claim to the Confederate Anthem
    Howard L. Sacks and Judith Rose Sacks
The Bluegrass Reader *Edited by Thomas Goldsmith*
Colin McPhee: Composer in Two Worlds *Carol J. Oja*
Robert Johnson, Mythmaking, and Contemporary American Culture
    Patricia R. Schroeder
Composing a World: Lou Harrison, Musical Wayfarer *Leta E. Miller and
    Fredric Lieberman*
Fritz Reiner, Maestro and Martinet *Kenneth Morgan*
That Toddlin' Town: Chicago's White Dance Bands and Orchestras,
    1900–1950 *Charles A. Sengstock Jr.*
Dewey and Elvis: The Life and Times of a Rock 'n' Roll Deejay *Louis Cantor*
Come Hither to Go Yonder: Playing Bluegrass with Bill Monroe *Bob Black*
Chicago Blues: Portraits and Stories *David Whiteis*
The Incredible Band of John Philip Sousa *Paul E. Bierley*
"Maximum Clarity" and Other Writings on Music *Ben Johnston, edited by
    Bob Gilmore*

Staging Tradition: John Lair and Sarah Gertrude Knott   *Michael Ann Williams*
Homegrown Music: Discovering Bluegrass   *Stephanie P. Ledgin*
Tales of a Theatrical Guru   *Danny Newman*
The Music of Bill Monroe   *Neil V. Rosenberg and Charles K. Wolfe*
Pressing On: The Roni Stoneman Story   *Roni Stoneman, as told to Ellen Wright*
Together Let Us Sweetly Live   *Jonathan C. David, with photographs by
    Richard Holloway*
Live Fast, Love Hard: The Faron Young Story   *Diane Diekman*
Air Castle of the South: WSM Radio and the Making of Music City
    Craig P. Havighurst
Traveling Home: Sacred Harp Singing and American Pluralism   *Kiri Miller*
Where Did Our Love Go? The Rise and Fall of the Motown Sound   *Nelson George*
Lonesome Cowgirls and Honky-Tonk Angels: The Women of Barn Dance
    Radio   *Kristine M. McCusker*
California Polyphony: Ethnic Voices, Musical Crossroads   *Mina Yang*
The Never-Ending Revival: Rounder Records and the Folk Alliance   *Michael F. Scully*
Sing It Pretty: A Memoir   *Bess Lomax Hawes*
Working Girl Blues: The Life and Music of Hazel Dickens   *Hazel Dickens and
    Bill C. Malone*
Charles Ives Reconsidered   *Gayle Sherwood Magee*
The Hayloft Gang: The Story of the National Barn Dance   *Edited by Chad Berry*
Country Music Humorists and Comedians   *Loyal Jones*
Record Makers and Breakers: Voices of the Independent Rock 'n' Roll Pioneers
    John Broven
Music of the First Nations: Tradition and Innovation in Native North America
    Edited by Tara Browner
Cafe Society: The Wrong Place for the Right People   *Barney Josephson, with Terry
    Trilling-Josephson*
George Gershwin: An Intimate Portrait   *Walter Rimler*
Life Flows On in Endless Song: Folk Songs and American History   *Robert V. Wells*
I Feel a Song Coming On: The Life of Jimmy McHugh   *Alyn Shipton*
King of the Queen City: The Story of King Records   *Jon Hartley Fox*
Long Lost Blues: Popular Blues in America, 1850–1920   *Peter C. Muir*
Hard Luck Blues: Roots Music Photographs from the Great Depression
    Rich Remsberg
Restless Giant: The Life and Times of Jean Aberbach and Hill and Range Songs
    Bar Biszick-Lockwood
Champagne Charlie and Pretty Jemima: Variety Theater in the Nineteenth
    Century   *Gillian M. Rodger*
Sacred Steel: Inside an African American Steel Guitar Tradition   *Robert L. Stone*
Gone to the Country: The New Lost City Ramblers and the Folk Music Revival
    Ray Allen
The Makers of the Sacred Harp   *David Warren Steel with Richard H. Hulan*
Woody Guthrie, American Radical   *Will Kaufman*
George Szell: A Life of Music   *Michael Charry*

Bean Blossom: The Brown County Jamboree and Bill Monroe's Bluegrass
  Festivals   *Thomas A. Adler*
Crowe on the Banjo: The Music Life of J. D. Crowe   *Marty Godbey*
Twentieth Century Drifter: The Life of Marty Robbins   *Diane Diekman*
Henry Mancini: Reinventing Film Music   *John Caps*
The Beautiful Music All Around Us: Field Recordings and the American
  Experience   *Stephen Wade*
Then Sings My Soul: The Culture of Southern Gospel Music   *Douglas Harrison*
The Accordion in the Americas: Klezmer, Polka, Tango, Zydeco, and More!   *Edited by*
  Helena Simonett
Bluegrass Bluesman: A Memoir   *Josh Graves, edited by Fred Bartenstein*
One Woman in a Hundred: Edna Phillips and the Philadelphia Orchestra
  Mary Sue Welsh
The Great Orchestrator: Arthur Judson and American Arts Management
  James M. Doering
Charles Ives in the Mirror: American Histories of an Iconic Composer   *David C. Paul*
Southern Soul-Blues   *David Whiteis*
Sweet Air: Modernism, Regionalism, and American Popular Song
  Edward P. Comentale
Pretty Good for a Girl: Women in Bluegrass   *Murphy Hicks Henry*
Sweet Dreams: The World of Patsy Cline   *Warren R. Hofstra*
William Sidney Mount and the Creolization of American Culture
  Christopher J. Smith
Bird: The Life and Music of Charlie Parker   *Chuck Haddix*
Making the March King: John Philip Sousa's Washington Years, 1854–1893
  Patrick Warfield
In It for the Long Run   *Jim Rooney*
Roots of the Revival: American and British Folk Music in the 1950s
  Ronald D. Cohen and Rachel Clare Donaldson

The University of Illinois Press
is a founding member of the
Association of American University Presses.

University of Illinois Press
1325 South Oak Street
Champaign, IL 61820-6903
www.press.uillinois.edu

.